Modernity and Its Other

Number Three
Studies in Architecture and Culture

Malcolm Quantrill and
Bruce Webb, Series Editors
(Center for the Advancement of
Architecture and Culture—CASA)

Modernity and Its Other

A Post-Script to Contemporary Architecture

Gevork Hartoonian

Texas A&M University Press, College Station

Library of Congress Cataloging-in-Publication Data

Hartoonian, Gevork.
    Modernity and its other : a post-script to contemporary
architecture / Gevork Hartoonian.
        p.   cm. — (Studies in architecture and culture ; no. 3)
    Includes bibliographical references and index.
    ISBN 0-89096-729-6
    1. Architecture, Modern—20th century—Philosophy.   I. Title.
II. Series.
NA680.H368   1997   96-38406
724' .6–DC20   CIP

for
Kenneth Frampton
and in memory of
Manfredo Tafuri

Contents

Illustrations

Acknowledgments

I am grateful to the many authors, architects, and artists whose work contributed to the formation of my ideas. I am especially indebted to Stanford Anderson, Kenneth Frampton, and Joan Ockman for their constructive comments. I have no words to thank Malcolm Quantrill for his unreserved intellectual support during publication of this book. He is a gifted person, and I hope that one day soon I will have the chance to break the ice of long-distance communication and meet him in person. I am grateful to Donald Kuspit for publishing the early drafts of chapters one and two in *Art Criticism*. Finally, I must also acknowledge Shaowen Wang's intellectual and emotional support.

Modernity and Its Other

Introduction

The essays collected in this volume grew partly out of notes for a seminar in "Contemporary Theories of Architecture" and partly out of a personal commitment to reflect on issues I raised in my previous book, without having the space to elaborate, about the vicissitudes of postfunctionalist architecture.[1] Those of us who began rethinking the premises of modern architecture, during or even before the inception of the journal *Oppositions,*[2] could not have fully anticipated the kind of "complexity and contradiction"—implied in Robert Venturi's discourse—awaiting us.[3]

This book explores the language that each major postfunctionalist architecture used to address the thematics of postmodern culture. Postmodernity here is defined not as a stylistic trend but as a historical unfolding informed by the failure of the project of the historical avant-garde and the nihilism of technology. I see the specificity of postmodernity in the coincidence between the historical avant-garde's strategies to demythify conventional values and the current technological drive for fragmentation and the loss of essence and meaning.[4] I will discuss different tendencies of postmodern architecture in the context of Mies van der Rohe's problematization of the architectonic potentialities of the modern language of architecture, and will also consider the perceptual horizons opened by a media technology that probes an architecture of simulacra.

My thesis does not explore the historical conditions of postmodernity. It rather suggests that postfunctionalist architecture is historical through and through. I view postfunctionalist architecture not as various stylistic choices in architectural production taking place since the 1960s but as the gestalt of certain sociopolitical events, including the student uprising of May 1968 in

France, the antiwar movement in the United States, the failure of the welfare society in the West, and the fall of the Berlin Wall. These developments marked the beginning of a new world order, or chaos, if you wish, and had a great impact on the philosophical and literary content of the debate on postmodernity that has been going on between Jurgen Habermas and the French poststructuralists. Poststructuralism questions every attempt to isolate general structures of human activity. It is a critique of semiological characterization of meaning as form, the structure of which assures the presence of the subject. Yet according to Habermas, the subject might have a claim on meaning only if she/he engages in the rational process of a communicative action taking place within a given structure of human activity.[5]

This modern/postmodern debate, which has continued for almost three decades, also points to the presence of some disagreement about the kind of relationship we maintain with our immediate past. Even Habermas in "Modernity: An Incomplete Project" implicitly acknowledges the crisis of modernity.[6] Implied in the word "incomplete" is the persistence, if not the domination, of a belief in grand narratives. After the historical avant-garde's failure to integrate art with different facets of the life-world, Habermas hopes to do so by reinforcing a parallel development and constructive mediation among science, morality, and aesthetics.[7] However, from a poststructuralist point of view, postmodern discourse debunks the importance of master narratives and incorporates themes such as gender, race, and ethnicity into various disciplines.[8] A major result of this is a shift from modernist understanding of artist/architect as Author/Guardian—one who would take care of her/his subject matter according to a canon and the latter's material realization—for an operator whose primary interest is the immediacy of the effects of the work.

There is a paradox in linking the architectural and philosophical issues implied in the word "post," as it occurs in the title of this volume. One line of postmodern discourse is indulged with the temporal connotation of "post." It sees the failure of the utopias of modernity as a rupture that perpetuates a historicist vision of periodization. Here, contemporary culture is only another step in the linear progression of history. As in the traditional debate between the ancients and the moderns, participants of this line of thinking perceive its superiority in temporal terms, as well as in the ability to quote history extensively, thereby subduing modernity's lack of concern for tradition. Charles Jencks's "radical eclecticism" is meant to reinforce tradition in architecture and to disrupt the very idea of periodization. Subdividing the entire architecture produced since the 1960s, Jencks questions the idea of *zeitgeist* and advocates a pluralism whose scope is limited to the convention of symbolism. On the philosophical front, Jean-François Lyotard, who has contributed to the discourse of postmodernity enormously, has recently argued for a more comprehensive understanding of the term. According to him, the "post" of postmodernism opens a visuality through which "rewriting of modernity" becomes possible.[9] Understood in this way, "post" is an analytical procedure uncovering themes and concepts suppressed by the modernist drive for universality.

Motivated by the perceptual horizon framed by mass media technologies, another line of thinking attempts to revitalize the historical avant-garde's inclination to overturn every tradition, including that of modernity itself. This tendency has evolved in reaction to the failure of the project of the historical avant-garde as discussed by Peter Burger.[10] In this context, Venturi's claim for an architecture of complexity and contradiction, dressed with the garment of historicism or articulated with the language of abstract formalism, endorses Manfredo Tafuri's position that the failure of the historical avant-garde connotes the death of architecture. What makes this unwanted symmetry between Tafuri and Venturi plausible is the idea of the "death of the subject" (the axis around which one can differentiate the synchronic dimension of postmodern historicism from its nineteenth-century twin) and the neo-avant-garde's use of deconstruction theory to block the return of the Cartesian subject.[11]

In addition to its temporal connotation, "post" recalls some aspects of Marc Antoine Laugier's architectural thinking as well. His departure from classical wisdom invigorated the nineteenth-century revivalist debate on Gothic and Greek architecture and attained a new momentum in Hendrik Petrus Berlage's criticism of Peter Behrens's interest in the "appearance" rather than the "intrinsic lawfulness" evident in Gothic architecture. The same horizon also separates Mies's tectonic constructs from Le Corbusier's Purism: while Mies saw geometry as a structural construct disclosing an empty space, Le Corbusier saw geometry as the language of an architecture whose plastic appearance should impress the senses. This contrast between the tectonic and aesthetic is important for current architectural theory and practice, and throughout the present work I will demonstrate the ways in which postmodern architecture benefits from Le Corbusier's vision. For example, postmodernism enjoys the architectonic implications of Le Corbusier's Dom-ino House, providing a deep structure over which one can paste simulated forms, or—in the manner of Cubism—camouflage the building's horizontal-vertical skeleton (its tectonic structure) with fragmented and rotated planes presenting a visual spectacle.

The proponents of postmodern architecture have turned the sharp edge of their criticism toward Mies. From Venturi to Leon Krier, Mies's minimalism has been reduced to a logo picturing modern architecture as a homogeneous discourse. Postmodernists' reversal of the Miesian idea of "less is more" into "less is bore" or "more is less" expresses the existence of a schizophrenic subject that cannot stand up to Mies's "deterritorialization" of the modern language of architecture.[12] To recast Gilles Deleuz, one might claim that Mies, similar to Andy Warhol, exhausted the tradition of the new to the point that his tectonic articulations soon became "ready-made" objects to be consumed by corporate and commercial architecture. The muteness of his architectural space mirrored the silence of what Theodor Adorno called the "culture industry."[13] Mies did not restore a nostalgia for bygone symbols, nor did he set out to make free forms. His architecture plays on the differences between tradition and modernity, and between interior and exterior. Compared to the infatuation of modern architecture with the "new," in Mies the notion of difference speaks for the invisible life of tradition. Like Adolf Loos he saw no way of saving the craft of architecture except to pursue the process of secularization to its conclusion.[14] Uprooting form from its traditional enclave, Mies left no choice for postfunctionalist architecture but to return to two major tenets of modern architecture: historicism and avant-gardism.[15] Only through these two strategic choices could postmodernism avoid the boredom of the absence of the new. Indeed, Venturi's attraction to Las Vegas and current interest in virtual reality and an architecture of image-making are responses to a historical "closure" caused by the crisis of modernity.[16]

In addition to the debate on the historical avant-garde, the importance of the question of technology should be stressed. Lyotard's reading of *The Postmodern Condition* is touched by a sense of technological determinism.[17] And he sees postmodernism as a historical delay within the project of modernity. This reading addresses at least two significant points: First, the delay is pictured as partly owing to a shift in the function of technology. The latter has expanded its operative domain from the technical into the cultural, radicalizing the process of secularization. This move is similar to the one that, in the early nineteenth century, extracted the traditional means of production from the guilds and subjected them to the forces of mechanization. Second, if we empty the project of modernity of its metaphysical content, its grand narratives, then postmodernism is nothing but the cultural logic of late capitalism, which at its best functions as a means to level the road for the progression of the process of secularization. In fact, the historicality of postmodernism rests in the intensity of this process, by which the whole culture is on the verge of being transformed into a commodity—a total metamorphosis of the organic into the second nature.[18]

Although most postmodern critics mark the 1960s as the time when the technological shift gave its cultural fruits, nevertheless one must agree with Fredric Jameson, for whom the vicissitudes of postmodernity go back to the late 1940s. Since then America has emerged as the leading Western superpower paving the road for a dynamic culture that would change itself according to the structural needs of late capitalism.[19] Most recently, Hal Foster has ramified historical shifts occurring in this century and the ways these moves are registered in postmodern discourse.[20] These readings of postmodernity have merit, and one might draw parallel developments for architectural discourse. The beginning of the end of modern architecture, for example, could be associated with the exhibition of the international style held at MoMA in 1932. The drive to formulate an "international" language was indeed a temporary answer to the loss of identity (subject) introduced by the eruption of Metropolis. It also testified the demise of the classical language of architecture registered in the nineteenth century's yearning for style. Yet fifteen years after the exhibition of the international style, MoMA sponsored a seminar with the telling title of "What Is Happening to Architecture?" In this gathering, Lewis Mumford's presentation on regionalism was a reaction against tendencies that would want to totalize architecture and deny a marginal identity for American architecture. It is true that history does not repeat itself, but are not current historicism and avant-gardism struggling to fabricate a cultural identity for America?[21]

The fourth decade of this century is also important for painting: Serge Guilbaut and J. Clarck see the abstract expressionism of those years as the last hurrah of the historical avant-garde and the beginning of a consumerist culture whose "vulgarity" (to use Clarck's word) matched the thirst of international corporations for a commodification the scope of which would soon surpass the territories confined to the early European bourgeoisie.[22] In retrospect, one might suggest that those years are crucial to our understanding of America's journey toward an architectural culture independent of the project of modernity. Yet the early authors of postmodern architecture could not conceive their objectives in "writing at the zero degree,"[23] to allude to the title of Roland Barthes's text of 1953. Instead, their attention was turned back to a history whose problematic was already registered in the modern language of architecture.

These hasty remarks on the conditions of postmodernity are important to my argument in this book, which primarily focuses on some thematics of modern architecture seen from the vantage point of the present situation. I chose this paradigm not to debunk modernity but to stress the historicality of postmodern architecture: The presence of Le Corbusier's Dom-ino House, the absence of Mies's *Baukunst* (the building art), and finally the temptation to make analogies between Louis Kahn's "What the Building Wants to Be" and the idea of the death of the author.

The historical process of secularization is a critical factor in taking architecture beyond the project of modernity expressed in progressivist and romanticist ideologies. While the latter sought to revitalize the bygone aura of craftsmanship, the former worked toward a utopia where conflict and difference are eroded. One can also argue that, in spite of their extreme differences on the essence of technology, these two discourses left the core of Western metaphysics intact: Western thought has concealed the fact that the *logos* is itself an aspect of metaphysics. However, one important contribution of postmodernity is its relentless criticism of modern logocentrism, to the point that the foundation of the arts, as a subsystem, is taken apart either by intrusion of themes that were secondary for modern discourse or by questioning the very internal logic of each discipline. Yet, in pursuing this process of deconstruction to its extreme, one might be faced with no choice but to endorse de-historicization, undermining the historical departure of art from its traditional cult and religious values. About this aspect of postmodernity, Martin

Jay has this to say: "we should be more sensitive to the enlightening as well as obscuring implications of much-maligned modernity whose promise is still greater than is assumed by those who counsel a leap into the postmodernist dark."[24] Simulation of historical forms by postmodern architecture comes to terms with that facet of the nihilism of technology that in surpassing all boundaries and localities transforms reality into image.[25] This is not a verdict against history but an attempt to stress the affinity between humanism and the world of technology, which, ironically, would never have resurfaced without the sociocultural developments of late capitalism.

In this context, rethinking architecture means recoding its limits, which involves the historical-cultural disarticulation of sign. A "weak thought" theory of architecture indeed emerges from a dialectical understanding of "the conditions of a given moment of capital"; it will prepare its subject, as Jameson argues, "to occupy a future real world where the work of art has already brought them to imagine, a world restructured not through the present but through the next moment in the history of capital."[26] This domain of the not yet conquered (by the forces of commodification) is the Other of the city, a fertile site where the limits of architecture should be recoded.

Obviously, this relationship between architecture and the city differs from Venturi's contextualism implied in his lessons from the mainstream architecture of Las Vegas, or expressed in his understanding of tradition—especially the classical language of architecture—as a totality that prevails within the purview of an unsuccessful project of modernity. However, whether one likes or despises the architecture of Venturi and Denise Scott Brown, one should acknowledge the fact that their discourse spoke for a particular historical time. The same historicality, with a different perspective, characterized the work of the Five Architects exhibited at MoMA in 1969. Pursuing the formalistic implications of the Dom-ino House, the Five underlined the alienation of architecture from the city. We are also reminded of Aldo Rossi's morphological studies of the relation between architecture and the city. Despite its strategic avoidance of the forces of commodification, Rossi's architecture remains disarmed against metaphysics. Both Venturi and Rossi see architecture mirroring the city, and yet their work falls short of deterritorializing the established limits of architecture. Rossi's typologies intend to modify the fabric of the city by silent recollection of the collective memory.

Venturi, instead, redimensions architecture to accomodate itself to the forces of commodification.[27] It is to the credit of Rem Koolhass that he saw the New York City of the first half of this century as the mirror reflection of the project of the historical avant-garde.[28] However, at his best, Koolhass registers the "innocent" moment of early modernity experienced in Raymond Hood of New York, Mies of Berlin, and, most important, Ivan Leonidov of postrevolutionary Russia. Again, one thinks of Lyotard and the idea of the "post" as a delay in rewriting modernity.

Since the Renaissance, architecture has been seen as a single coherent phenomenon whose aesthetic is either inherent or is derived from the compositional rules of its twin sisters (painting and sculpture). While such an architecture could legitimize itself up to the industrial revolution and during the early days of Metropolis, the failed utopias of modernity attest to the fact that a coherent vision of the lived space, as presented in Le Corbusier's "Plan Voisin," for example, could no longer stand up against the nihilism of technology. On the other hand, the experience of postmodernity tells us that apart from the view that takes the forces of commercialization of the life-world for granted, one still can draw some critical conclusions from Mies's work at *Friedrichstrasse*. Le Corbusier's vision of the city managed to unite the fragmentary character of modernity and clothe the metaphysics of humanism in clean, coherent geometries. Mies's glass architecture, on the other hand, incorporated the formative themes of Metropolis such as "shock" and "stranger" (observed and discussed by George Simmel and Walter Benjamin) to open a path toward renunciation of what was expected to be an organic evolution arisen out of the ashes of a medieval city.[29] This is not to historicize Mies but to propose that in rethinking architecture one needs to search for the thematics of a postmodernity that will anticipate the next aesthetic and formal horizon at which capital might aim.

Does the absence of the idea of Metropolis from present-day architectural discourse endorse Benjamin's prophecies about the end of experience? And does this lacuna suggest to accept the prevalence of virtual reality as the real—the realm that embodies (embodied?) the political dimension of life?[30] And "if this important frontier [public space] is displaced," Jacques Derrida reminds us, "it is because the medium in which it is instituted, namely, the medium of the media themselves (news, the press, tele-communications. . . . that which in general assures and determines the *spacing* of public space, the very possibility of the *res publica* and the phenomenality of the political), this element itself is neither living nor dead, present nor absent: it spectralizes."[31] The loss of the sense of nearness and its importance for our bodily experience of space may well affirm the fact that, in the face of current technological illuminations, one has no choice but to accept a state of total alienation. But, current technologies of communication can initiate a significant step toward a rupture that Martin Heidegger would have enjoyed addressing. One of the major contributions of new technologies seems to be their drive to overcome "distance" by furthering distanciation. It would be tempting to think that this process would satiate our thirst for infiltrating every phenomenon at our distance and diffusing everything solid into the air, so that we, the next gifted generation of modernity, might "for the second time" dwell in and experience the idea of nearness. These are questions that address the extent of the current process of secularization and that are topical for architectural discourse. The search for these answers defines the scope of this volume.

In the first part of chapter one I discuss postfunctionalist architecture in the context of American postwar culture. Within the broad theoretical work of postfunctionalist architecture, three tendencies are recognized: postmodernism (historical eclecticism), neorationalism, and deconstruction architecture. This is not meant as an all-inclusive discussion of theories of postmodern architecture; the primary attention is given to Robert Venturi, Aldo Rossi, and Peter Eisenman, who have contributed enormously to postfunctionalist architecture. The second part of chapter one presents a theoretical framework whose concrete architectural implications are discussed in the last chapter. Following the first chapter, the reader will note my inclination to place the thematics of an architecture of the Other in Tadao Ando, Louis Kahn, and Kenneth Frampton's concept of critical regionalism respectively. My own theoretical assessment on this subject is presented in the last chapter. However, throughout the book I have drawn on the works of diverse thinkers such as Theodor Adorno, Walter Benjamin, and Martin Heidegger whose influence on Gianni Vattimo's discourse on secularization and weak thought need no additional emphasis.

In chapters two and three I explore the impact of Le Corbusier's experience on postmodern architecture. Today, it is commonly agreed that the New York Five architects reexamined Le Corbusier in light of themes that have been formative for postmodern discourse. I contend that, without dismissing Le Corbusier's experience, Tadao Ando and Louis Kahn present an alternative to the architecture of the Five and Robert Venturi. Chapter two takes the case of the Dom-ino frame and examines the perceptual implications of technology for architecture. The Dom-ino armed Le Corbusier with a conceptual tool by which he could restructure the formative themes of classical discourse and work toward an architecture whose aesthetic was perceived along the spirit of machine and the technical exigencies of mechanization. The Dom-ino also framed a window through which postfunctionalist architecture could recapitulate those elements of Le Corbusier's thought that would endorse the inconsistency between appearance and construction. I discuss the architectonic implications of the duality between construction and appearance in light of Venturi's discourse on "both-and." I conclude this chapter by reading Ando's work within the purview of the parody of modernity and tradition and the phenomenological dimension of minimalist art of the 1960s. Dispensing with the Dom-ino frame as a concept, Ando's tectonic constructs close the gap between construction and appearance, unfolding a nonreferential architecture. The meaning Ando invests in his work is neither representational nor self-reflective: the work is understood in the collective lived experience of a cultural space that itself is distorted by the universal aspects of modernization. Kahn's contribution to postmodernity, instead, is an architecture that hopes to bridge the gap between modernity and tradition. No one can deny that Kahn's distinction between cutout openings and window openings were not already at work in Le Corbusier's Villa Savoye. But unlike the latter, Kahn did not celebrate the liberation of facade from both the plan and the structural frame; a distinction that gave the chance to Le Corbusier and the Five to perceive the facade in terms of the aesthetic of pictorialism. Finally, focusing on Kahn's Salk project, in chapter three I discuss the uncanny connotation of "what the building wants to be" for postmodern discourse on the death of the subject. Against abstract formalism, anonymity in Kahn's work evolves out of his interest in the tradition of architecture: Kahn surpassed historicism by subjugating the received historical types and the tectonic of masonry construction to a Corbusian distinction between appearance and construction. At the same time, he distanced himself from a semiological discourse that sees architecture as a sign. Kahn endorsed the idea of the death of the subject by a tectonic that speaks for the poetics of revealed construction. Nevertheless, I contend that at Salk, Kahn's tectonic discloses a discourse on anonymity that comes short of a critical apprehension of the antinomies of modernity: A theme topical for a postmodernity that has to thrive on the void left by the failure of the project of the historical avant-garde.

The failure of the project of the historical avant-garde does not necessarily bring to an end the possibility of a neo-avant-garde practice. Peter Burger does not share this position. However, his seminal text on this subject makes important contributions to distinguishing the thematics of the nineteenth-century vanguard artistic practice from the historical avant-garde. Following Burger's premises, in chapter four I stress the importance of the eighteenth-century separation of architecture from classical wisdom. This rupture paved the road for modernist discourse on autonomous architecture and enticed the avant-garde to launch a contestant discourse against an unassociated concept of art and the need to reintegrate art with the conditions of life. I wish to argue that, in postmodernity, the move of technology from the technical into cultural has opened a paradigm to discuss the thematics of postmodern architecture. It has also consolidated the failure of the historical avant-garde and the need to rethink architecture beyond the modernist oppositional and transgressive strategies. One implication of this reading of the failure of the historical avant-garde is to stress the importance of the cultural for postmodern discourse. Another is the criticality of technology for postmodern architecture and the importance of Heidegger's belief that the work of art is the last bastion to confront the nihilism of technology. In this conjunction one cannot dismiss Frampton's concept of "critical regionalism": it advocates a dialectical entertainment of modernization and tradition. Frampton's position is unique among postmodern and deconstruction architecture: it is antimodern and postmodern simultaneously, and yet vulnerable in its assumption of culture as an autonomous enclave, independent of the nihilism of technology.

If we accept Vattimo and other critical thinkers' reflections on the nihilism of technology, then one should depart from an architecture of time and place in favor of a discussion of the culture of building. The spatiality disclosed by telecommunicative technologies suggests to think of architecture within the spatiality of architectural discourse, a line of thinking to which Rossi came close but whose seeds he failed to cultivate. His journey into history was framed by a structuralist view and made stops only in the "constants" that are instigated by metaphysics. In the last chapter I examine the thematics of the culture of building and the relationship between architecture and the city. These two levels of architectural knowledge are critical for articulating the theoretical vicissitudes of a weak thought architecture. I believe that themes such as column-and-wall have already entered into the history of architecture. Like a released informational byte, these themes belong to anyone and yet defy place and time. I discuss these two textual levels of architecture from a historical point of view, and certainly the reader would notice my inclination to historicize architectural discourse: my conviction that Mies deterritorialized the language of modern architecture and my understanding of the spatiality of architectural discourse as an enclosed "total space." These assumptions are informed by the return of historicism, the neo-avant-gardism, and the scopic regime implied in tele-communication technology. My stress on the criticality of the return of these themes should not be interpreted as the impossibility to realize a different project; rather they postulate a void, the not-yet-construed, and the magic of its beyond. The conclusions I draw accordingly have merit if one agrees that postmodern discourse folds and unfolds utterances that in one way or another address the idea of the death of the author, the nihilism of technology, and the failure of the project of the historical avant-garde.

Postmodernism 1
The Discrete Charm of the "Other"

The Crisis of Culture, Then and Now
Adolf Loos is well-known for his critical discourse on culture
and architecture. His ardent criticism of the aristocratic tendencies of the late Viennese bourgeoisie should be discerned from his
criticism of the progressivists of the Bauhaus School. The latter
sought to close the historical division between art and the crafts.
Loos, on the other hand, emphasized purposefulness of architecture and kept a hopeful eye on the pragmatic aspects of a different culture emerging in America. During a short visit to Philadelphia and New York City, Loos was amused with the practical
implications of a Weberian discourse on secularization.[1]

Now, after almost a century, this promising beginning has become the so-called "new reality," the billboards that remind us
we are at the threshold of another cultural rift. Indeed, Loos was
not speaking into the void; the major line of his criticism is still
viable in the context of a postmodern *fin-de-siecle* and an avant-
gardism that has put everything at stake of simulacrum.

Within the last two decades, Western societies have seen the for-
tieth anniversary of the atomic attack on Hiroshima and celebrated the fall of the Berlin Wall; one disclosed the dark side of
technology and the other inaugurated the promised land of democracy. In retrospect, we can assert that these historical events
have marked decisive points in our historical awareness of contemporary culture.[2] Prior to that, the positivistic canon projected
that the Enlightenment would bring emancipation and social
betterment through its technological development. This written
and spoken telos was (is?) the ideological cornerstone of both a
welfare state and a socialist utopia. On the threshold of leaving
behind a conservative dynasty in America, and facing the per-

petual revisions of Russian state capitalism for perestroika, we can argue that the project of the historical avant-garde has come to an end and its formative themes have been absorbed by the culture industry.[3] In the whirlpool of cultural commodification, the concept of the "new" is pushed to its extreme banality, and themes like collage and montage have acquired institutional support.[4] Montage is commonly seen in the advertising industry and in Hollywood movies, and photomontage, the political cutting edge of dada, is reduced to mere technique serving the commercial intentions of magazines of any kind.[5] And the overuse of the concept of "shock" has blurred the line between art and kitsch. Yet in its most modish version, postmodern architecture has established kitsch as a major theme for its practice exemplified in Charles Moore's "Piazza d' Italia."

It is quite clear that the magnitude of the current cultural crisis differs from that of Loos's time. The present cultural discourse is characterized by commodification of the totality of the life-world, including the "void" left by the failure of the historical avant-garde's sociopolitical contest. Indeed, it is wrong to speak of a void in a culture where nothing is immune to the logic of capital. Whatever is said, or to put it in Martin Heidegger's words, whatever is brought out of the darkness of the earth and tossed into the light of the sky, is subject to the rules of commodification. One thinks of Karl Krauss's skepticism, that, if a person has something to say, he or she should step forward and keep silent. The profound metaphorical significance of silence for Mies van der Rohe's and Loos's architecture needs no further stress here.[6] Loos's plain and (so to speak) dumb exteriors, and Mies's minimalism attest to "the limits of late bourgeois emptiness."[7] To camouflage this void, postmodernism reversed Mies by advocating "more is less." One popular example of making things more meaningful and communicative was to regress into the history of architecture. Proliferation of historical forms, uprooted from their historical necessities, secured the theoretical ground for an early postmodernism that arose out of semiotic discourse. But this was not a free choice, rather, the only possible choice for the 1960s. With no aversion for the actual process of commodification of architecture, simulation of historical forms endorses the spatial excursion of a late capitalism that has gained the physical and metaphysical means to break into all localities and pass through all boundaries, including the historical ones. On the other hand, the demise of the grand narratives has left postfunctionalist architecture with no choice but to promote historicism.

There are many responses to the question "Where Do We Go From Here?" asked by Mies in the late 1950s. Mies's response to his own question is intriguing: "Sometimes confusion holds even great men in its grip—as it did around 1900. As Wright, Berlage, Behrens, Olbrich, Loos, and Henry van de Velde worked, all did so in different directions." And he speculated that "we are not at the end but at the beginning of a new epoch. This epoch is being determined by a new spirit and driven by new technological, sociological, and economic forces, and they will come up with new tools and new materials. For this reason we will also have a new architecture." Here, it seems that Mies is expressing a fatalistic understanding of history. Later in the same passage he warns us that the "future does not come about by itself. Only if we do our work properly."[8] The ethical and ideological weight of the word "proper" separates Mies from modern progressivists and from some advocates of postmodern architecture who in the wake of a sociological approach perceive postmodernism as the culture of present-day society, labeled "postindustrial." Robert Stern, for example, speaks for his architecture in the purview of a linear view of history. For him, postmodernism is the continuation of the modern in the way that post-Renaissance succeeded Renaissance.[9] Charles Jencks, on the other hand, formulates an antimodern reading. For him the destruction of the Pruitt-Igoe housing project in St. Louis in 1972 was a declaration of the death of modern architecture.[10] These two views are exemplar in representing a conception of history in which the present secures a safe haven for the promised future. In this regard, the early postmodern polemics against modernity might be associated with the thematics of the literary quarrel between the ancients and moderns. Yet a closer inspection of the modern and postmodern debate reveals the fact that the situation now is radically different. Postmodern architecture manipulates industrial building techniques and covers modern sectional and planimetric organizations with scenographic references to history.[11] I will discuss Le Corbusier's contribution to this aspect of postmodern architecture in the next chapter. Here I wish to underline its ideological implication—its reduction of the classical language of architecture from its tectonic quality, a state of representation by which one grasps the world as picture.[12] This analogy to Heidegger has less to do with the idea of imitation; it rather points to one's noncritical motivation in getting "into picture," a celebratory acceptance of the process of rationalization that is intensified by current technologies of simulation.

One plausible answer to the question raised by Mies might be formulated based on the proposition that we are at a historical standstill. In the last four hundred years we have carved out too much from history. The past is dark, and in place of utopia, a lacuna. God is dead, and those who see the void have nothing to put in its place. The metaphoric characterization of *telos* has been the major impetus of modern architecture. Yet the current debate on modern vs. postmodern rests on the detritus left by the loss of center. The drive to eliminate any thematic remnant of a grand narrative is indeed a formative theme for various theories of postmodernity. If this observation is correct, then I would like to suggest that, by lightening the weight of nineteenth-century historicism, it is possible to discuss the "post" of postmodern as a standstill concept of time through which a critical rewriting of modernity comes forward. In this rewriting, the projective vector of time is bent over and attention is given instead to space and "geographies":[13] *topos* that were excluded by and from modernity. On this level, race, gender, and ethnicity and some cultural aspects of the developing countries should be considered. Yet in order to avoid the pitfalls of any grand narrative, one should have no illusion that the current thematic shift of interest for the mentioned spatial horizons are nothing but the attributes of late capitalism itself. (The international character of current financial corporations and the penetrating rays of media technologies together have changed the balance between space and time.) Our current inclination for spatial geographies suspends the concept of time that in the context of the project of the Enlightenment would have jeopardized the very premises of capitalism itself. This paradox is theoretically convincing if one accepts the fact that the project of the historical avant-garde has failed and technology is drastically changing the cultural domain.

Before further ramification of the above proposition for my reading of postfunctionalist architecture, I need to stress the importance of technology for modern architecture. For example, would the futurist discourse on architecture have any significance without its teleological problematic? Let us hear them tell their tale:

> We had been awake all night, my friends and I, under the mosque shaped chandeliers which, starry like our souls, were lit by the inner radiance of an electric heart. For hours. . . . we were alone before the hostile stars. . . . Suddenly we heard the roar of the starving cars, let us go, I cried, let us

depart. Mythology and mystic idealism are defeated at last. We are in at the birth of the centaurs, we shall see the first angels fly. . . . Let us go. There on earth is the first dawn of history and there is nothing to match the red sword of the sun, slashing for the first time through the shadows of a thousand years.[14]

Following Renato Poggioli, we can claim that the futurists' discourse on architecture is "valid" only in the context of its continual adherence to the potentialities of the future. The dawn of a "new age" and its implications for architecture also attained a modest trajectory in the Bauhaus's idea of total design. The school hoped to bring art back to life, promoting a harmony between civilization and the aesthetics of art. This quest for the "formation of an international unity in life, art and culture"[15] was, indeed, the epitome of an instrumental vision that saw in technology *"the possibility of overcoming* the conflictual-dynamic essence of Metropolis."[16]

Ironically, the idea of global unity in life and art has fallen into conformity with the tendency of capital toward a universal culture of consumption. Manfredo Tafuri acutely observed that the failure of a quest for homogeneous culture can be traced in the avant-garde's desecration of utopian content in their planning for the real world. According to Tafuri, the liberation of an ideology's potentialities has no other outcome but being assimilated into the general process of rationalization led by capital.[17] This process has expanded its function even to the colonial territories, eliminating ethnic and cultural diversity in favor of secularization.[18] Parallel to these developments, the international style closed the door on every other possible style.[19] The exhibition of the "International Style" at MoMA was also an occasion to introduce America as the new home for a culture whose foundation had been shaken by the cultural politics of Nazism and Stalinism. The implication of this cultural transplantation for regional and national cultures should be stressed, too. The international style enforced a departure from heterogeneous buildings for a uniformity induced by industrial building techniques and the aesthetics of abstraction. In a very Promethean sense, the early modernists conceived of technology and its rapid cycle of transformation as the appropriate media for closing the gap between the present and the *telos* of the future. Nevertheless, in less than half a century, the "red sword of the sun," the myth of redemption, disappeared in the cool silence of virtual reality.

The discussed historical closure is probed by philosophers, literary critics, historians, and theoreticians of architecture. Yet the problematic of architecture remains untouched. Perhaps we should ask, instead, if there has ever been a period in history when architectural discourse was not considered to be problematic. While this might be true, the peculiarity of the crisis of postfunctionalist architecture should not be neglected. We are experiencing a historical condition in which the demise of the myth of history has become the subject matter of every cultural discourse.[20] If the utopian content of a linear vision of history has come to an end, then it is reasonable to explore the implication of this historical unfolding for architecture. However, this is not the case in the mainstream of architectural practice today. Why, one is prompted to ask, does this disarray exist; and (if the above hypothetical proposition is accepted) what should the state of architecture be?

Gianni Vattimo has a good deal to say about the current cultural crisis. In "Myth and the Fate of Secularization," Vattimo identifies three discourses on myth.[21] His methodological inquiry will be used here to conduct a critical reading of postfunctionalist architecture.

A detailed reading of the complexity and diversity of post-1960s architecture requires thorough research that is beyond the scope of this volume. However, following Vattimo's argument, and at the risk of oversimplification, I wish to propose that a general discussion of post-1960s architecture can be mapped in the following three discourses: postmodernism, neorationalism, and deconstructivism.

According to Vattimo, in their diverse approaches to myth, "archaism," "cultural relativism," and "limited rationality" express a common dislike for the modern idea of history as a unitary linear progress. Archaism, for example, attributes most of the sociocultural shortcomings of modernity to the latter's positivistic understanding of science and technology. As an alternative scenario that does not draw its thematics from the realm of technology, archaism formulates its discourse around the fiction of origin. This renewed contact with other cultures, and especially with Greek mythologies, hopes, according to Vattimo, "to discover a possible way out of the errors and contradictions of current scientific and technological society."[22] Cultural relativism, by contrast, suggests that our civilization possesses its own myth.

This idea is motivated by a structuralist interpretation of myth in which signification is seen as inherent in the relationships among different elements of the structure of a text, toys, and even a wrestling match, as discussed by various schools of semiology. The most articulated of them is Roland Barthes's *Mythology*.[23] The third discourse on myth, limited rationality, bases its argument on the importance of the narrative and the ways in which a narrative legitimizes its discourse. We are reminded of Jean-François Lyotard's proposition that narrative knowledge discloses a mode of legitimization appropriate to our postmodern culture. His conviction is based on the idea that scientific knowledge is exclusive in terms of its addressee, while narrative knowledge is inclusive and prescriptive: it is a prescientific knowledge that makes "someone capable of forming 'good' denotative utterances, but also 'good' prescriptive and 'good' evaluative utterances."[24]

Vattimo's pointed analysis does not stop here. Disclosing the problematic of these discourses on myth, he argues that these positions stop short of articulating their assessment within the historicality of modern experience.[25] Each position conceives of and reflects on myth outside the modern *episteme*. And each seems to undermine, first, Max Weber's observation that the sociocultural values of modernity are nothing but a secularized version of Christianity, and second, that our very understanding of myth itself is inseparable from the experience of modernity. Otherwise, how could one be an adamant critic of capitalism, for example, and at the same time advocate to return to the authentic values of, say, Greek culture? Thus, Vattimo concludes, "if we want to be faithful to our historical experience, we must realize that our relationship with myth, once demythification itself has been proven to be a myth, will not be restored to its original state, but will remain marked by this very experience."[26]

There may be, in Vattimo, some traces of negative thinkers such as Sigmund Freud, Karl Marx, and Friedrich Nietzsche who believed, in one way or another, that our best intentions flourish within certain limitations.[27] For me, however, the merit of Vattimo's argument is the point that Western epistemology has suffered from its inability to see the present as a gestalt of unresolved historical problems. This ideological blindness posits one set of positions against another without taking responsibility; phenomenology considers its discourse to have nothing to do with positivism, and poststructuralism justifies its radicalism by debunking structuralism. Interestingly enough, the desire to dispose of one set of discursive paradigms for another is itself a symptom of modernity. Until the seventeenth century's famous battle between the ancients and the moderns, the hermeneutics of culture were nothing but a generic variation on the permanent prototypes disclosed in a cyclical understanding of history. Since then, however, the spatiality introduced by the advent of capitalism, and the latter's ever-increasing interest to surpass national boundaries, has motivated European writers and thinkers to engage in a process of negation of one set of ideas for another, analogous to what commonly occurs in the world of commodities.[28] If we have reached the end of a linear concept of history, where no grand narrative can hold its ground, then we should see Vattimo's historicism in a different light. And more important, we should question the motive behind those schools of thought that attempt to legitimize a particular brand of narrative.[29] The implications of this last point for architecture might be phrased in this way: how could one avoid modernism and at the same time practice an architecture relevant to the experience of modernity? I am advocating not pessimism but an acknowledgment of the fact that to grasp the present state of the architectural problematic we need to avoid legitimizing propositions derived from traditionalist or avant-gardist paradigms. This point of view is supported by a post-Hegelian thought, which perceives the present as the eternal return of the Same within a different relation of forces; neither the unproblematic continuity of tradition nor a total rupture with the near past.[30] The "responsibility" I mentioned in passing is meant to be the ethical content of a critical thinking that in each turn of the eternal return (secularization?) attempts to save the unfulfilled utopian content of tradition.[31] To save the claim of the past, one should place tradition in the bedrock of secularization.

What would be the result of Vattimo's argument about "myth and the fate of secularization" for architecture? As a general premise, regardless of their different languages, postmodernism, neorationalism, and deconstructivism refuse to address dualities such as tectonic/construction or ornament/structure that are crucial to understanding the antinomies of tradition and modernity disclosed since the nineteenth century. Postfunctionalist architecture departs from modernity only by expanding the purview of architecture to include science, literature, and the fine arts.[32] In fact, the prefix "post" reveals a desire to avoid discussing those topics within the context of modern experience.

Now consider Robert Venturi's *Complexity and Contradiction,* which has correctly marked a turning point for contemporary theory and practice. The text justifies its objectives by underlining the importance of tradition and the positivistic inclination of modern architecture. Against the monofunctionalism of late modern architecture, Venturi advocates a mannerism that would juxtapose various thematic dualities together to generate meaningful architecture. Yet he fails to draw a line "between complexities which are intentional and those which are the result of accretion over time."[33] In support of his argument, Venturi presents examples of complexities not only in the work of an architect like Frank Furness but also in Le Corbusier and Mies. If the work of the latter two architects could cross over the homogeneous language of the international style, then is not Venturi's criticism mainly concerned with the absence of figurative language in modern architecture? This is a plausible charge if one agrees that the political and cultural dimension of Venturi's position is embedded in his discourse on the idea of "both-and." Against the contemporary avant-garde's political polarization of modern society into proletariat and bourgeois interests, and against the monofunctionalist inclination of "form follows function," Venturi did his best to articulate the aesthetic valorization of a populist taste.

The idea of "both-and" discloses the cultural interest of an already growing middle class whose values could be nurtured by different sources. Moreover, Venturi advocates a stylistic understanding of tradition that is supported by the image-making potentialities of electronic technology and the kitsch content of pop art. According to Venturi, "Pop Art in the sixties turned our sensibilities toward the commercial Strip as the painting of the decade before it [Abstract Expressionism] confirmed our interpretation of the piazza." Furthermore, pop art discloses the value of "familiar and conventional elements by juxtaposing them in new contexts in different scales to achieve new meanings perceived alongside their old meanings."[34] I will return to the idea of popular art shortly, but first I would like to explore the proposition that technology has broadened the ideological gap between high art and popular art.

According to Jean Baudrillard, the functional rationality of the Bauhaus "gives birth to an irrational or fantasy counter discourse which circulates between the two poles of kitsch and surrealism."[35] By invoking the "repressed," or the outmoded, surrealists, on the other hand, attempted to bypass the synthesis of aesthetics and utility in design and to counter the socio-political intentions of the Bauhaus to reconcile technology with the craft of building. While surrealism was successful in its drive to question the perspectival visuality of realist painting and an art institution that codified bourgeois ethics and aesthetics, it did not unfold an architectural discourse that could overcome the functional and technical rationality of the Bauhaus.[36] Only a minor part of modern architecture was touched by the idea of juxtaposing the old and new, a strategic position that could be associated with Andre Breton's idea of "the crisis of the object."[37] The arcades, the exhibition halls, and the interiors of bourgeois houses are architectonic examples that recall Walter Benjamin's "wish-image," a concept that also drew his attention to surrealist dreamlike objects. In the absence of such a historical unfolding, functionalism found a posthumous refuge in kitsch. However, one might speculate whether the kitsch-image was not already at work in the surrealist intoxication with technological phantasmagoria.

This was a major facet of Benjamin's belated criticism of surrealism, which was partly motivated by his paradoxical position on technology. John McCole calls it an anti-instrumental affirmation of technology.[38] Benjamin argued that after the loss of aura the new techniques of reproduction would provide the ground for contemplation and reception of art different from the humanist perception of aesthetics. Benjamin saw an emancipatory power in mechanization that if utilized correctly could evoke the historically unfulfilled collective experience. Certain aspects of Benjamin's observation are still valid; particularly, his critical understanding of the moment of awakening through which one recodes the past in the context of the present. Yet as Susan Buck-Morss reminds us at the end of *The Dialectics of Seeing,* one should not immortalize Benjamin. His discourse was formulated in a historical conjunction that was unable to see the shock element, and other techniques important for his ideas on phantasmagoria were being channeled into kitsch.[39]

Kitsch is mostly defined as a decadent popular art evolved through the early century's mass-produced artifacts. Around the 1930s, Clement Greenberg launched the concept of the high art as a strategic position to resist the proliferation of kitsch into the domain of art. Those years are also important because of the Western intellectual's disillusionment from Stalinist cultural policies, which for good reasons induced a debate on the crisis of culture and the sociopolitical function of art in America. Greenberg saw the solution in pursuit of the tradition of avant-garde, suggesting to the artists to do critical work within the work itself. According to Greenberg, this focus on the autonomous character of art will rescue the "quality" of the work, which otherwise is threatened by kitsch. For Greenberg, kitsch had already become "an integral part of our productive system in a way in which true culture could never be except accidently."[40] Now, as we surpass the modern discourse on aesthetics and politics, kitsch "is simply that which, in the age of plural ornamentation, still wishes to stand like a monument more lasting than bronze and still lays claim to the stability, definitive character and perfection of 'classic' art."[41] In other words, in the absence of the thematics of the high art, kitsch has appropriated the aesthetic norms and institutional support that once were attributed to classical and late modern art. In addition, the weakening of the dichotomy between the high and low art has to do, as mentioned before, with the emerging middle class whose destructive potentialities are articulated by Giorgio Agamben. It is worthwhile to quote him here at full length:

> The petty bourgeois nullify all that exists with the same gesture in which they seem obstinately to adhere to it: They know only the improper and the unauthentic and even refuse. . . . That which constituted the truth and falsity of the peoples and generations that have followed one another on the earth—differences of language, of dialect, of ways of life, of character, of custom, and even the physical particularities of each person—has lost any meaning for them and any capacity for expression and communication. In the petty bourgeoisie, the diversities that have marked the tragicomedy of universal history are brought together and exposed in a phantasmagorical vacuousness.[42]

T. J. Clarck has also underlined the formative position of "vacuousness" for the formation of the middle-class values. Discussing American abstract expressionism of the 1940s, Clarck borrows the term "vulgarity" from John Ruskin and argues that a kind of nothingness prevails when subject matter is totally brushed away from abstract painting. Clarck sees this transgression determinant for the class consciousness of American petty bourgeois culture.[43] However, he is not saying that Jackson Pollack's painting, for example, is populistic. Clarck rather alludes to the absence of representation and the end of meaning in pictorial art.

Implied in his argument is the need for rewriting the history of the 1960s in terms of what he sees as the "art's withdrawal from Abstract Expressionism's impossible class belonging." And he continues, "Art had to go on, and that meant returning art mainly to normal avant-garde channels."[44] Seemingly Clarck invokes the idea that pop art brought meaning back to art by infusing some elements of popular culture, such as advertising industry, and banal elements of everyday life into painting. Therefore, "the flatbed picture plane accommodates recognizable objects, it presents them as man-made things of universally familiar character."[45]

This reading is applicable to architecture too: Venturi's interest in some features of the main stream of Las Vegas[46] and comparisons he made between "decorated shed" and a "duck house" are desperate acts in search of meaning for architecture, a potentiality suspended by the failure of the project of the historical avant-garde.[47] The search for meaning was also meant to be a search for an architectural language appropriate to American postwar culture. Alan J. Plattus sees Venturi's rhetorical juxtapositions of historical forms with some elements of modern architecture as a process in which "American culture passes from modernity to postmodernism, bypassing 'modernist' altogether."[48] A proposition that when applied to art and architecture, again, recalls Greenberg's suggested strategy: in order to save art from the threats of kitsch, one has to liberate form from its historicality and subject art to a formalistic enterprise whose emphasis on process would eventually make the process itself as the source of meaning.

There are other facets to my interest in drawing parallels between postmodern discourse and American cultural formation during the last four decades. One might argue that kitsch (the popular) finds its legitimacy in the inability of American bourgeoisie to generate its own ideological apparatus. Part of this impotency has to do with the fact that, contrary to its European counterpart, the bourgeoisie in America, while holding the economic and political power, has never enjoyed the historical baggage of a humanist culture. This line of discussion has been recently taken up by Michael Hays. Discussing Mies's architecture in America, Hays sees the process of American class formation not in "the destruction of the last remnants of surviving aristocratic forms" but in the latter's autonomy from "the class struggle with an aristocratic *ancient regime,* as had been the case in the Old World."[49] This historical void was subsidized by Fordist massification of production, a phenomenon that was followed by a series of massification in cultural products to generate the concrete situation for the evolution of the "culture industry": a social system in which "what happens at work, in the factory, or in the office can only be escaped from by approximation to it in one's leisure time."[50]

To put everything said in the context of architectural history, kitsch can be associated with the term "fabrick" used by Henry Russell Hitchcock to describe the character of romanticism in architecture. "Ruins were definitely more sublime as well as more picturesque than solid buildings. Architecture as subsidiary to landscape was seen through a double screen produced by painting and literature." Hitchcock continues, "Good construction became generally to be considered, if not a matter without importance, at least of no particular interest to the connoisseur."[51] Parallel to the picturesque interest in painting and literature, an analogy between kitsch and fabrick is not far-fetched: both concepts are formative for an architectural discourse in which the tectonic is excluded. Yet the historical process of such an exclusion is accelerated by industrial building technology. Under the overall thrust of commodification, the building industry constantly introduces new materials and products into the process of construction, at such a rate that any sense of mastery of crafts, that is, detailing, is unattainable. On the other hand, the same materials and techniques provide a vast background of fake formal reproduction. In this context, postmodernism promotes a perception of architecture that makes belief in former ways of doing things obsolete. The fallen blocks at the foot of the wall of the parking area in James Stirling's Neue Staatsgalerie demonstrate the kitsch character of postmodern construction (figure 1.1). And yet such a simulation of ruins convincingly supports our analogy between a picturesque lamentation for ruins and the postmodern interest in fragmentation. Replication of historical forms directs architects' attention away from the depth and toward the skin, from the tectonic to the appearance.

This analogy between kitsch and "fabrick" has further connotations for architecture. Being itself nonreal, architectural kitsch does not leave room for imagination; it reduces architecture to image per se.[52] The advocates of postmodern architecture conceive of historical form as a metareality; a state of objecthoodness that is ready to be put into another cycle of significa-

FIG. I.I. James Stirling,
Neue Staatsgalerie,
Germany. From
Charles Jencks, *The
Language of Post-
Modern Architecture*
(Academy Editions,
1977).

tion. Robert Venturi was the first to formulate this position in
architecture. According to him: "Conventional elements in architecture represent one stage in an evolutionary development, and
they contain in their changed use and expression some of their
old meaning as well as of their new meaning. What can be called
the vestigial element parallels the double-functioning element. . . .
This is the result of a more or less ambiguous combination of the
old meaning called up by associations, with a new meaning created by the modification or new function."[53] In practice, modification takes historical forms as given and leaves their contingencies dormant. Thus, architecture loses the memory of making,
embedded in the tectonic. History evaporates and form is reduced to a sign. Consider the Vanna Venturi House whose plani-

metric and facade organization are supposed to deploy the idea of complexity and contradiction (figures 1.2 and 1.3). Here the overall symmetrical composition of the main facade is contradicted by few architectonic elements placed asymmetrical in regard to the central axis. The latter is further stressed by a relatively large opening that leads to a small entrance door. The idea of a nondirect access to the interior space goes back to Frank Lloyd Wright and Kahn, from whom we also inherited the architectonic distinction between an opening and the window or door frames. These aspects of complexity and contradiction are entertained by most postfunctionalist architecture. My criticism, however, is reserved for an architecture that dismisses the tectonic and represents form as a communicative sign in full accord with a populist expectation of what tradition should mean to architecture. In fact, the late 1960s were very receptive to this kind of aesthetic valorization.

FIG. 1.2. Vanna Venturi House, Chestnut Hill, Philadelphia, 1962. Courtesy Venturi, Scott Brown and Associates, Inc. Photograph by Rollin La France.

The demise of the modern utopia, the failure of the project of the historical avant-garde, and finally, the institutionalization of the modern language of architecture together prepared the situation

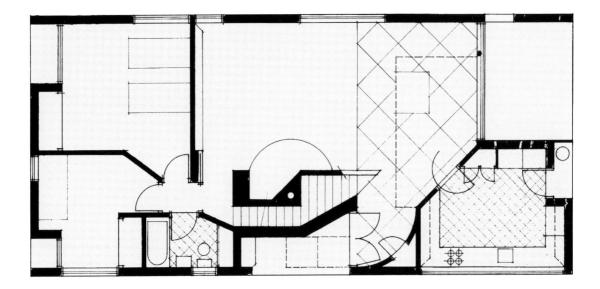

FIG. 1.3. Ground floor
plan, Vanna Venturi
House, Chestnut Hill,
Philadelphia, 1962.
Courtesy Venturi, Scott
Brown and Associates
Inc.

for the post-1960s architects to dismiss the historical avant-garde's political contentions and yet eagerly utilize the latter's techniques to replicate historical forms. Here, I am taking a position parallel to Serge Guilbaut's observation that American painting from the late 1940s intended to depoliticize the avant-garde as a necessary step before incorporating abstract art into the realm of politics.[54] Nevertheless, one should not dismiss postmodernity's contribution in elevating our awareness of the one-dimensional thrust of modern architecture on progress and the pitfalls of its rational planning. While addressing these problems, postmodernists make a giant leap back, bypassing the architectural problems of the nineteenth century, and turn their attention to the symbolic and aesthetic values of classical architecture. This esteem for archaism is the common denominator of Venturi's populism, Jencks's symbolism, and Leon Krier's interest in the tectonics of the classical architecture.

This said, I would also like to draw the reader's attention to the political delusion of some advocates of postmodern architecture. Jencks's presentation at the "International Symposium" at the Tate Gallery is a case in point.[55] Here, with a confidence worthy of the futurists, Jencks lumps deconstructivist architecture (including, of course, the so-called late and new modern architecture) together with bourgeois values to convey the project of modernity. The question about his own stand within the present sociopolitical realities remains unnoticed. This is not the first time, and probably will not be the last, that modernism has been questioned. John Ruskin and other moral romanticists have written the preface to this antimodern position. However, the nineteenth-century critics of modernization openly advocated the ethical and aesthetic values of the medieval age; the revival of the sociocultural organization of the guild system, and a belief in homology between truth and beauty. The theoreticians of postmodernity, instead, neglect the aesthetic experience of modernism and attempt to sustain humanist values by a concept of social engineering worthy of modernist planners. Krier's project for *Atlantis,* for example, discloses a passion for harmony and total planning equal to Le Corbusier's *Plan Voisin.* In his ardent criticism of modernism, however, Krier remains a romantic revolutionary who believes that the spirit of humanist democracy could be restored by reconstruction of his version of the Acropolis. In support of this project, Demetri Porphyrios asserts: "measured against the aesthetic of voyeurism of contemporary postmodern and neo-modern cultures, classicism appears to be the only possible critical and progressive stance."[56] Both Krier and Porphyrios are reluctant to accept the crisis of ideology and the fact that the problematic of the utopian content of modern architecture was not owing to its abstract language but to its attempt to harmonize the contradictions evolved out of Metropolis. Moreover, Krier's insistence on classical archetypes as a theme for an architecture of resistance is politically naive. The culture industry has reached a level of transparency that can internalize any subsidiary alternatives, including Krier's *Atlantis,* to accelerate its cycle of production and consumption.

Again, one might argue that the strategy of "both-and" theorizes the replacement of the metaphysics of the new with the metaphysics of tradition. In Vattimo's words, current right-wing traditionalism transforms the myth of progress into a myth of origin.[57]

This predicament opened a middle ground for the structuralist theories of the 1960s and a synchronic vision of history. Instead of the traditionalist's esteem for the myth of origin, structuralism conceives the "structure" of those myths itself as the site of meaning. "Myth is not defined by the object of its message, but by the way in which it utters this message,"[58] Barthes says. It is the grammatical organization of a literary work, for example, that discloses the poetics of a text and not the author's intention. The absence of the theme of the author in structuralist discourse has further connotations. It suspends the linear projection of history, bending its vector into a synchronic horizon where one can explore various cultural themes independent of a centralized subject. A spatial explosion, indeed, that not only shed light on suppressed issues like ethnicity and gender but also incorporated these themes into other discourses. Losing its humanist agenda, the body (building) was thus seen from different planes, the intersection of which became the home for postmodern schizophrenic subject. In the same vein, some architects argued that, surpassing its historical contingencies, type and its morphological structure are the source of signification in architecture.

This position prevailed in almost every cultural discourse, including the *Tendenza,* a movement founded in Italy during the 1960s. To find new grounds for a meaningful architecture, *Tendenza* came up with variety of propositions.[59] Among these, Aldo Rossi's discourse has merit, mainly because of its acknowledgment of the loss of the center and the importance of memory in architecture. His projects and writings contributed enormously to the language of neorationalist architecture.[60] Concerning the utopian content of modern planning, Rossi stresses the import of typological and morphological structures and their role for understanding and transforming the city.[61] For Rossi, any intervention in the city's fabric is modified by two constants: First, by those buildings whose history is experienced in the present (meaning that certain buildings could work for different functions and yet maintain the autonomy of their original structure, or fabric). Second, by those sites or buildings that could be called critical zones, sites that integrate the individual and collective memories of the city. These two constants are essential for Rossi's discourse on type and for the architecture of monument and cemetery.

One might argue that Rossi's morphological exploration was one of the fruitful results of the structuralist discourse. The criticality of Rossi's constants for the city, indeed, embody spatial structures (sites) whose importance came to light by the collapse of history. They are also accountable for Michel Foucault's concept of heterotopia: sites where the simultaneity of individual and collective is sustained (figure 1.4). It seems Rossi had read Foucault saying that the cemetery "is a space that is however connected with all the sites of the city state or society or village, etc., since each individual, each family has relatives in the cemetery." Foucault defines heterotopia as a spatial structure that in certain circumstances invert "the set of relations that they happen to designate."[62] This I believe alludes to Rossi's first constant: a structure whose void could be charged with new function, while its "shell" recalls history through memory.

Type is a formal structure in which the knowledge of making meets the object itself. Similar to an artifact—say, a basket—an architectural object possesses an "inner formal structure" that evolves out of use and through production. Giulio Argan argues that type "is formed through a process of reducing a complex of formal variants to a common root form." The latter, he continues, "has to be understood as the interior structure of a form or as principle which contains the possibility of infinite formal variation and further structural modification of type itself."[63] Nevertheless, this formal structure attains a particular figuration through technical potentialities and tactile sensibilities of the material used. In this process, form transcends its geometrical and functional dimensions and becomes a basic unit of architectural language. In Rossi's architecture, type represents a state of architectural discourse that surpasses the boundaries of empiricism and touches the domain of memory.

Rossi's work discloses two strategies for understanding architecture through memory. His early work possesses a quality analogous to the surrealist idea of found-object: timeless geometrical

FIG. 1.4. Aldo Rossi, Modena Cemetery, plan. Courtesy NACASA.

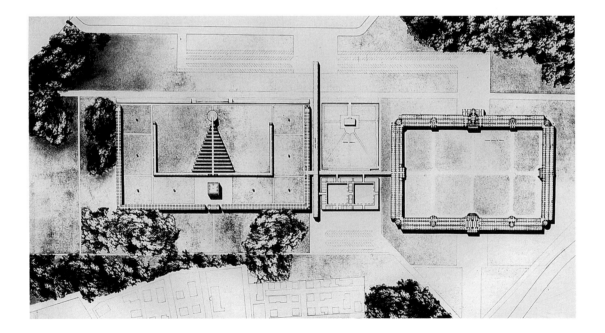

constructs whose autonomy from any single system of communicative language alludes to an ideal but a lost architecture. Everything becomes possible, Rossi wrote, "when desire is dead. . . . Almost paradoxically, at the moment when there is a loss of desire, form, project, relationship, even love are detached from us and can therefore be represented" (figure 1.5).[64] One might read in Rossi a nostalgia relevant to modernist discourse. But more important, one should read him in the context of the failure of the project of the historical avant-garde, the absence of which has offered Rossi the possibility to see things as they used to be, that is, to see the archaic in a space of mist compressed between life and death. By juxtaposing artifacts with architecture, Rossi charges his drawings with a poetic vigor palpable to the dream qualities of a displaced object. According to Peter Eisenman, Rossi's drawings "like the surrealist limp watch which combines the precision of the mechanical world with the dough-like softness of the edible work . . . become the negative image of positive reality."[65] Indeed, "L'Architecture Assassinee," a 1975 drawing dedicated to Manfredo Tafuri, discloses the material reality of a modernity whose project was supposed to generate not coherent totalities but fragmentation and constant reconstruction of the city under the spell of capital (figure 1.6). More important, his entry for "Modena Cemetery" interlocks the idea of "the house of the dead" with elementary objects, disallowing an easy association with the repertoire of architectural history, except the architecture of the Enlightenment, which is formative for Rossi's concept of autonomous architecture.[66] Here the reference to the architecture of the Enlightenment is meant to be not symbolic but indexical. Ironically, Rossi's later work moved from index to sign, from objectification to figuration, charging his forms with tactile and semantic potentialities. It is not far-fetched to associate this later body of Rossi's work with Giorgio de Chirico's paintings. The association has merit if one agrees that Rossi's entire endeavor enjoys a kind of critical dimension that one would have expected from surrealism.

Insisting on architectural métier, Rossi resists the commodification of architecture enforced by building industry. This strategy is more tangible when his design economy disappoints popular expectation from a particular building type. I am thinking of his Il Palazzo Hotel in Fukuoka, Japan, where the adjacent river would have encouraged both the conventional wisdom and the corporate architecture to provide each room with vast exposure to its scenic surrounding (figure 1.7). Rossi cancels this expecta-

tion and instead refers to the excluded windows by recessions made on the surface of the wall facing the river. There is a kind of cynicism, if you wish, at work here marking Rossi's approach to the city different from Venturi's celebratory embracement of the commercial strips of Las Vegas. According to Tafuri, Rossi's "*poiesis* refused to compromise with the reality, since the only way to return to the 'ancient house of language' was by maintaining an attitude of surly indifference."[67]

However, at the expense of accepting the metaphysical truth of body and power, Rossi's typological approach breaks the ice of the "grand plan." His vision of a fragmented city is a critique of Krier's belief that the "whole" still sustains the truth. Moreover, Rossi's analogical architecture undermines the postmodernist acceptance of the gap between signifier and signified. Yet in neorationalist architecture, metaphysics harks back through the empty floating structure of type, and through the square-shaped window frame, a Rossian device to open a different vista into the horizon of humanism.

FIG. 1.5. Aldo Rossi, "Monument to Partisana at Segrate." Courtesy NACASA.

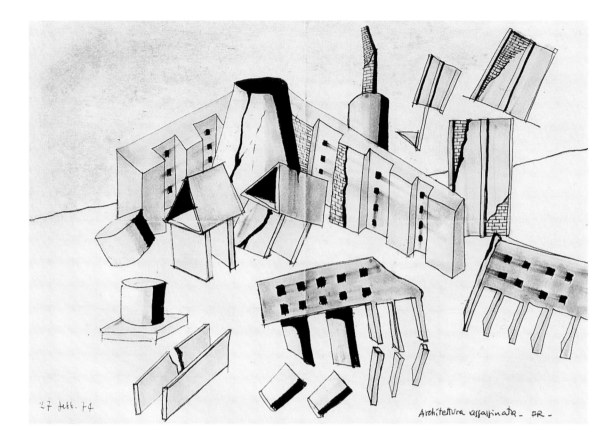

27 febb. 74

Architettura assassinata _ AR _

FIG. 1.6. Aldo Rossi,
L'Architecture
Assassinee, 1975.
Courtesy NACASA.

The postmodernist interest in replication of historical forms suggests that those forms contain the truth of prehistory, a state of innocence that is not touched by scientific and rational thinking. Structuralism arrived at the same point by closing the gap between form and content; the space where the subject is supposed to play a meaningful role. The void left by nullification of the subject is filled with a concept of type whose meaning resides in the elements of its structure. Jacques Derrida's metaphoric characterization of the structuralist understanding of a sign as "somewhat like the architecture of an inhibited or deserted city, reduced to its skeleton by some catastrophe of nature or art," is intriguing.[68] The structuralist's intention to pacify the subject became the point of departure for poststructuralist discourse. According to poststructuralists, the problem of subject is not inclusive to the discourse of the Enlightenment; it rests primarily in the textual structure of Western metaphysics.

For deconstructivists, structuralism is a veil preserving the ethos of humanism intact. At stake was—and still is—the ability to part the veil of metaphysics without revitalizing the classical tale of representation. To this end, Derrida's oeuvre offers the architect a chance to maintain a different relation with his/her work. In deconstructivist architecture, the architect functions as an operative "critic" rather than a planner. This development has made the task of architectural critic more difficult. Rather than analyzing the concrete formal and compositional aspects of a work, the critic now has to develop a metanarrative in order to disclose the architect's operative mode of thinking.[69] From now on, architecture will be the formal result of one analytical procedure among many other possible ones by which an architect can deconstruct the metaphysics of architecture.[70]

FIG. 1.7. Aldo Rossi, Il Palazzo Hotel, Fukuoka Japan. Courtesy NACASA.

In this junction, it is helpful for my argument to consider Diego Velazquez's *Las Meninas* (figure 1.8) as a precedent to the architect's operative relation to his/her work. By depicting himself in the nonpresent space of the painting, Velazquez questioned the Renaissance perception of a "spatial continuity between the space in the painting and the viewing space outside it."[71] He also undermined the established scopic regime of perspectivism. Dispensing with the perspectival convention, which resumes a one-to-one correspondence between the eye of the beholder and that of the painter, Velazquez debunked the narrative essence of the pictorial image.[72] Ironically, the importance Foucault assigned to this particular painting speaks for his interest in operative structures.

Peter Eisenman's writings and projects can be cited here as the best architectonic barometer for the above pictorial development. As early as 1969, Eisenman drew our attention to the structure of form as a fertile source for pumping meaning into architecture.[73] Cardboard architecture, a term he used to characterize his early formal experimentation, draws its theoretical strength from several sources: First, Eisenman utilizes Le Corbusier's experience in Dom-ino House and explores the virtual and implied layering produced by a particular configuration of surface (figure 1.9). Second, he nurtures his analytical reading of Le Corbusier with the plastic and spatial inventions of Cubism, Noam Chomsky's discourse on transformational linguistics, and the phenomenalogical interest in meaning and perception. These theoretical horizons are formative for Eisenman's discourse for what he calls formal structure and the deep structure of architecture. Eisenman wrote, "While formal relationships can exist in an environment at a real, actual level, where an individual is aware of them through his senses—perception, hearing, touching—they can also exist at another level in which though not seen, they can be known."[74] Without any intention of generalization, I would like to suggest that the formal implications of the Dom-ino House, the spatiality explored by Pablo Picasso and Mondrian, and finally, an understanding of architectural object as phenomenon are the common cord bringing together the very diverse formal investigation undertaken by the Five Architects (figure 1.10).[75]

In his introduction to the catalog of the Five's exhibition, Colin Rowe mapped the differences of these architects in the heroic context of the experience of modern architecture. Instead of con-

16460 - MADRID - Velasquez - Las Meninas - Gall. del Prado - Ripr. interdetta - Anderson, Roma

FIG. 1.8. Diego Velazquez, *Las Meninas*. Courtesy Art Resources, New York.

stantly endorsing the revolutionary myth, Rowe suggested that "it might be more reasonable and more modest to recognize that, in the opening years of this century, great revolutions in thought occurred and that then profound visual discoveries resulted, that these are still unexplained, and that rather than assume intrinsic change to be the prerogative of every generation, it might be more useful to recognize that certain changes are so enormous as to impose a directive which can not be resolved in any individual life span."[76] Rowe's reservation stems partly from the fact that, by the time modern architecture touched the shores of this country, its utopia content was already evaporated. Yet the desire for cultural identity, a subject that occupied many American intellec-

FIG. 1.9. Peter
Eisenman, House II,
Falk House,
Hardwick, Vermont,
1969. Courtesy
Eisenman Architects.
Photograph by Dick
Frank Studio.

tuals since World War II, had to be saturated too. This last point
is critical for Tafuri's reading of the Five. For Tafuri, the work of
the Five discloses a nostalgia for *Kulture* that America has always dreamed since recognizing herself as the Other of Europe.
Tafuri assures us that the work of the Five is not a "betrayal of
the ethical ideals of the Modern Movement. On the contrary, it
records the mood of someone who feels betrayed and reveals
fully the condition of those who still wish to make 'Architecture.'"[77] To give a new turn to this wish, the later work of the
Five departed from phenomenology in favor of either a semio-

logical reading of architecture[78] or an Eisenmanesque emphasis on text as the deep structure of form. The latter found its thematics in the space opened by poststructuralist critique of both semiological understanding of social structures and the phenomenological obsession with vision.[79] In fact, Rowe's disenchantment with deconstructive architecture also has to do with the latter's strategic shift from object to the process, a move undermining the formalistic reading of architecture that was at the heart of Rowe's discourse.

Eisenman's shift can be checked in his project for "Biocenter for the University of Frankfurt."[80] Here, following the Cannaregio project, the site is one of the two important factors informing the significatory process (figure 1.11). Another factor is the geometry of DNA, the deep structure, which for Eisenman possesses the potentiality to reduce the gap between function and representation. In the process, Eisenman utilizes themes and notions instrumental for synthetic cubism. Frontality, cutting, and fragmenta-

FIG. 1.10. Piet Monderian, *Composition in White, Black, and Red*, 1936. Courtesy Museum of Modern Art, New York.

tion (not fragment) provided the critical groundwork for the formation of this project. With its rational organization, the front or public elevation is compatible with the contextual character of the rear side. While the existing buildings and the underground service core induced Eisenman to consider disjunction as an appropriate theme for generating meaning. The fragmentation of the main unit opens a space for the spine; together, they initiate a different compositional unity. The complex relationship between the labs and the spine might be associated with Louis Kahn's concept of served and service spaces. While Kahn used the idea of served/service spaces to express the myth of Order, Eisenman sees it as a syntax for the fiction of disjunction. The aesthetic voyeurism of the Frankfurt project, and the linear posture of the spine, later would become important marks for Eisenman's architecture (figure 1.12).

Myth, fiction, and kitsch are three appropriate metaphors to characterize the state of postfunctionalist architecture. This proposition has a merit when one considers the fact that myth, fiction, and kitsch each speak for the loss of the real through a metalanguage. Moreover, these metaphors unfold a discourse that at best could be characterized as a remedy to the deterritorialization of the language of modern architecture. In the paradox of Rowe and Tafuri's reading of the Five, Kahn and Venturi surprisingly present the two poles of a reasonable and modest approach to the experience of modernity, a direction Rowe expected postmodern architects to pursue anyway.[81] Eisenman, instead, explores the potential unfoldings of a decentered subject through operative techniques.

The idea of the architect as an operative critic has further connotations. The esteem for the childhood of history, so dear to structuralists, is mediated radically by deconstructivist architecture. One might argue that the archaism implied in deconstructivist theories is motivated by the concept of "play":[82] a narrative structure pushing the foundations of rational thinking to its limit. It is also a reminder of the elementarist logic at work in John Hedjuk of the Five, and in Eisenman's search for the logical structure of form, the result of which was to characterize the relationship between actual structure (consciousness?) and the deep structure (unconsciousness?) as "quiet primitive." One thinks of Georges Bataille's writings, or the interest of early modern artists in primitive art. Yet, as an ideological aspect of postmodernism, this "play" ignores the materiality of meaning

FIG. I. II. Peter
Eisenman, "Biocenter
for the University of
Frankfurt," presenta-
tion model, View
from East, Eisenman
Architects. Photograph
by Dick Frank Studio.

and registers an abstract state of myth, although on a different
level.[83] To do this, deconstructivist architecture "disturbs" the
purity of traditional forms and the everlasting structure of type.
In his introduction to MoMA's catalog on deconstructivist architecture, Mark Wigley emphasizes this aspect of their work:

> It [deconstructivist work] exploits the weaknesses in the
> tradition in order to disturb rather than overthrow it. Like
> the modern avant-garde, it attempts to be disturbing, alien-

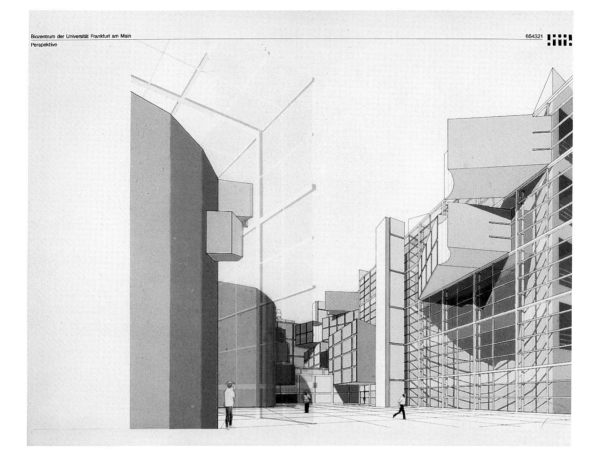

FIG. 1.12. Peter
Eisenman, "Biocenter
for the University of
Frankfurt," courtyard
perspective, Eisenman
Architects. Photo-
graph by Dick Frank
Studio.

ating. But not from the retreat of the avant-garde, not from
the margins. Rather, it occupies, and subverts the center.
This work is not fundamentally different from the ancient
tradition it subverts. It does not abandon the tradition.
Rather, it inhibits the center of the tradition in order to
demonstrate that architecture is always infected, that pure
form has always been contaminated. By inhabiting the tradition fully, obeying its inner logic more rigorously than
ever before, these architects discover certain dilemmas
within the tradition that are missed by those who sleepwalk
through it.[84]

This line of thinking could be interpreted as a radical critique of
modernism, especially those architectural theories that rejected
tradition in its totality. It also could be read as an attack on the
neoconservative esteem for reappraisal of tradition, attributed to
Jurgen Habermas.[85] It is true that Habermas's criticism arises out

of his belief in the possible completion of the project of modernity. Nevertheless, there are other concerns related to Wigley's statement that should be addressed here.

Architecture has always been subject to the metaphysics of religion or the state. Indeed, there has never been, and may not exist, any "pure" architectural form. But, on what basis could one be convinced that beyond the Derridian problematization of a given text, deconstruction of the metaphysics of architecture can really take place? And second, what would guarantee that the neo-avant-garde's act of subversion of the "center" itself remains immune from the metaphysics of the system? Interestingly enough, speaking of deconstruction as a strategic position, Derrida discloses that deconstruction might "confirm, consolidate, or 'relever,' at a depth which is ever more sure, precisely that which we claim to be deconstructing. A continuous explication which precedes the opening risks falling into a close autism."[86] One thinks of dadaism and the very fact of its nihilism, a strategy that eventually turned into an appendage to what it intended to negate in the first place.[87]

Beyond its ideological problematic, one also wonders how to justify the deconstructivist's relative and unpredictable formal play. Is theirs the return of the historical avant-garde—emptied of its political content—which in its attempt to entertain a prehistoric mode of thinking has no choice but to cultivate the fruits of a rationally organized technology of simulation? I will discuss the significance of technology for architecture in the context of the project of the historical avant-garde; however, it is important to stress the point that technology "appears as the cause of a general process of dehumanization that includes both the displacement of humanistic cultural ideas in favor of a modeling of the human subject based on the science and on rationally controlled productive capabilities, and a process of accentuated rationalization at the level of social and political organization that reveals the features of the wholly administered and regulated society that Adorno describes and criticizes."[88] If technology is a threat to metaphysics only in the realm of appearances, then deconstructivist architecture is nothing but euphoria. One might modify this charge by recalling Benjamin's words and conclude that the neo-avant-garde architecture is nothing but a "wish-image" in which there is "a positive striving to set themselves off from the outdated—that means, however, the most recent past." But for Benjamin, the collective consciousness internalizes the new to "produce the utopia that has left its traces in thousands of configurations of life from permanent buildings to fleeting images."[89] The apparent formal similarities between deconstructivist architecture and Russian constructivism suggest that, having no other choice, deconstructivists set their work apart from the late modern architecture to "return" to the collective unconsciousness of the historical avant-garde.[90] This strategic move, however, fails to respond to Benjamin's demand from the surrealists, whose work was supposed to "win the energies of intoxication for the revolution" and to evoke the hope embedded in the early childhood of modernity. In this paradox, one could argue that the return of postmodern architecture to the experience of modernity is empty of any political dimension and leaves current architecture disarmed against the forces of commodification.

What brings postmodernism, neorationalism, and deconstructivism together is the idea of the "death of man," to use a phrase coined by Foucault.[91] In this lacuna, the architect takes refuge in the autonomous body of type, or becomes the agent of an operational form. Apropos of this, two developments take place. The first is the way in which the idea of "the death of man" affects architectural discourse. Postfunctionalist architecture demonstrates a sharp turn of interest from Le Corbusier's idea that "the plan is the generator" toward an analysis of the final product. This development started with the work of the Five, where the plan is reduced to a compressed two-dimensional composition of lines and points, the configuration of which dispenses with any three-dimensional reading of the lived-space. In the absence of "man" as the embodiment of a constructed space, the plan is turned into the site of a complex process of decomposition and disjunction. The second development concerns the deconstructivists' theoretical justification of the above metamorphosis. Deconstructivism locates the metaphysics of architecture within postmodern historicism, and in the self-referentiality of modernism. However, accepting the impossibility of surmounting metaphysics, deconstructivism allocates its energy to "dislocation." According to Eisenman, "to dislocate" means to question the institutional limits of architecture.[92] In practice, this strategy pumps new blood into the old body of formalism and discards significant themes such as the relationship between architecture and the city, and the tectonic. At this point, the critical edge of deconstructivist discourse turns into its problematic: Relieved from the fiction of humanism, architecture becomes the subject matter of the architect's operational analytic.

By restoring a place for the subject, deconstructivist architecture overcomes the structuralist synchronic understanding of history. But the price architecture pays for this resolution is significant. In deconstructivist discourse the architect performs a twofold function: at one level, he/she is engaged in a process of self-criticism, a critique of the historical subject; he/she is seen as the mirror image of the authoritarian self-centered humanist subject. Reciprocally, the subject resumes a critical relation with the "object" and with the cultural artifacts and texts as well. At this level, the subject aims to deconstruct the metaphysical grounds of architecture, including the Renaissance belief in the centrality of the body, and the scopic regime of perspectivism. Moving in between these two critical zones, the architect dismisses Kahn's idea of "what the building wants to be" and reduces architecture to a reflective image displaying epistomological debates, a text that, as Barthes would say, is "a multi-dimensional space in which a variety of writings, none of them original, blend and clash. The text is a tissue of quotations drawn from the innumerable centers of cultures."[93] The result for architecture is a state of parody analogous to the predicament of a fugitive who enters a dead-end alley. Peculiar intellectual skills are needed in order to turn the situation to advantage. As Eisenman has come to realize, architecture (among other disciplines) may not be a fertile realm for the operational rules of deconstructivism.[94] It is not by chance that at the end, the better choice is the "Thin Blue Line," that is, a constant oscillation between the realm of truth and untruth, a dead-end premise in itself.

The "Other"[95]

At present, with our situation bringing to mind the historical debate between Benjamin and Adorno,[96] we need to ask whether it is desirable to distance art and architecture from the aesthetic values of the culture industry. Of course we are speaking of a sense of autonomy that is potentially different from "l'art pour l'art." The latter was seen by Adorno as a resistance against the nihilism of technology; however, as far as the dialectical continuation of modernism is concerned, a semiautonomous position for architecture does have its merits.

For Adorno, art has a twofold essence, "being both an autonomous entity and a social fact."[97] Indeed, one might argue that in the context of capitalism, where the cutting edge of commodification is in command, a critical discourse has no other choice but to set forth the dialectics of rupture and reconciliation. This position recalls Benjamin's anti-instrumental affirmation of technology; a subject whose relevance to the thematics of postmodernity could be mapped in the present concern for the death of the author and the liquidation of the historical ground for grand narratives. This reading is significant for an architecture that avoids both repeating the tale of classicism and replaying the Prometheus myth of technological redemption. It also questions the predilection of Western thought, conceiving truth as a function of time. Again, Jencks's polemics against modern architecture could be presented here as one manifestation of this phenomenon. Another example is implied in Krier's esteem for the classical and his criticism of both the modern and postmodern architecture. However, a standstill perception of time displays another kind of orientation: its dynamism neither points forward nor backward. In regard to the question of "temporal distance," we can agree with Giambattista Vico that the externality introduced by time can be excluded through the power of imagination and memory.[98] By the same token, in dissociating itself from the so-called spirit of time, architecture can sustain a critical position by recollecting the idea of "inhabiting"—discussed by Martin Heidegger—a theme whose absence in post-1960s architecture is problematic.

Designating the formal traits and canonic rules of classical architecture as the only subjects of architecture, postmodernism remains in the domain of classical discourse: it separates architecture from building and crowns it with metaphysics. Reduced to a single edifice, architecture falls short of its critical role as the harbinger of the construction of the life-world. Such is the state of architecture revealed in postmodern simulation of historical forms, in the neorationalist emphasis on typology, and in the theoretical vigor of deconstructivist architecture. In these three architectural tendencies, the weight of classical discourse precedes the idea of inhabiting. Although Heidegger spoke of the Greek experience of dwelling, one should not associate "inhabiting" with the primitive or vernacular state of architecture where totalization is in command.[99] This word of caution is necessary because in thinking of Heidegger, and in Heidegger himself, as Derrida reminds us, there is the risk to suppress the desire for the other in favor of totality.[100] The aim rather should be directed toward a dialogue between location and spaces, or, in Piero Derossi's words, to demonstrate the interplay between locality and district through disjointure.[101] Somewhat similar to Adorno's discourse on "particular,"[102] our interest in locality focuses on the ways that it holds a picture of the district (totality). In this dialogue between locality and totality, we are also informed of the transitoriness of the idea of inhabiting. Meaning that, rather than preserving the elements of inhabiting, one should transform them in a process of negative affirmation. In Vattimo's words, one should recode locality by exposing it to the general process of secularization.

For Heidegger, the thematics of inhabiting precede architecture, in the same way that language precedes a child. Language provides a sense of belonging to a place or community. It also enables human beings to relate to the broader horizon of life, encompassing the spheres of sky, divinity, mortals, and earth. Heidegger evokes the dialogue between location and space when he reflects on the way a building relates to dwelling. In his text, "dwelling and thinking," Heidegger suggests that, place making is revealed in "the act of gathering of the bridge." Yet Heidegger's bridge is empty of any specific references to its technical or functional aspects, and even of its symbolic or textual dimensions. For Heidegger, the bridge becomes a dwelling when it brings to our attention the separateness of the two banks and the way the land stretches along the stream. "A location comes into existence only by virtue of the bridge," when *construction* gathers the sky, divinity, mortals, and earth around the stream. One can take Heidegger and lament for the metaphysics of place and the genius loci. One rather should take Heidegger and reconstruct a given place according to the ways we postmoderns experience Heidegger's fourfold. Again I am thinking of the process of demythification of values through secularization and understanding architecture not through its form but through the mental structure of a given time.

Thus, location designates proximity but not the idea of home. While contextualism and historicism, for example, imprison the concept of proximity in the metaphysical truth of a place, and deconstructivism attracts the eye to its playful forms, Heidegger draws one's attention to the dialogue between nearness and distance, even to the question of homelessness and the impossibility of dwelling. "What if man's homelessness," Heidegger asks, "consisted in this, that man still does not even think of the real plight of dwelling as the plight?"[103]

Heidegger's text offers no solution to the question of how to articulate the architecture of dwelling. But he introduces a way of thinking that, without undermining the importance of technology, is radically different from the nineteenth-century discourse on the truth of material and construction. It also saves architecture from the analogies that functionalists would draw between architecture and machine, as part of their response to the crisis of the object.[104] Vattimo's concept of "project" is among the theoretical works closest to Heidegger. Vattimo contends that a building becomes a dwelling when it is revealed as a dis-joint, "an intermediary zone between an enrootedness in a place—in a community—and an explicit consciousness of multiplicity."[105]

Again, in the dialectical relationship between the particular and the whole, the particular does not encapsulate the "truth of tradition" in type, nor in the symbolic pastiche of contextualism. Rather, it articulates the tectonic by recollecting the culture of building.[106] The latter encompasses themes that have accumulated in the historical work, both in theory and in practice. These include thematic dualities such as inside/outside, structure/ornament, column/wall, and so forth, as well as the hermeneutics of their construction.[107] Here, recollection does not intend to correct what went wrong with a certain theme in such a place and time, or to construct a nostalgic remembrance of some forgotten past. Instead, recollection is a counter memory that distorts—to use Vattimo's word—the unified cultural experience of the West, or any other region intending to represent a source of authority and harmony.[108] In this process of recoding, architecture accommodates itself to the existing subjective and objective conditions of life, making room for openness to hold sway, a process that "among other things, grants the appearance of things present to which human dwelling sees itself consigned." On the other hand, "making-room prepares for things the possibility to belong to their relevant wither and, out of this, to each other."[109] Accordingly, the idea of project provides an architectonic expression through which "one recognizes oneself, not only in the sense that there is a perception of shared values, but also in the sense that one recognizes where one is, that there are distinguishing marks."[110] These marks function like a dis-joint, relating a constructed form to a greater whole in which the context of contemporary life is experienced.

The dialogical relationship between locality and totality is better understood if one recalls Heidegger's reading of the Greek temple. The temple portrays nothing, Heidegger says; it "stands there, first gives to things their look and to men their outlook on themselves."[111] Thus, the meaning of the temple is perceived not in the semantic content of its language nor in the moral and ethical values of its dormant living conditions. Rather, the "thingness" of the temple repudiates the representational discourse and touches off the conflict between the setting up and the setting forth of the work. I would suggest that the thingness of the temple alludes to a process of nihilism through which the darkness of the earth is revealed within the domain of the light and the sky. Here the light and the sky speak for the life-world, which, in our epoch, is defined and redefined by the process of secularization. Thus, a critical thinking of architecture is possible only if one subjects the culture of building to the process of secularization. By doing so, one also avoids harmonizing the dialectics between structure and ornament, for example, and yet is able to "weaken" the architect's subjective intentions. Discussing Mies and Loos, Massimo Cacciari reminds us that "truth of a project cannot be understood as a manifestation of the agent's intention. . . . the work does not produce truth either in or by itself."[112] Rather, the work achieves its truth and "thingness" only when the architect, similar to the artifex-constructor of the Greek state, is at the service of both the work and the *polis*. The concept of architect/servant is more promising for a critical theory of architecture than a postmodernism that simulates historical forms, or a deconstructivism that indulges in formalistic operations. In this paradox, the architect abandons the operative strategies of deconstructivism and engages in a rescue mission to save the Ur-forms, the suppressed elements of history.[113] This is indeed the only project that my critical reading of the thematics of postmodern architecture pursues in this book.

Yet, in the rift between the setting up and setting forth of the work, the metaphysical content of the concept of inhabiting is drained while at the same time it is accepted with resignation.[114] This tension suggests a different reading of the modern experience; instead of a dialectical harmonization, one is driven to believe that conflict is never dialectically reconcilable. In this horizon, architecture rejects any set of a priori rules, even the ones resulting from the process of deconstruction. As Vattimo contends, this line of thinking posits a "weak thought" architecture, one that remains aloof from the bankrupting of the metanarrative and the resurfacing of the bourgeois state through its own problematics.

There is nothing exciting or nostalgic about this architecture. Nor is there any futuristic credo, shouting, "Down with the past!" However, it illuminates the continuous perception of the surviving structure of architecture residing, not in a coded form, but in the culture of building. The culture of building makes it possible to see tradition as "vestiges, models that are hidden and distorted and yet profoundly present."[115] More important, it leads us to come to terms with what dwelling is. This is a weak-thought architecture that, without imposing a grand narrative or merging into the logic of technology, provides the opportunity to appropriate architecture through a human being's experience of the life-world. It is a sort of therapeutic architecture, if you wish, by which one might heal the rift caused by the crisis of the object. Only in this paradox could I risk accommodating the next two chapters to a discussion of Le Corbusier and Kahn respectively. Le Corbusier for the obvious importance of the Dom-ino House for postfunctionalist architecture, Kahn for a body of work that simultaneously bridges and separates the banks of modern and postmodern architecture. Kahn's is an artifice of disjoint whose importance remains hidden from the spectacle it brings together.

Dom-ino and Its Trajectory   2
Metamorphosis Deconstructed

During long periods of history, the mode of human perception changes
with humanity's entire mode of existence.

—Walter Benjamin,
"The Work of Art in the Age of Mechanical Reproduction"

Walter Benjamin's essay discloses the profound impact of technology on our perceptual experience and the ways the dialectics
between visuality and construction nurture architecture. I do not
intend to analyze Benjamin's seminal piece here but to underline
his ambivalent approach to technology. Contrary to contemporary architects' gratification with the formal and optical potentialities of modern technology, Benjamin believed that "buildings
are appropriated in twofold manner: by use and by perception—
or rather, by touch and sight."[1] And he related the tactile aspect
to habit or use in such a way that it becomes determinant for the
optical appropriation of architecture. Discussing film and the
visual distraction caused by montage, Benjamin again stressed
the importance of distracted habit over sight. What drives me
into Benjamin is his belief in the presence of a kind of collective
experience in technology that should be given equal attention
along the technical one. I would like to discuss the criticality of
this subject for modern architecture as well as for the impact of
Le Corbusier's Dom-ino House on postmodern architecture.

According to Benjamin, "Only a thoughtless observer would
deny that there are correspondences between the world of modern technology and the archaic symbol-world of mythologies."[2]
Stressing the anthropomorphic dimension of machine products,
Benjamin's statement also alludes to a methodology for historical
work already present in Sigfried Giedion's *Bauen in Frankreich*.
For Giedion, the basic feature of the architecture of early twentieth century could be found in buildings of the 1850s, especially
in arcades and exhibition halls. Giedion stated: "We read today's
life, and today's forms out of the life and apparently secondary,
forgotten forms of that era."[3] Benjamin's reflection on modern
architecture in general and the avant-garde in particular has

some affinity with Giedion, and I would like to associate these considerations with Le Corbusier in two ways:[4] First, the grave attention Le Corbusier gave to the work of engineering, the exhibition halls, bridges, and grain silos, and his speculation on the aesthetic significance of these buildings for modern architecture.[5] Second, the idea of "mechanical selection,"[6] through which Le Corbusier saw the continuity of the logic of craftsmanship in modern technology. Reducing the historicality of modern technology to the technical, Le Corbusier dismissed Benjamin's remark on the loss of aura: the empathic connection between the body and the material world, and the craft quality of a cultic art that embodies the work's ability to return the gaze of the spectator.

Benjamin's argument on the loss of aura alludes to the crisis of the object caused by the mechanization of production process. To avoid a simple affirmation of technology, Benjamin "espoused the technique of the work of art as a sobering antidote to mystifications of creativity"[7] and questioned the positivistic reading of technology so dear to most architects of this century. Yet, no contemporary architect has articulated the implications of machine for architecture better than Le Corbusier. This subject occupies such an important place in *Towards a New Architecture* that most historians could not avoid seeing Le Corbusier and the entire modern architecture apart from it. Le Corbusier's indulgence with technology and Purism need no emphasis here. I would rather confine myself to the ways that some historians— Colin Rowe the most consistent among them—have turned Le Corbusier's pictorialism into a critical tool for reading architecture. This methodology dismissed other topos of modernity that might have nurtured Le Corbusier's architecture.[8]

I also intend to discuss Le Corbusier's contribution to postmodern architecture. To this end, I would like to examine the thematic sharing between modern and postmodern architecture with those of the classical architecture. My analysis of these three architectural discourses arises from a point of view originated by architecture itself. Le Corbusier's Dom-ino has not only set up a critical criterion by which a different reading of classical architecture has become possible but it has paved the way to formulate the vicissitudes of postfunctionalist architecture as well. Accordingly a discussion of the implications of technology in contemporary architectural debate is instrumental for mapping the thematics of an architecture different from postmodern simulative language.

Since the 1960s, some have put into practice what Charles Jencks once prematurely celebrated as "the death of modern architecture." The general fascination with this prophecy was so strong that few architects and theoreticians were able to maintain a different position. In addition to the drastic changes taking place in global sociopolitics, technology has played a significant role in establishing such a claim, one major result of which was to pull architecture further into the ostentatious whirlpool of cultural commodification. In the era of mass communication and political conservatism of the early 1980s, there was less room left to expose the affinity of postmodern architecture with its immediate past.

While purposely avoiding a philosophical discussion of the implications of "modernity," it is appropriate to stress the point that, for me, modern architecture is not merely synonymous with the use of new materials or techniques. Nor do I agree with those scholars who conceive and theorize modernity from within the purview of the crisis of modern science.[9] Instead, I share the view that locates the genealogy of our modern perceptual world in the domain where the mythical distance between gaze and object was obscured by what Martin Heidegger called "world picturing."[10] Certain aspects of Heidegger's ideas on "picturing" were already present in perspectival representation: the fact that the image stands between the viewer and the object viewed and that the object must be positioned in front of a subject (frontality), these considerations, together, constitute a visual system by which one not only sees the picture but "gets the picture" as well. Realist painting and its contemporaneous architecture were seen and constructed, or composed, according to figure/ground relationships in which the depth issue was essential for the corporeality of the work. Leon Battista Alberti's discourse in *De Pictoria*[11] established a visuality assuring the prevalence of perspectivism in painting. An early idea of "world picturing" in architecture can be associated with Alberti's transplantation of the image of a triumphal arch over the facade of an existing masonry building. This was certainly a leap toward the modern discourse of representation.

As in painting, so in architecture, a drive to overcome the phenomenon of depth was entertained by cubism and by the aesthetics of a concept of making that is pertinent to steel frame structure. While cubist painting charges the surface with depth, the frame provides architecture the possibility to tear apart the consistency between a load-bearing wall and its function as a spatial enclosure. Besides denying the coherency between space and structure (typical of masonry structures), the frame in Le Corbusier's architecture is a conceptual means by which one can articulate architecture in the index of modernity. The plan in his work, however, did not make a total break with perspectivism; both in cubism and Dom-ino, the Cartesian grid sustains its life under planes covered and occasionally laid in between the structure of the frame. The De Stijl group also approached the idea of frame as a means to eliminate the limits separating architecture from painting. For them the time was ripe to seek a unity between architecture and painting. This proposition was based on the belief that architecture and paintings are now conceivable in terms of their essential elements, walls and painted planes respectively. Yve-Alain Bois reminds us of the ways in which the De Stijl architecture treated vertical and horizontal planes to camouflage the anatomical (tectonic?) aspects of building.[12] But the exchange between painting and architecture attained its critical dimension in Le Corbusier's Dom-ino, the result of which provided a new formal repository for post-Corbusian architecture.

Frame structures were used in buildings by the 1920s both in this country and in Europe. Colin Rowe correctly differentiates the Chicago frame, for example, from the Dom-ino. For Rowe, the former system evolved in response to multifarious pragmatic needs, including the problem of density and technical efficiency enforced by the Chicago fire. Dom-ino, instead, "is not so much a structure as an icon, an object of faith which is to act as a guarantee of authenticity, an outward sign of a new order, an assurance against lapse into private license, a discipline by means of which an invertraterressionism can be reduced to the appearance of reason."[13] In architectural discourse, Le Corbusier's Dom-ino assigns a particular depth to architectural representation. Like most artistic trends in this century, Dom-ino is a point of view, a way of seeing and making (figure 2.1). Designed in 1914, Dom-ino is the best manifesto of the modern attitude toward nature, technology, and cultural life. Dom-ino is not merely a solution to the problems imposed by new building techniques; it discloses Le Corbusier's obsession with painting and his praise for technology. In this context, the Dom-ino frames a perceptual horizon influenced by analytical cubism and machine aesthetics. Through his paintings, Le Corbusier came to share the figure-ground relationship essential for cubism.[14] Dwelling upon the notion of simultaneity, the cubist figure-ground relationship chal-

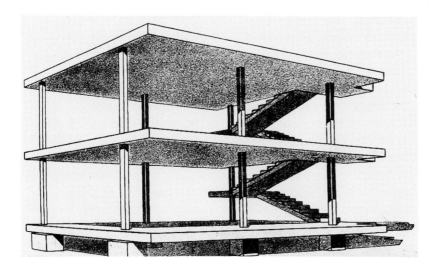

FIG. 2.1. Le Corbusier, Dom-ino Frame. © 1995 ARS, New York/ SPADEM, Paris.

lenged the conventional body of representation. Maurice Merleau-Ponty, in "Phenomenology of Perception," suggests that some modern painting alludes to a primordial unity between various senses.[15] An analogy between the phenomenal transparency of Villa Garche, noticed by Rowe,[16] and the ambiguous play of different layers in Picasso's 1919 *Guitar* also speak for the same point. However, the transplantation of a pictorial experience into architecture could not have been possible without the potentialities offered by technology.[17]

Novel achievements in engineering gave Le Corbusier the chance to conceive Dom-ino as the "deep structure" over which one could hang the planes representing the aesthetics of purism and the precision of machines. Le Corbusier solidified a purist vision of architecture, the properties of which are implied in what he called "object-type"—a neutral structure molded with the stylistic needs of machine technology. Object-type "condense natural needs and actions into the streamlined tools of single functions in actuality."[18] This was indeed Le Corbusier's answer to the crisis of the object and its implications for painting and architecture. It was a concept by which he and Ozanfant could distinguish the underlying structure of any given object—the logical economy of a form—from its ephemeral and outward dressing: "If we eliminate from our hearts and minds all dead concepts in regard to the houses and look at the question from a critical and objective point of view," Le Corbusier said, "we shall arrive at the 'House-Machine,' the mass-produced house, healthy (and morally so too) and beautiful in the same way that the working tools and instruments which company our existence are beautiful."[19] Again one thinks of the idea of mechanical selection and the continuity of the logos of manual fabrication in machines.

The specific implications of the Dom-ino for architecture should be stressed, too: the piloties, and the setback of columns from the edges of the concrete slab, and their affects on architectural form. Peter Eisenman was the first to discuss these aspects of the Dom-ino frame. Pointing to the traces of humanism in Rowe's reading of Le Corbusier, Eisenman's early work consolidated the thematics of a postfunctionalist architecture. For Eisenman, the Dom-ino is a self-referential sign whose basic elements, three horizontal slabs, six boxlike footings, the six linear columns, and one staircase, disclose "a Modernist condition of architecture."[20] In this context the Dom-ino is seen as a diagram where every other intentionality is brushed aside except its objecthoodness. Eisenman's correct criticism of Rowe, however, leaves us with the question of whether a "formal" analysis is the only way to avoid the humanist discourse on representation. An alternative point of view might flourish if one examines the ways Le Corbusier's architecture differs from the classical. The Dom-ino opened a perceptual field the horizon of which discards the classical concern for a one-to-one correspondence between planimetric organization and the limits of masonry construction, a subject I will further elaborate shortly. This development gave Le Corbusier the opportunity to treat horizontal and vertical surfaces as "contour," which according to him is free of all constrains, and there is no longer "any question of custom, nor of tradition nor of construction nor of adaptation to utilitarian needs."[21]

Le Corbusier saw the relationship between the plan and the facade in a different light. In classical architecture, the overall correspondence between the compositional order of a building and the major axis of its plan was part of the logos of making. Most of Le Corbusier's villas acknowledge the ordering logic of the classical planimetric organization. Reflecting on ancient architecture, he stated: "from the very start the plan implies the method of construction to be used; the architect is above all an engineer," and he continued, "a plan proceeds from within to without, for a house or a palace is an organism comparable to a living being."[22] Le Corbusier's belief that "the plan is generator" could be associated with some aspects of classical architecture. Following Rudolf Wittkower, Rowe investigated the impact of mathematics for architecture to disclose the consistency between formal logic of Le Corbusier's plans and that of Andrea Palladio's.[23] Rowe's analysis, however, dismisses the point that by emphasizing the mechanical selection, Le Corbusier engulfed his thought in the perspectival regime in which the ground-plan is the plane from which every compositional element, including the vertical ones, are projected. The grid expressed in the horizontal and vertical axis of the Dom-ino induces a perception of space analogous to "straited space." Recalling a woven fabric, Gilles Deleuze argues that a straited space "is constituted by two kinds of parallel elements; in the simplest case, there are vertical and horizontal elements, and the two intertwine, intersect perpendicularity."[24] While every other frame structure is coordinated and structured by the two axes of a Cartesian grid, Le Corbusier's use of frame enforced a diagonal directionality that is absent in most of the Renaissance architecture. In fact, every major plan of Le Corbusier's villas is organized according to the Deleuze's characterization of the straited space. The plans of both the Villa Savoye and the Villa at Garche, for example, are similar to a woven fabric in that they can be extended only along their lateral grid axis (figure 2.2). In Le Corbusier's utilization of the Dom-ino, the facade in one side of the building is attached to the columns, while on the opposite direction, the facade is hung from the suspended part of the slab. The projective position of the slab here is not meant to question the constructive rules of perspectivism; it rather frees the exterior enclosure from the vertical datum of the column. Therefore, enclosure in Le Corbusier's architecture is subject to a design strategy totally different from those initiated by the exigencies of the plan and its structural datum, or for that matter from the utilitarian needs of the space behind.

Moreover, Le Corbusier's concept of the facade undermines the classical notion of *techne* whose aesthetic is disclosed in Andrea Palladio's recommendation for the design of villas. According to Palladio:

> The rooms ought to be distributed on each side of the entry and hall, and it is to be observed that those on the right correspond with those on the left, so that the fabric may be the same in one place as in the other, and that the walls may equally bear the burden of the roof; because if the rooms are made large in one part, and small in the other, the latter will be more fit to resist the weight, by reason of the nearness of the walls, and the former more weak, which will produce in time very great inconveniences, and ruin the whole work.[25]

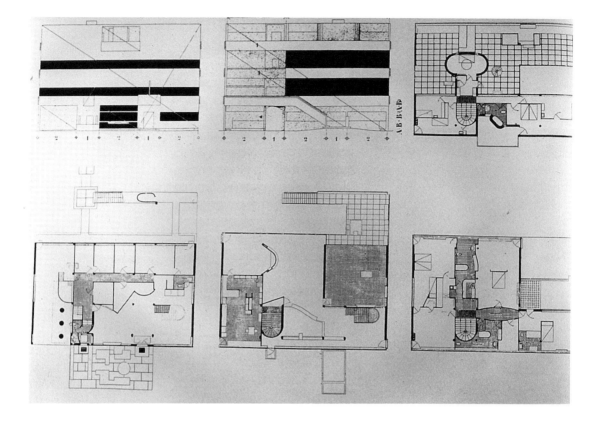

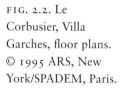

For Palladio, the integrity between aesthetic valorization and structural rationality is imperative for the classical discourse on composition. This point was also addressed by Alberti. It is appropriate to present the ideas of Palladio and Alberti here because their discourse is important for understanding of not only Le Corbusier but the continuity of humanist discourse in the work of postfunctionalist architecture in general, and that of the New York Five, in particular.

In his discourse on lineaments, Alberti argues that the "whole matter of building is composed of lineaments and structure" and that their purpose "lies in finding the correct, infallible way of joining and fitting together those lines and angles which define and enclose the surface of the building."[26] Here, "the surface of the building" refers to a constructed mass that must wait to be covered and finished by lineaments. Thus, indifferent to purpose and structure, the lineaments become the sole content of an atectonic form "conceived in the mind, made up of lines and angles, and perfected in the learned intellect and imagination."[27] Since then, a distinction between construction and appearance remains problematic. Le Corbusier's contribution to this problem is articulated in his reflections on "the regulating lines." One might also interpret Alberti's thought on lineaments in association with the distinction he made between architecture and building, or between architecture and the geometrical mass. As noted above, it is part of the architect's imagination to elevate and translate a constructed form into "architecture." However, within a masonry construction there exist certain predetermined limitations to the scope of lineaments. These limitations have to do with the metaphysics of masonry construction, if you wish, through which a load-bearing wall must follow the lines of its foundation. The congruity between the facade and the plan of a Renaissance church, or the sectional organization of a villa, as discussed by Palladio, are in part an architectonic expression of this limitation, too. The desire to escape from this confinement was fulfilled, not in the interior space of a church—lit by the light pouring from its dome—but in the horizontal section, the plan, where the form and direction of its masonry walls and their final volumetric expression recall the general outlines of a cross. This relationship between the mass and the plan anticipated Le Corbusier's dictum that the plan is the generator. It also relates Le Corbusier to an Albertian distinction between appearance and construction.

To recode the duality of construction and appearance, Le Corbusier had to do more than just repeat Alberti. After all, Alberti's thought was conceivable only in the analogies that one could make between the divine life and the everyday life of the Renaissance. Moreover, Le Corbusier had to rearticulate Alberti's association of architecture with the body. These are the general outlines of a project visible "between the lines" of Le Corbusier's *Towards a New Architecture*.

Against the compositional monism of the classical architecture, Dom-ino discloses a dialogue between disintegration and composition. This paradox finds its architectonic language in the sectional organization of both the Villa Savoye and the Carpenter Center (figure 2.3). In these buildings the ramp disintegrates the Platonic corporeality of the building. As a design economy, *promenade architectural* unfolds a perception of architecture in which the mass is dissolved in favor of the volume and a dynamic sense of visuality.[28] *Promenade architectural* empties the internal solid body of the mass and generates a spatiality unprecedented in the classical architecture. In the Villa Savoye the ascending person along the ramp is driven one step further from

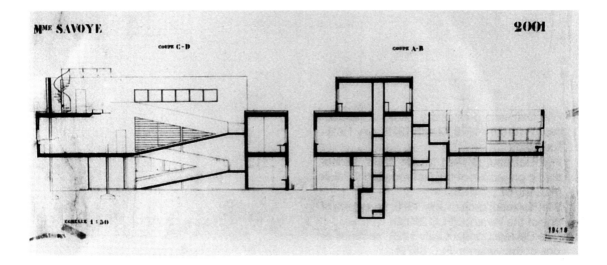

COUPE C-D   COUPE A-B

ECHELLE 1:50   19418

FIG. 2.3. Le Corbusier, Villa Savoye, section. © 1995 ARS, New York/ SPADEM, Paris.

the concept of frontality so dear to classical architecture. A person entering this villa, instead of pulling his/her body along a path perpendicular to the main facade of the building, emerges into the building from below along a vertical axis. This upward movement dematerializes the volume connecting the piloti to the roof garden.[29] The body also experiences a sense of lightness stimulated by the piloti and the fact that the mass is perceived through the surface enclosure. These design strategies hollowed out the volume and disintegrated the mass but came short of deconstructing the plan where a perspectival view of making is laden. However, the architectonic elements of a disintegrated object, held together loosely in Le Corbusier's stress on plan could have no destination except idle drifting in the fragmentary spatial images induced by current microchip technology. Eisenman was right to remind us of the "futility of objects,"[30] permissible in the process of disjunction and decomposition, and its eventual turn into the modus operandi of the post-Corbusian discourse. And yet Le Corbusier seems to be aware of this transgression. His later work took some steps away from the Purist implications of the Dom-ino frame. The body of work invested in most of his architecture of the 1930s, such as Maison Week-End and Vacation House, and more so in the Ronchamp, are devoid of the duality of appearance and construction I have presented here (figures 2.4 and 2.5).[31] In Ronchamp, for example, there is a homology between the mass and the plan peculiar to the classical logic of making, if not analogous to vernacular buildings. Here Le Corbusier utilizes the idea of "mechanical selection" to transpass the historical boundaries posed by the experience of modernity and the loss of the aura. The Ronchamp entertains a kind of symbolism that Tafuri could consider as an "encounter between purism and surrealism." For Tafuri, the late Le Corbusier "practically discovered the crisis of the crisis of the object."[32] Again one is reminded of Eisenman's "futility of the object" whose work in the absence of a Corbusian lyrics ends up in cultivating the artistic and formal potentialities of the Dom-ino. This aspect of postfunctionalist architecture has also to do with architecture's own oscillation between craft and art. This subject is discussed in the last chapter, and here I would like to make the point that in the mentioned paradigm, Le Corbusier distanced himself from the craft nature of architecture and thought of the latter as a plastic art. His inclination was strong enough that his postmodern followers could not deviate from the master.

The experience of the Five Architects supports the idea that ar-chitecture is a self-referential entity. They took Le Corbusier's discourse on the object-type for granted and conceived of archi-tecture as a field subject to formal and intellectual exercises. They intended to break the ice of high modern architecture by deconstructing the metaphysics of humanism. In this context, it is not far-fetched to associate Eisenman's House III (figure 2.6) with Picasso's 1937 *Portrait de Dora* (figure 2.7). Leo Steinberg

FIG. 2.4. Le Corbusier, Maison Week-End, St.-Cloud, near Paris, 1934–35. © 1995 ARS, New York/SPADEM, Paris.

FIG. 2.5. Le Corbusier, Church of Motre Dame du Haut, Ronchamp, France- view from southeast. Courtesy Foto Marburg/Art Re- sources, New York.

sees this painting as Picasso's attempt "to pass beyond the banal, ninety-degree dichotomy of front and side."[33] Eisenman, on the other hand, implements Picasso's intention by rotating the core of his building forty-five degrees. The formal configuration of the house initiates a step toward deconstruction of the Platonic geometry. However, fixed by its outer edges, the rotated square could be read as a representation of the separation between construction and appearance or signifier and signified as discussed in the semiotic theories of the 1970s.[34] Eisenman's later works confirm that through the process of decomposition, the signified disappears and the signifier emerges as the formative theme for architecture. To the same end, Michael Graves, whose early work was primarily influenced by Le Corbusier, dwells on the notion of simultaneity and takes a step toward the "erosion" of the surface.[35] In most of his houses, the vertical face of the front column defuses into the surface of the side partition wall. These works integrated the experience of the Dom-ino with a body of theoretical work solidified in Robert Venturi's discourse on complexity and contradiction.

In retrospect, we might argue that the Five initiated two parallel architectural practices that metaphorically confirm Venturi's notion of "both-and."[36] In the wake of a historical consciousness, one line of thought dwells on the problematic of "contradiction." Postmodernism covers its modern planimetric and sectional organization with the garment of a "history whose meaning and limits they skillfully keep hidden from themselves."[37] This esteem for historical forms is a mask. And its architectonic figuration should be discerned from Palladio and Alberti's discourse on the duality of appearance and construction.

We have come far enough not to be obliged to put together the broken kinship of things and words.[38] However, the specificity of postmodern historicism lies in its apologetic position in relation to the two major vectors of the "culture industry," that is, kitsch and the nihilism of technology. Through Venturi and Jencks, this attitude initiated the "pseudo-sign"—the simulated historical forms. The postmodern voyage into the labyrinth of history is in fact a reaction to Mies's deterritorialization of the language of modern architecture. Mies's speechless constructs demythified

FIG. 2.6. Peter Eisenman, House III, Miller House, Lakeville, Connecticut, 1971.

FIG. 2.7. Pablo
Picasso, *Portrait de
Dora*, 1937. Courtesy
Art Resources,
New York.

tradition and left no territory to be emancipated from its representational burden. More important, he exhausted the tectonic potentialities of the glass and steel architecture. In return, postfunctionalism sought to utilize the Dom-ino frame as a conceptual means to escape this historical impasse.

Deconstructivists, on the other hand, posit metaphysics as the problematic of our contemporary architecture. Criticizing postmodern historicism, deconstructivists build their discourse on "complexity" and apply the theory of deconstruction to a field in which construction is its formative theme. Of course deconstructivism does not deny construction, but as part of their criticism of the nineteenth-century discourse, deconstructivists dispense with the tectonic dimension of architecture. Yet their claim for autonomy of architecture lacks the critical content of the historical avant-garde's project. By pushing the thoughts of the historical avant-garde to its limit, deconstructivists conceive the "non-sign" as the threshold of the western concept of the metaphysics. Holding on to the self-referential nature of architecture, they shifted the postmodern emphasis from history to "text."

For Eisenman, architecture is a text when it contains "something else," an "approximation or simulation of another object."[39] In the process of simulation, two things take place. First, relieved from the fiction of humanism, the architectural object becomes a formal entity subject to the architect's operational analytic. Second, by simulating another object, architecture attains a state of "hyperreality," where its formal configuration is drawn by the textual power of other discourses.[40] Eisenman's triad of deconstruction—that is, history, reason, and representation—implicitly disclose the theoretical premises of the historical avant-garde.[41] But the avant-garde's critical edge rested in the position they maintained within the cycle of production and consumption.[42] Their contention that art must be integrated with life was, in fact, a yearning for the re-construction of the social conditions of life. Such a position is different from current debate among the dominant theories of architecture that, in one way or another, dispenses with the relationship between architecture and the city. This issue will be raised again later, but taking into consideration all the apparent differences between deconstructivist and postmodernist architecture, these works inaugurate a design economy indulged with the "principle of the absolute absence of reality,"[43] a cardboard architecture.

In passing, one should differentiate the line of criticism presented here from Demetri Porphyrios's claim that both "Neo-Modernists and Post-Modernists thrive on convention: the first by dismembering conventions in the name of deconstructionist critique; the second by saturating the market with instant conventions in the name of pluralism."[44] One might agree with the content of Porphyrios's criticism and yet reject his exclusion of the modern experience from contemporary architectural knowledge. This erosion is the basis of his and Leon Krier's belief in the exclusivity of tectonic figuration to classical language.

Putting aside this esteem for convention, my intention here is to locate the problematic of postmodernism and deconstructivism in the index of an architectural language immanent to Le Corbusier's experience. Interestingly enough, the formal dimension of such a potentiality is dramatized by the perceptual field opened by today's media technology. Nevertheless, machines "are social before being technical." Or, rather, as Deleuz argues, "there is a human technology which exists before a material technology."[45] Long before disjunction and fragmentation became "visible" through technology, its human aspects were already being expressed in Analytical Cubism.[46] One cannot help but agree with the claim that design strategies framed around these concepts welcome the nihilism of technology. More important, the theoretical drive to reconcile architecture with the negative aspects of technology dismisses Theodor Adorno's point that the avant-garde's utopia did not have practical functions; it was rather a critical move to challenge the status quo.[47]

The nihilism of technology is not a new subject; however, "the new technologies are giving this process a new momentum insofar as they submit any kind of inscription on any kind of medium—say visual images, sounds, speeches, musical scores, songs and the like, and, finally, writing itself—to an exact computation."[48] At the end of his piece, in a movie titled *Aria*, Franc Rodmann presents a vivid cinematographic image of this computation. In the plot, the disappearance of Las Vegas's shiny billboards is followed by their replacement with an image of an old woman walking out of a casino with an empty bowl in her hand. The plot, as it develops, frames the suicide of a young couple who came to the city at the very beginning of the episode. Interestingly enough, the movie ends with a scene depicting another young couple, also departing from the same point for Las Vegas. This apocalyptic vision reflects a kind of radicalism that in postmodern debate emphasizes the debacle of the Enlightenment in order to bring forth the dawn of the absolute absence of cultural life.[49] Are we to conclude that the "violence," once transforming nature into culture, now intends to devour the culture itself? Or is the current interest in the theme of violence, entertained in both architecture and other fields, recalling the Promethean myth of yearning for a prehistoric era of plenitude (pluralism?) in which a "both-and" situation comes to life through a nomadic life juxtaposed with the aesthetics of classicism? Robin Evans's response to the need for resuscitation of primitivism in postmodern architecture discloses another facet of the idea of both-and—that is, the conflict between the real and the imaginary. "As always, we dream of making of architecture what it is not, and the dream finds its way into the look of things."[50] The problem with postmodern architecture rests in its inability, as Evans reminds us, to accept this inconsistency and to avoid reducing architecture to the "reality" of the billboards of Las Vegas or the virtual reality of media technology.

Yet there is more to Venturi's idea of "both-and." In an orthodox modernist discourse, the term could have been interpreted as a revisionistic concept endorsing the metaphysics of Western epistemology coded in modern and classical architecture respectively. Implicit in the concept of "both-and" is the idea of the death of the author and the end of any utopian ideology. "Both-and" addresses this historical paradigm in an architecture of parody or simulacra, which, ironically, raises an important question. Should we take the fantasies of a cardboard architecture as a means to forget the anguish caused by the failure of the project of the historical avant-garde? Or should we articulate an architecture that assimilates that anguish into itself, producing a dark image that can be experienced only in Adorno's writings? Given such a paradox, one wonders whether there is any room left for a critical discourse. In the present theater of architectural theories, a discourse concerning the idea of architecture and the city still deserves attention. Interestingly enough, current work on this subject underlines both the historical avant-garde and Le Corbusier's experience.[51]

In retrospect, one might question whether Le Corbusier's ambiguous remarks on "architecture or revolution" were not his way of mapping the vicissitudes of a critical discourse. Beyond the constructivist tendencies of his time and the formal potentialities of Dom-ino, Le Corbusier turned his attention toward the core of the project of the Enlightenment: that is, total reconstruction of the modern conditions of life. His obsession with the city might be associated with the Bauhaus's drive for total design.[52] Yet regarding our experience of postmodernity, one might conclude that Le Corbusier's ideas on the city fell short of anticipating the logic of capitalism. Le Corbusier's vision encompassed a city "where life would become intelligent, educated and clean, in which social justice would be established and political issues resolved—the city was not to be built."[53] Rowe's observation is correct. Ville Radieuse could not have been realized, even today, as long as architecture thrives on the weight of classical forms and the aesthetic of fragmentation perceived through the media technology. On the other hand, the culture industry has reached a point that can disarm and abrogate any project initiated from outside of the process of commodification of the built environment. At stake is the dialectical relationship between a cultural product and the exigencies of its social reality. Otherwise, how could architecture sustain its autonomy in the power struggle running through cultural constellation? And more specifically, how could one retain Le Corbusier's experience without ending with an architecture of both-and?

Tadao Ando, along with a few other contemporary architects, offers a plausible alternative to the experience of the Five. Obviously Ando does not provide solutions for most of the problems discussed above. Yet it is useful to stress the point that his interest in the tectonic of column and wall, and his avoidance of using frame structures—a line of thinking he inherited from Louis Kahn[54]—have resulted in an architecture that dismisses the allure of the concept of the "world picturing." It seems Ando is aware of this phenomenon when he says that, in postmodernity "the value of architecture in itself is given little credence, and much is made of flashy buildings designed to look attractive."[55] The idea of "both-and" is also absent from his work, and this has to do with the fact that Ando saw Le Corbusier through Kahn, whereas the Five implemented Le Corbusier's experience through Venturi. More important, one has to emphasize Ando's minimalism, which discloses the phenomenological inseparability of the temporal and the spatial. Ando does not deny meaning but, similar to minimalist art of the 1960s, the meaning is seen arising "from a public, rather than a private space."[56]

Cut into the rift between Japanese traditional culture and the forces of civilization, Ando unfolds a poetic construction recalling the tectonic of a classical wisdom and specifically the correspondence between the plan and the mass on the one hand and the section on the other. The absence of stylistic historicism and the Albertian aesthetic of lineaments (representation), or for that matter, a Loosian cladding, is suggestive to argue that Ando, like Mies, leaves no room for a discrepancy between signifier and the signified. This aspect of Ando's architecture alludes, again, to the issues evolved in minimalist art. Besides its nonrelational composition, the disappearance of figure-ground in minimalism not only undermined the illusion of depth but also endorsed the hegemony of shape, or that which Michael Fried has termed "objecthood,"[57] a nonreferential construct that undermines the duality between construction and appearance. The meaning of an architecture of objecthood is neither in itself nor outside, but stems from the tectonic. In this context, I would like to suggest that the postmodern inclination for a self-referential sign does not do enough: it does not depart from pictorial illusion and semiological understanding of sign. Against a postfunctionalism that is touched by the technology of image making, Ando's constructs are spatially meaningful through haptic experience, discussed by Benjamin. On the other hand, his architecture embodies a spatial construct that in a way deterritorializes the totality of a putative Japanese sense of space. His ruminations on wall, column, and colonnade are neither formalistic nor simulative. For him, the wall and the column are common constructive elements drawn from the repertory of an architecture whose meaning is meshed with the life-world. In this way, as Ando describes, "space can restore the relations between human beings and things."[58] For him, the monolithic compositions of column and wall are indissociable from the figurative aspects of the tectonic.

Ando's simple geometries are not timeless. They unfold a spatial ensemble evoking the experience of difference. Indeed "difference" is a formative theme for Ando. Take his concrete walls, for example, where the same rough, heavy, and nonclad surfaces are experienced both in the climatic transformations of the outside—light and wind, but also rain, snow, fog[59]—and inside spaces. The latter is saved from total darkness by laserlike lights seeping through slits staged between the wall and the roof (figure 2.8). Today, Ando stresses, "the major task is building walls that cut the interior off entirely from the exterior. In this process, the ambiguity of the wall, which is simultaneously interior and exterior, is of the greatest significance. I employ the wall to delineate a space that is physically and psychologically isolated from the outside world."[60] Through its surprising weight, the wall in Ando's work also reflects, as Kenneth Frampton notes, "not only the Seismic conditions of country, but also the 'storm of progress' which rages throughout Tokaido megapolis."[61] The heaviness, however, evaporates as soon as these concrete walls are exposed to light, marking the edges of a space that seems to precede its massive enclosure. Again Ando explains this metamorphosis: "the concrete I employ does not have plastic rigidity or weight. Instead, it must be homogeneous and light and must create surfaces. When they agree with my aesthetic image, walls become abstract, are negated, and approached the ultimate limit of space. Their actuality is lost, and only the space they enclose gives a sense of really existing."[62]

Similar to minimalist sculptors, Ando sees concrete beyond the early modernist belief in "truth to material." For him the form is

not found in the alleged nature of material (figures 2.9 and 2.10).
The association with minimalism is instrumental for stressing the
difference between Ando and the Five, too. The latter's fascination with the death of the author recalls pop artists' desire for
anonymity. The pop artists gave the look of anonymity to their
work by employing commercial techniques, introducing the politics and aesthetics of commodification into various art forms.[63]
Are not the Five's abstract formal anonymity and postmodern
communicative forms the two sides of the same coin: the commodity fetishism and its quality to attract our attention and yet
simultaneously remain anonymous about the work's actual place
in one's collective memory? I will further elaborate the association between commodities and current architecture in the remaining chapters, but here I would like to recall Francis Colpitt's
assertion that, for minimalism (figure 2.11), anonymity is the
result of fabrication and not the initial motivation.[64] It is the concept, or in Ando's words, "my aesthetic image," and its spatial
constructs that restore anonymity in the collective domain of
lived-experience defusing the naturalness of material. In passing I

would like to credit Ando for codifying the tectonic of concrete in architecture, an achievement, if I do not exaggerate, equal to what architects have done with marble throughout history.

The dialogue between culture and technology is another factor that informs Ando's discourse on difference. Jun'ichiro Tanizaki's aspiration for Japanese ethical and aesthetic sensibilities is sug-

FIG. 2.9. Tadao Ando, "Festival." Courtesy Tadao Ando Architect and Associates. Photograph by Tadao Ando.

FIG. 2.10. Tadao
Ando, "Festival."
Courtesy Tadao Ando
Architect and Associ-
ates. Photograph by
Tadao Ando.

gestive to read Ando's interest in dim interior spaces as a strategic retreat against the inevitable forces of civilization.[65] These
semidark interiors are not sanctuaries of loss but trajectories for
"mourning," and they affirm "difference." The insinuated sublime monumentality and stillness in Ando's work is the result of
a marriage between modernization and tradition that takes place
outside of history. His is different from a postmodernism that
appropriates pastiche as the language to justify the separation

between signifier and the signified. However, the peculiarity of current historicism lies in its skillful juxtaposition between a modernist technology (Dom-ino frame) and an envelope that simulates historical forms that have nothing to do with the frame behind these forms. The communicative potentialities of this simulated surface disclose postmodern obsession with information technologies.[66]

Following Fredric Jameson, I would like to stress my proposition, once more, that the possibility for architecture to simulate historical forms was already at work in Le Corbusier's idea of the Dom-ino. This is a plausible charge if one agrees with the idea that steel-frame is the ultimate architectural contribution of a social mode that is identified with heavy industries. The departure of late capitalism from old industrial production system for electronic technologies, instead, has marked the closure of mo-

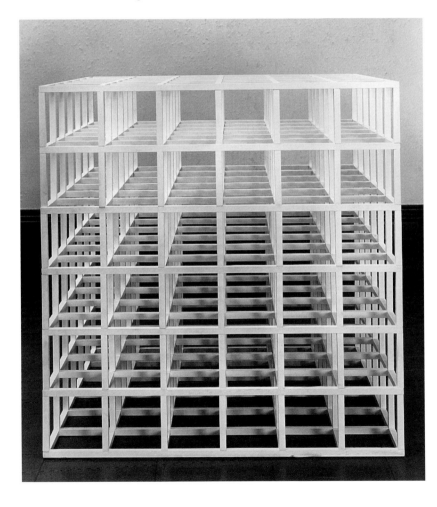

FIG. 2.11. Sol LeWitt, *Open Modular Cube*, 1928. Courtesy Art Gallery of Ontario, Canada.

dernity and a shift of interest from construction to appearance. In this context, Ando's strategic importance rests in his choice of concrete wall, itself a modern technology, to address cultural themes relevant to our very postmodern conditions.

And yet, Ando's work merges in the fabric of the city as its Other and sustains a topological relation between architecture and the city. In Ando's spaces the relation to oneself is homologous to the relation with the outside and the two are in contact through intermediaries such as beamlike lights, bare concrete walls, and silent courtyards. Here, the wall is a measure of enclosure against the hostile metropolis, and it emerges, metaphorically, as a critique of the rigid-frame system. No one has spoken for this aspect of his work better than Ando: "The rigid-frame has robbed the post of its myth and the colonnade of its rhythm."[67] But the trabeated concrete frame in the Wall House (Matsumoto

FIG. 2.12. Tadao Ando, "Wall House– Matsumoto House," Courtesy Tadao Ando Architect and Associates. Photograph by Masao Arai.

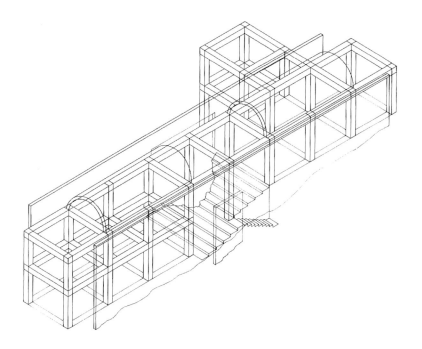

FIG. 2.13. Tadao Ando, "Wall House–Matsumoto House," axonometric. Courtesy Tadao Ando Architect and Associates.

Residence), for example, differs from the pragmatic essence of the Chicago frame and the Dom-ino frame, which, in the last analysis, functioned as a conceptual tool paving the way for a new architecture (figure 2.12). The frame in the Wall House is not utilized for pictorial ends but like Sol LeWitt's *Open Modular Cube* it establishes meaning between the internal body of the frame and the cultural space (manmade nature) surrounding it. Here, the tectonic juxtaposition between volume (wall) and void (frame) opens a diaphragm through which one could see the nature as the mirror image of the space occupied by the observer. According to Koji Taki "the frame prepares the whole 'site' to be architecturalized—that is to say, the frame prepares the ground for the generation of space. Through the uniformity of the frame, a 'place' is already set apart from the random order of reality"(figure 2.13).[68]

Of the greatest significance is Ando's intention to retain the tactile and haptic experience of architecture, a phenomena rubbed by the formalistic products of the Five. They reduced meaning into a private enterprise stressing the formal autonomy of architecture. Ando, instead, insists on the externality of meaning, the sources of which are laid in the tectonic of column and wall, and a negative affirmation of Japanese tradition. Finally, we can claim that Ando transcends the formal implications of the discourse of "both-and." His constructs spring up in the cracks left

FIG. 2.14. Tadao
Ando, "Church of the
Light." Courtesy
Tadao Ando Architect
and Associates.
Photograph by Mitsuo
Matsuoka.

(opposite page)
FIG. 2.15. Tadao
Ando, "Forest of
Tombs Museum."
Courtesy Tadao Ando
Architect and Associ-
ates. Photograph by
Mitsuo Matsuoka.

by the textual power of deconstructivist and postmodern architecture. Within the chaotic cycle of production and consumption,
Ando recollects the silence of waiting for the unrealized Miesian
desire of an architecture of almost nothing, that is, an architecture of objecthood. On the other hand, the formal dynamism
and expressionistic dimensions he implements in recent projects
are signs of his struggle to recapitulate the logic of a restless and

FIG. 2. 16. Tadao
Ando, Forest of
Tombs Museum.
Courtesy Tadao Ando
Architect and Associ-
ates. Photograph by
Hiroshi Ueda.

self-transgressive culture industry (figure 2.14). It also discloses
the intersection of modern technology with the thematics of
postmodern culture, charging architecture with a "theatrical"
quality.[69] To put it differently, Ando's theatricality refers to an
artifice whose distance from tradition allows its techniques of
construction (the tectonic) to be exhibited (figures 2.15 and
2.16). This emphasis on technique is essentially a modernist
theme prevailed in painting, film, and in Mies's architecture, too.
However, theatricality in postmodern discourse alludes to a moment when architecture's dissociation from tradition is replaced
by allure of fetishism, which for Adorno characterizes "the
blindness of the art work to the reality of which it is a part. And
it is this fetishism that "enables the work of art to break the spell
of the reality principle and to become a spiritual essence."[70] It is
this transgressive dimension in Ando that makes him different
and puts his architecture in a more complex relationship with its
sociocultural context than postmodern simulation of history, or
the neo-avant-garde's total assimilation into the nihilism of
technology.

Louis Kahn
at the Salk Institute

3

What the Building Wants to Be

Every contemporary architect has, at least once in his or her career, given thought to Louis Kahn's famous phrase, "what the building wants to be."[1] This statement could be read in different ways. Before presenting my interpretation of Kahn's words, I would like to discuss two other readings instrumental for placing Kahn in the twilight of modern architecture. Kahn's work has been mostly seen from a phenomenological perspective, the architectonic implications of which are not too difficult to trace in his writings.[2] Whether Kahn had read Martin Heidegger or other thinkers of the school of phenomenology is not the point; to take Kahn's writings at face value and read his architecture accordingly is to dismiss its historicality. Kahn was situated between modern and postmodern discourse. Although there is a strong sense of typological roots in Kahn,[3] his architecture acts like a joint; it brings two things together and yet maintains their separateness from each other. In the context of contemporary architecture, it happened to be Kahn who had to bridge the gap between Mies van der Rohe's poetics of construction and a postmodernism that has put its trust in simulacrum.

One might see in Kahn's aphorism a way of revising the fiasco of "form follows function." We are well aware of the mechanical and utilitarian concern of functionalism. And we also know how different Kahn's architecture, especially his later work, is from modern functionalism. But the aforementioned hypothetical association has merit if one interprets functionalism outside of themes formative for the early modern architecture. From this point of view, the two aphorisms, "form follows function" and "what the building wants to be," could be seen as two different enunciations of the same problem; that is, the crisis of the object.[4] The debate on postmodernity also indicates the fact that

Mies's architecture exhausted the tectonic potentialities of modern building technology. Being unable to offer any substantial contribution to "construction," current telecommunicative technologies have forced architects to work mainly with the surface or appearance of buildings. This has created a situation radically different from the time before eighteenth century when technology was indissociable from the craft of building.[5]

The departure of architecture from its classical wisdom was already at work in the eighteenth century where geometry was conceived as the internal structure of a speaking architecture. This historical unfolding separated architectural discourse from the metaphysics of the divine world. We will return to this subject shortly, but here, it suffices to say that the eighteenth-century architecture was critical to a functionalism that would substitute the remains of a symbolic architecture with the exigencies of utility. Kahn, instead, ascribed meaning to architecture by veiling the absence of the subject with a poetic supplement.[6] This aspect of Kahn's short-lived experience is dismissed by most advocates of postmodernity. Take Robert Venturi's *Complexity and Contradiction* and his argument that "implicit in this (what a thing wants to be) is its opposite: What the architect wants the thing to be."[7] With such a stress on the role of the subject, one wonders if Venturi's dislike of modernity is not mainly concerned with its futuristic dimension. Why should Venturi open his text with the theme of "tradition" if he is not sympathetic to the regressive potentialities of the historical subject? In other words, a "return" to the historical past is not less problematic than the futuristic orientation of the modern movement.[8] Venturi's reversal of Kahn's statement, and his rhetorical treatment of the historical forms, take the narrow boundaries of historicism for the experience of modernity.

The second reading of Kahn's statement is implied in two consecutive editorials of *Oppositions*. In the fifth issue of this journal, Mario Gandelsonas reformulates the tendency of the 1960s to map the possibility of a symbolic dimension of a neofunctionalist architecture. According to him, neofunctionalist architecture intends to develop the progressive aspects of functionalism, "an action which implies the effective transformation of its idealistic nature, building a dialectical basis for architecture."[9] Detecting some humanist traces in Gandelsonas's pretext of the "Neo," Peter Eisenman, in the next editorial, proposed the vicissitudes of a "Post-Functionalist" discourse. For Eisenman, the

solution to the humanist ethics of form is in the uncritical acceptance of the death of the subject. Thus, architectural form must
refer to simple geometrical forms, or else it has to turn into "a
series of fragments—signs without meaning, dependent upon,
and without reference to, a more basic condition." For Eisen
man, both tendencies defined "the inherent nature of the object
in and of itself and its capacity to be represented." And they began, according to him, "to suggest that the theoretical assumptions of functionalism are in fact cultural rather than universal."[10] Here Eisenman correctly points to the historicality of the
experience of functionalism and rejects the fiction of the oneness
of form and meaning in favor of a form whose meaning is embedded in itself. If this is a plausible reading of Eisenman's text,
then, what Eisenman calls the form-in-itself could be associated
with Kahn's "what the building wants to be." In fact, both sides
of this unwanted equation suggest the idea of the death of the
author; itself a formative theme for theories of structuralism.

Certain aspects of Kahn's architecture and some recent deconstructivist projects support the above claim. Consider Eisenman's
Biocenter Building for the University of Frankfurt, where design
evolves out of the form of DNA (see figure 1.11). Or Daniel
Libeskind's new addition to the Jewish Museum in Berlin in
which the planimetric organization and ultimately its volumetric
expression can be associated with a fragmented Star of David
(figure 3.1 and 3.2). Kahn's "what the building wants to be" and
the tendency in some deconstructivist architecture to see building
as the architectonic realization of its subject matter (program?),
point to a discourse that was already at work in some avant-
garde painters. Rene Magritte's painting, *Philosophy in the Bou-
doir,* comes to mind: the shoes in the picture do not express a
particular style or function but instead assimilate themselves into
their subject, the feet Comparing van Gogh's well-known painting of the peasant shoes (figure 3.3) with Andy Warhol's dia-
mond dust *Shoes* (figure 3.4), Fredric Jameson reflects on the
differences between the high modernist and postmodernist moments. While the first painting, from Heidegger's point of view,
could express certain characteristics of the rift between the earth
and the world, Warhol's, instead, speaks primarily for simulacra.
What drives me to recall Jameson's brilliant analogy is his short
speculation on Magritte's painting, *Le Modele Rouge* (figure
3.5). In this painting a pair of shoes again assimilates the form of
the feet to itself. According to Jameson, "Magritte, unique
among the surrealists, survived the sea change from modern to

FIG. 3.1. Daniel Libskind, Extension to the Berlin Museum with the Jewish Museum, Berlin, 1989. From Daniel Lebskind, *Counter Sign* (Academy Editions, 1922).

its sequel, becoming in the process something of a postmodern emblem: the uncanny, Lacanian foreclusion, without expression."[11] To this I would add that the form of the shoes in Magritte's painting prevent any question concerning their subject; indeed the latter's prints are already there, in the form of the shoes. In this pair of shoes there is no gap between sign and signifier. In addition, the absence of the so-called subject in van Gogh's painting raises the following rhetorical question: To whom do van Gogh's shoes belong? A polemical trap that the famous exchange between Heidegger and Meyer Shapiro could not dismiss.[12]

The following conclusions are possible. First, the association between Kahn's "what the building wants to be" and Magritte's painting differentiates Kahn's work from high modernism and is suggestive of the presence of some traits of postmodern discourse in his work. Second, the gap between sign and signifier, or appearance and construction, implied in Le Corbusier's Dom-ino House, has paved the way for an architecture of "both-and." Finally, the possible link between Kahn and postmodernism makes one wonder whether Manfredo Tafuri was not correct in placing Kahn and Venturi in the void left by the failure of the project of the historical avant-garde. For Tafuri, Kahn and Venturi present that aspect of American culture which is pressed by the lack of history. If Kahn "could have produced a school of mystics without religions to defend," Venturi has in fact "created a school of disabused and disillusioned individuals without values to denigrate or violate."[13] If the absence of history and the

FIG. 3.2. Daniel Libskind, Extension to the Berlin Museum with the Jewish Museum, Berlin, under construction. Courtesy Ingo Herrmann.

FIG. 3.3. Van Gogh, *A Pair of Shoes,* 1886. Courtesy Van Gogh Museum Amsterdam/Art Resources, New York.

impossibility of articulating an authentic culture is the problematic of postwar America, then the question to ask would be—and this is the point Tafuri missed—whether in this circumstance architecture has any other choice but to assimilate itself into its subject. Tafuri's observation contains positive points and has made great impact on current theoretical work. However, in regard to the question of "what the building wants to be," I believe the answer lies neither in Eisenman's postfunctionalism nor within the limits of Tafuri's historicism.

A more profitable line of inquiry might be found in Theodor Adorno's discourse on "mimesis" and "linguistic quality," by which he articulates a critique of the extirpation of expression in functionalism—something Gandelsonas seemingly failed to accomplish. For Adorno, mimesis has nothing to do with superstition, it rather discloses a mode of behavior that assimilates the self to an other.[14] Adorno believed that mimesis is that aspect of the work of art that resists the totalization enforced by instrumental reason. Functionalism, instead, purified architectural form from its mimetic behavior, "expression," and reduced form to the imperatives of technology. It should be noticed here that by expression I mean the linguistic quality of architecture; the tectonic, which according to Gottfried Semper is rendered in "a *structural-symbolic* rather in a *structural-technical* sense."[15] The

FIG. 3.4. Andy Warhol, *Shoes*, 1980. Courtesy Andy Warhol Foundation, Inc., New York.

tectonic is the mimetic behavior of an architecture that escapes the dictates of structural rationalism and resumes a poetic relationship between appearance and construction. I will discuss the specific implications of mimesis for Kahn's architecture shortly and more so at the end of this chapter. For now, following Adorno's criticism of the matter-of-factness of functionalism, I would like to argue for the presence of numerous ideological sharing between functionalism and postfunctionalism (such as the drive for autonomy and the problematic place of the subject) that, ironically, justify their differences. To clarify these points further, we need to recall the implications of the experience of modernity for architecture, though this time from Adorno's point of view.

FIG. 3.5. Rene Magritte, *Le Modele Rouge.* Courtesy Giraudon/Art Resources, New York.

Adorno's mimesis refers to that quality of contemporary art whose expressiveness ties art to individual human experience. This experience speaks for the totality of modernism: in each turn of its development, capitalism intensifies the process of commodification of the life-world. Adorno's is a strategic position that is more radical than other theories that, in one way or another, have helped to define the relationship between art and "reality." According to Adorno, most of these theories ended either regressing into the past or indulged in the "arbitrary positing of a new order by the subject."[16] Here Adorno's criticism is directed toward expressionism and dadaism. Yet it is possible to apply Adorno's position to a postmodernism whose interest is limited to copying historical forms, or to a deconstructivism that, in its contention with metaphysics, has no choice but to stress on the autonomy of the object.

As I mentioned before, the modernist drive for autonomy was in part a response to the historical problem caused by the separation of technology from architecture. Anthony Vidler is correct in saying that in Ledoux's architecture, for example, "the traditional sense of a building that embodied beauty in its proportions and in its three-dimensional geometries was gradually subordinated to the idea of a geometrical order that followed the dictates of social or environmental needs."[17] As an heir to this tradition, modern functionalism canonized the dictates of social and environmental needs and the exigencies of technology. Postmodernism, instead, discards the concept of "expression" and focuses on semiotic understanding of signification and its implications for architecture. In a discrete way, these theories identify expression with the subject's intention. For Adorno, on the other hand, "expression is the non-subjective in the subject; it is not so much the subject's expression as it is its impression, in the sense of imprints." By suggesting that the language of expression is older than its significative counterpart, Adorno presents a critical understanding of the relation between expression and mimesis. He observes, "There is nothing more expressive than the eyes of apes, which seem objectively to grieve over the fact that they are not human."[18] Here Adorno pursues not the oneness of form and meaning but the mimetic impulse by which art "does not imitate something but assimilates itself to that something."[19] The same mimetic potentiality is embedded in Kahn's architecture; a potentiality that made his work different from both modern functionalism and postmodern semiotics.

Now, what is nonsubjective in the subject of architecture? And what is that nonsubjective entity that the building wants to be? Here, "nonsubjective" means not posited by the architect or by an ideal type. If we disagree with modern functionalism, and the formalistic interpretation of form in itself, then I would suggest that the linguistic quality of architecture is embedded in the construction of a purposeful space through which a building can assimilate itself into what it wants to be.[20] Of course, we are not concerned with an abstract space here but with a sense of space that, according to Adorno, is closely connected with purpose. For Adorno, architecture inquires, "how can a certain purpose become space; through which forms, which materials?"[21]

In associating Kahn's "what the building wants to be" with Adorno's ideas I intend to suggest that Kahn was responding to a set of unresolved historical problems, among others, the architecture's drive for autonomy, which started with the architecture of the eighteenth century and continues today in Eisenman's postfunctionalism. This aspect of Kahn's work convinces me that both Kenneth Frampton and Vittorio Gregotti were correct to see in Kahn the French and modern connection respectively.[22] Yet Kahn's statement pertains to an architectural imagination that departs from the eighteenth-century interest in the sublime and from modern aesthetics of abstraction. His architectural imagination also differs from the postmodern interest in replication of historical forms, and from the formal operatives of deconstructivist architecture. His work unites purposefulness and autonomy. His architectural imagination unfolds a tectonic form that permits purpose to become space. In this context, "space and the sense of space," as Adorno noted, "can become more than impoverished purpose only when imagination impregnates them with purposefulness." Adorno continues, "imagination breaks out of the immanent connections of purpose, to which it owes its very existence."[23] In other words, the significance of Kahn's theorem rests in its peculiar manner of molding imagination by means of the dialectic of space and purposefulness. This important part of Kahn's thought is undermined by those scholars who have canonized his architecture merely by institution (type) or the play of form and structure alone. "What the building wants to be" is the mimetic behavior of an architecture, which like the eyes of Adorno's ape, expresses itself in speechless construction. Sadly enough, for an ostentatious consumer culture like ours, the imprint of Kahn's tectonic for current architecture is brushed aside. One might speculate further that Kahn's esteem for order and geometry was as much rooted in history as it was in response to a technology that plunged architecture into the whirlpool of commodification.[24]

After these rather dense theoretical considerations, we can proceed to interpret Kahn's imagination as it is developed in the Salk Institute. It is always temptable to enter the site of the institute from the angle of the parking lot located next to the complex. However, I chose to enter the complex along its main axial composition and approach the site from its front garden. Standing in the middle of the courtyard and next to the water fountain, the first impression is typical of all perceptions of this place: it affirms those texts written on the silence and emptiness of the space (figure 3.6). After a second, one hears the sound of the water. The eye responds to the aural message and follows the path of the water all the way to its other empty end. The void before, the sound of the water, and the wings flanking the building, together set the stage upon which one can engage in haptic and optic dialogue with this contemporary sanctuary.

Elsewhere I have discussed the silence in Kahn's architecture as a heritage he received from Mies, and yet devoid of the latter's critical intentions.[25] Mies's was an architecture of renunciation in a double sense. In the first place, following the avant-garde of his time, Mies undermined the traditional understanding of dwelling: those picturesque architectonic articulations that would assure the rootedness of a building in the place. Also, those elements that even Adolf Loos would have appreciated in his early interiors in order to convey the idea of intimacy and the separation of the inside from the outside. Indeed, the warm interiors of the bourgeois were not yet touched by the *unheimlich* features of the emerging Metropolis. Second, Mies seems to be aware of Adorno's belief that the linguistic quality of art, whose importance for the survival of art he himself underlined, would be eliminated by the nihilism of technology. The tectonic of a frame construction whose void was enclosed by a fabric of steel and

FIG. 3.6. Louis I. Kahn, Salk Institute Laboratories, La Jolla, 1959–65. Photography by author.

glass—typical of Mies's later work—was indeed Mies's response to the limits of architecture and of the place, and his belief in a spiritual sense of responsibility. Each person needs to "give to each thing what intrinsically belongs to it, then all things would easily fall into their proper place; only there they could really be what they are and there they would fully realize themselves."[26] Only if one had the chance to stand inside of the 50×50 House could one have sensed the critical nature of Mies's silence and its significance for recollection of the idea of dwelling.

Wrapped in his language of steel and glass, Mies's silence discloses the architectonic impetus of salvation, which, according to Walter Benjamin, is based on a dialectical principle: that is, "on the overcoming of difficulty by accumulation of difficulty."[27] Such a negative dialectic is also at work in Mies's tactile sensibilities. The "poverty" of the glass in Mies was sought to overcome the metaphysics of inside/outside and radicalize their differences. According to Benjamin, "To live in a glass house is a revolutionary virtue par excellence. It is also an intoxication, a moral exhibitionism, that we badly need. Discretion concerning one's own existence, once an aristocratic virtue, has become more and more an affair of petit-bourgeois parvenus."[28] The absence of wall in the interiors of Mies's glass houses speaks for the idea of "void" and alludes to a nomadic sense of space: "ground emptiness in air and light, newly cosmic from nothingness."[29] The idea of "less is more," criticized by postmodernists, discloses the state of truth and meaning achieved not through communication but by accumulation of silence through speechless construction. I believe Kahn was aware of this aspect of Mies's work. And yet being already haunted by postmodern conditions, he had no choice but to retain Mies's silence within the archaic walls of a Roman architecture.

Kahn's search for the archaic should be differentiated from a postmodernism that, after Mies, was driven into historical forms as of a momentary relief from the fear of tumbling into the void he left. Kahn's architecture, instead, defines the idea of newness of the latest thing as itself an archaic pattern. But Kahn had to take another step away from modernity: Forgetting "the gap between the word and the thing" (that Michel Foucault considered essential for a departure from the Renaissance discourse of similitude),[30] Kahn entertained a Platonism at work in the distinctions he would make between *a* spoon and *the* spoon; as if

there is an ideal waiting for each artifact, including the building, to join with.[31]

Still the question of "what the building wants to be" awaits us. Standing in the courtyard of the Salk Institute, one is impressed by a sense of stoic space and absence of any excess (figure 3.7). The stone pavings, the concrete load-bearing elements and their wood in-fills, and finally the rhythmical articulation of two wings of the building toward the ocean, all together connote a kind of spirituality that might be experienced in the nave of S. Maria Novella (figure 3.8). The almost unadorned interior of this church unfolds a discourse of silence that would soon disappear in the architecture of the high Renaissance and the Baroque. In the nave of S. Maria Novella, the visitor's eye is drawn to the thick masonry wall and its windows, where the play of light and

FIG. 3.7. Louis I. Kahn, Salk Institute Laboratories. Photograph by author.

shadow obstructs the infinity behind it. To see the "other side" is not permitted. Only a glimpse of light, passing through the opaque spaces, provides visual comfort and endurance. Kahn's typological reconstruction, instead, breaks down the wall of theology and folds the "emptiness" of the other side into the silence of void.

At Salk, a person standing next to the springs wants to follow the stream. On arriving at the other end, the water again leads to a void. Here one experiences a flashback speculating, "perhaps it would have been better to stay there, keep waiting and staring at the ocean, as if waiting for Godot!" The analogy to Samuel Beckett's play has merit. One might say that his is a secularized version of the idea of waiting and hope so essential for Christian eschatology, whose legends celebrate the metaphoric nature of water and make allusions to the ocean as the harbinger of the

FIG. 3.8. S. Maria Novella, Florence, Italy. Photograph by author.

coming "unknown." There is another facet to Godot's discourse on waiting that underlines its differences from that of the religious one. The grand narrative of Christianity possesses a projective dimension through which one does not wait but is driven toward the promised destiny. Godot's tale, instead, speculates on the end of projective narrative. He reverses the perspectival canon into a vista through which one waits to receive. Again one thinks of a standstill concept of history discussed in chapter 1. One also is reminded of Ernest Bloch and his belief that in modernity "hope is not confident. If it is not to be disappointed it would not be hope."[32] And finally, one thinks of Federico Fellini's *La Dolce Vita,* where at the end of the movie, the ocean brings a strange creature to the shore. A cinematographic presentation of the end of utopia. Yet Kahn does not draw any conclusions of this kind: While staying within the discourse of modernity, he leaves us alone with the myth of redemption the power of which is not projective but must be awaited.[33]

The concept of waiting attains a concrete architectonic form in the design of research rooms. Beside the tactile articulation of concrete and wood—itself a reminder of what already is seen in the courtyard—one is also reminded of the existence of infinity through the window opened to the ocean.[34] In order to discover the poetry of Kahn's treatment of the window here (figure 3.9), it is useful to search for parallels in painting. The concept of waiting and the window, as an optical opening into nature, was topical for romanticist art. Contemporary European painting, indeed, is full of examples depicting the window as a means to express different psychological traumas such as melancholy and desire for harmony between the inside and outside worlds.[35] Interestingly enough, the dialectic of inside and outside is problematized by Magritte, who from 1933 on was preoccupied with the theme of the window. But Kahn's window at Salk does not follow Magritte. Rather, it seems to be more at home with the tradition of romanticism. The narrow and vertical shape of the windows at research rooms follow the anthropomorphic posture of the beholder and directs his/her gaze toward the ocean. The location of window inside this room draws one's attention to the ocean and interlocks the concept of waiting with the idea of "what the building wants to be." The window lifts "the ambiguity of distance, both removal and connection," and as Emmanuel Levinas reminds us, it "makes possible a look that dominates, a look of him who escapes look, the look that contemplates."[36] A

comparable poetic of window and waiting is palpable in Rainer
Maria Rilke's lines:

> You, window, O waiting's measure
> refilled so often
> when one life spills out and
> grows impatient for another[37]

It is to Kahn's credit that he employed an architectural form that
is analogous to the idea of waiting and looking for something to
come as the embodiment of the scientific mode of thinking.[38]
What is the verity of science if it is not a truth "coming" to a
researcher in a flash of insight as a revelation of a dormant reality? At the Salk Institute, science finds its textual body within a
space enclosed by walls, finished in concrete and wood, and
opened to the ocean through a window as it was an opening to
the distance.[39]

This reading is justified when one leaves the research cells for the
laboratories located in the first floor. Each lab is provided with
ample natural light pouring in from both sides of its rectangular
plan. Unlike the courtyard and the research rooms, these two
labs have no visual access to the ocean. The walls enclosing the
other two sides of the labs leave no room for the metaphysics of
contemplation. They are designed according to the purpose of
the experimental work performed within them. For Kahn, a lab
is a space where the mind must concentrate and verify the movement of hands and the motion of eyes. At the Salk Institute, the
idea of "what the building wants to be" evolves through Kahn's
imagination of the difference between the speculative dimension
of a scientific work and its empirical results in the laboratory.
The thematics of his imagination evolved around the idea of silence and waiting whose tectonic form is expressed in the design
of the windows at the labs and the research rooms. The latter
space directs the gaze toward the horizon through a window that
opens into the distance. The windows of the former, instead, are
conceived only as a sources of light without access to the ocean.

As an early comer to the end of modernity, Kahn reinterprets the
utopia of waiting. It is the stillness that recalls Bloch's "anticipa-
tory illumination," suggesting "how to complete the world without the world being exploded as in the Christian religious antici-
patory illumination, and without disappearing apocalyptically."[40]
Yes there are bits of mysticism in Bloch too. But in what ways
might one transgress mysticism in order to present a critical

reading of postfunctionalist architecture? There are two points in this quest that I would like to address: First, losing the modernist esteem for renunciation, and dispensing with the lexicon of the new objectivity, *Sachlichkeit* (which was central for the early modern discourse), architecture could avoid the abstract formalism of the Five only by reducing itself to a communicative sign. Postmodern interest in replication of historical forms and typologies are indeed classificatory modes that put architecture in dialogue with both history of architecture (itself an enclosed labyrinthine space), and with the tradition of the life-world of a particular region. Postmodernity relegates identity and meaning into the realm of simulation (formal and contextual), or to the tradition of the tectonic. Second, modern departure from history stipulated artistic forms that had nothing to do with classical vocabulary, and remained anonymous if not surreal. The anonymity of modern architecture could be better understood by the picture Karl Marx depicts from commodities: "A commodity is therefore a mysterious thing simply because in it the social character of men's labor appears to them as an objective character stamped upon the product of that labour."[41] But modern architecture resisted anything that is not useful and thus aligned itself to the imperatives of the production line. In this historical background, and with the present proliferation of commodification, it is suggestive to think of the ways by which the idea of the death of the author can bear positive fruits. Paradoxically, a critical response to my quest would demand to think of a tectonic that affirms both anonymity and the mystics of commodities.

I would like to speculate further that the entire body of postmodern architecture can be classified according to the degree of its response to the dialogical relation between anonymity (difference?) and communication (identity?). Consider the architecture of Venturi and Aldo Rossi where simulation of historical forms by the former and revitalization of typologies by the latter have produced a body of work that are strong in communication but weak in anonymity. Whereas Eisenman's work places "the observer in a perfect state of alienation with respect to the real, corresponding to the absolute estrangement imposed on the forms."[42] Kahn too invested in anonymity but not from a formalistic point of view. Indeed it is not easy to read at one glance the invisible tectonic line in some of his buildings. How should one read, for example, the communicative dimension of the brick facade at Exeter Library except through the tectonic of a void and solid that, almost like a Gothic buttress, robs the wall of any

FIG. 3.9. Louis I. Kahn, Salk Institute Laboratories. Photograph by author.

structural function (figure 3.11)? This tectonic articulation is intensified by the cutouts at corners to abort any reading of the tectonic drives mainly on the logic of masonry construction. These tectonic considerations speak for the nonstructural character of the brick wall of the facade, anticipating the void at the center.

I contend that, in regard to postmodern reduction of architecture into a communicative sign, Kahn maintained an ambivalent position. Kahn's break with modernity is not total: he dispenses with the theme of renunciation and pumps a new blood into the late-nineteenth-century discourse on the tectonic. This in-betweeness is revealed in the opaque and heavy thingness of his tectonic figuration, resisting postmodern temptation for animation and automaticism.[43] However, the historicality of Kahn's design economy has to do with Mies's deterritorialization of the language of modern architecture, and the fusion of technology into the cultural domain. To put the latter point rhetorically, how could any cultural product, including architecture, remain immune from the mystical character of the fetish where the whole culture is at the brink of commodification?

Indeed, one important facet of the current crisis of the object has to do with our awareness of the ghost of what Marx coined a century ago as fetishism, or the mystical character of commodities. The point is not to discredit the ghost that is truly haunting us today but to stress the ways that Marx's speculation might offer a critical tool to renew our classificatory mode for differentiating modern architecture from postmodern, and the various tendencies within the latter. Therefore, one should not condemn the mystical nature of commodities; the phenomenon is not external to the experience of modernity. One should rather seek in the chaos generated by commodification the elements that might induce a rigorous recoding of the metaphysics of architecture.[44] In this paradigm, one major differences between Kahn and Venturi account for the degree of their willingness to absorb "mysti-

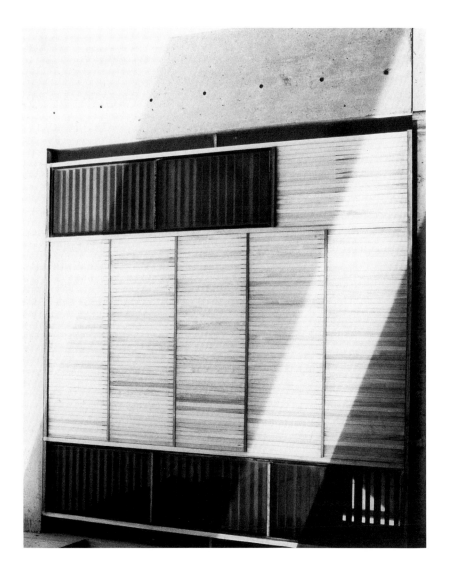

FIG. 3.10. Louis I. Kahn, Salk Institute Laboratories. Photograph by author.

FIG. 3.11. Louis I.
Kahn, Exeter Library.
Photograph by author.

cism" into architecture. The wonder Kahn frequently spoke about might have to do with his own wonder at what a building would have wanted to be if it could speak at all.[45] I do not intend to speculate on this subject further. I like, however, to suggest that Kahn's dialogue with brick is a residue of the early modernist desire to work with the nature of materials, whereas in postmodernity, one is indulged with the phantasmagoric world of commodities. In Kahn there is an aesthetic dimension that is at once nostalgic and critical; nostalgic in its tactile sensibilities that remind us of the auratic stage of the material used; and critical because the brick in most of his work, like marble in the Kimble museum, is cut and shaped for a tectonic that is supported by its concrete frame structure. Again one thinks of Adorno's contention that mimesis "bears the marks of regression, of being *passe,* of having been left behind by the general progression of things."[46] The brick, the travertine, and the slate panels occasionally used by Kahn allude to tactile sensibilities belonging to the auratic experience of architecture (figure 3.10).

The difference between Kahn and Venturi also leads one to wonder why in this country, where the speed of commodification competes with the ever-increasing rate of national deficit, not many American architects have pursued Kahn's tradition, whereas Venturi's discourse, if not his architecture, has been formative not only for postmodern architecture but for its adversary, the deconstruction architecture. The case of the latter is unique: In the spirit of the historical avant-garde, deconstructivism seems willing to finalize the process of total internalization of the fetish of commodities into architecture. Interestingly enough, there is a sense of "cuteness" in deconstruction architecture that is not visible in the most vigorous constructivist work of the early century. This makes us think of the concept of "return" and the ways the neo-avant-garde and postmodernism entertain the theme of difference, and how the difference in their work is motivated by the mystics of commodities. The phenomenon is also relevant to Kahn's typological modification and a tectonic whose theatricality is the result of folding the mystics of the logos of making into the current profusion of fetishism. Yet we might speak of theatricality as a moment when "the time is out of joint"; that is, when a commodity breaks away from its use-value and enters the world of fetishism. Interestingly enough, Benjamin spoke of the "exhibition value" of an art, the aesthetic of which is dominated by the process of economic exchange. When the various arts are emancipated from cult value, their products are ready to be exhibited. Benjamin contends that eventually the work of art will internalize exhibition value as their new nature. I am not presenting a dark view of theatricality here. In *Ontology of Construction,* I have spoken for a theatricality whose "playfulness" is rendered according to the tectonic; the structural-symbolic articulation of the dialogue between appearance and construction.[47] What I am emphasizing here is that architecture is construction plus something else. This surplus is the source of a theatricality that is emulated not by the intentions of the architect but by his/her imaginative engagement with technique. Discussing stereotomy in Gothic architecture, Robin Evans argued: "in architecture, technique and effect do not stand in a simple casual relation. Neither is determined exclusively by the other. Sometimes a technique will produce unexpected but desirable effects; sometimes, as probably with the west country lierne vaults, the desire for a particular effect will impose on technique, demanding of it more than it can easily deliver."[48] Therefore, theatricality plays at the threshold of absorption and impermeability: it dwells on artifice (fabrication) to reveal the dialogical relationships between imagination and the logos of making. A messianic contact between the present and the specific moments of the past, as Benjamin would have liked to say, is the content of Kahn's rear-garde architecture.

Avant-Garde

4

Re-Thinking Architecture

The Blossoming of a Failure

Peter Burger's important work on the *Theory of the Avant-Garde*[1] is critical for understanding current architectural discourses. His argument that dadaism and constructivism failed to reintegrate art with life relegates the discourse of the avant-garde to the abyss of history. And his distinction between the political and aesthetic implications of modern art from those of the historical avant-garde are equally significant. Although written in the context of German academic inquiry about the state of art in 1960s, one can draw critical lessons from Burger for present architectural theory and practice. Besides addressing the question of autonomy, Burger reminds us of the historical avant-garde's programmatic differences with the sociopolitical vanguard of the nineteenth century on the one hand and the present neo-avant-garde on the other. Equally important is the "question concerning technology," coined by Martin Heidegger. Recalling the significance of technology for the historical avant-garde, a second thought on the nihilism of technology is unavoidable: what possessed a magical power and critical edge for the avant-garde has turned at the order of the culture industry.

Prior to Burger, most works on the avant-garde framed their problematics around concepts such as "aestheticism," "anti-tradition," and "futurism." These themes have made it difficult if not impossible to distinguish some tendencies within the modern movement from those of the historical avant-garde. Matei Claniscue, for example, pictures the avant-garde as the radical wing of the modern movement: "There is probably no single trait of the avant-garde in any of its historical metamorphoses that is not implied or even prefigured in the broader scope of modernity. There are, however, significant differences between the two movements. The avant-garde is in every respect more radical than modernity. Less flexible . . . naturally more dogmatic—both in the sense of self-assertion and, conversely, in the sense of self-destruction."[2] For Burger, on the other hand, the historical avant-garde's discourse comprises, first, an attack on art as an institution, and second, the need to reintegrate art into the life-world. This second point makes it clear that unlike the modernists' negative view on history, the historical avant-garde did not abolish "an earlier form of art (style), but an unassociated concept of art."[3] Confronting the drive for rationalization and for the autonomy of architecture, Manfredo Tafuri suggests that the avant-garde did not have many choices: "either the self-recognition of intellectual work as essentially work pure and simple, and therefore not something able to serve a revolutionary movement," or "an intellectual work that negates itself as such, claiming a position of pure ideology . . . Its objective, however, is always to get out of productive work and stand before it as its critical conscience."[4] Before analyzing Kenneth Frampton's and Tafuri's remarks on the dilemma of the avant-garde, the dialectic between the avant-garde and modern architecture needs consideration.

The esteem for simulating historical forms, and their exaltation by advocates of postmodern architecture, championing the end of modernity, is a farce. Certainly the last three decades testify to sociocultural and technological transformations that are critical for any revision of contemporary architecture. This observation is touched by poststructuralist discourse and does not agree with those postmodern tendencies who argue for an epochal break with modernity. Indeed, recalling the transformative content of the project of the historical avant-garde, it is possible to place the beginning of the end of modernity back in the sociocultural space opened by the failure of the 1874 Paris Commune. Kenneth Frampton has already spoken about this subject without explicitly identifying it with the end of modernity. In reference to the Fourierist artist G. D. Laverdent, Frampton concludes: "This initial avant-gardist thrust, unity in exuberant movement, both art and social protest, ceased to prevail as a phenomenon after the mid-1870s."[5] This reading rescues the idea of modernity from the political and cultural content of humanism. It also fosters modernity's critical dimension and puts the work of art beyond the vicissitudes of its autonomy and the current interest in periodization. In this context, the project of modernity designates the sociocultural aspirations of that brief period of time, around the 1870s, when the artistic avant-garde was in alliance with the political.[6] However, since the victorious advent of the resurgent bourgeoisie, the road toward concrete realization of autonomous art has not been interrupted.

The idea of autonomous architecture had already blossomed in the eighteenth-century episteme, anticipating contemporary formalism that will find its compositional logic in the subdivisions and dissociations introduced by socioeconomic imperatives of modernity. This proposition is convincing in light of Jean-François Lyotard's association of avant-garde art with the aesthetics of sublime discussed by Emmanuel Kant. According to Lyotard, sometime around the eighteenth century the unquestionable continuity of classical discourse came to a halt and the artist could ask him/herself "and what now?" The pleasure and pain of this historical moment found its aesthetic dimension in sublime. "It is around this name that the destiny of classical poetics was hazarded and lost; it is in this name that aesthetics asserted its critical rights over art, and that romanticism, in other words, modernity, triumphed."[7]

In *The Order of Things,* Michel Foucault suggests that the two notions of "character" and "structure" were instrumental in causing a break with the classical discourse of representation. Foucault argues that in the eighteenth century, "The area of general knowledge is no longer that of identities and differences, that of non-quantitative orders . . . but an area made of organic structures, that is, of internal relations between elements whose totality performs a function."[8] The concept of organic structure was not a totally new theme. But according to Foucault, the idea of organic structure, as a method of characterization, was new to the discourse of knowledge. Paralleling Foucault, one might claim that, by conceiving geometry as the internal structure of architecture, Etienne-Louis Boullee took a significant step toward overcoming the classical discourse of architecture. Obviously, to assign importance to Boullee on these grounds goes against those historical readings that present Claude Perrault as one of the first moderns. It is true that Perrault discussed architecture from a positivistic point of view; yet he saw and built within the paradigm of classical language of architecture.[9] In order for architecture to crumble from the weight of classical order, it had to do more than speculate in the problematic realm of positive and arbitrary beauties. Perrault's revolt from "classical doctrine" remained in the realm of ideas: no *epistemic* horizon had been opened to permit him to see arbitrary and positive beauties outside of the classical language of architecture.[10] Certain conceptual discontinuities and scientific horizons were needed in order to distill architecture from its classical wisdom.

In this paradox of formal expression and conceptual representation, Boullee's work maintained a unique place. The geometry so dominant in his architecture touched areas different from those of the Renaissance. In classical architecture, geometry sustained the similitude between everyday life and the divine order. For Boullee, on the other hand, geometry was an expressive means. The arrangement of a volume should be such, Boullee maintained, "that we can absorb at a glance the multiplicity of the separate elements that constitute the whole."[11] The result is an architectural object whose "character" can be effectively received by an observer. Anthony Vidler understands this aspect of Boullee's architecture to be a major advance in the transgression of classical wisdom. Independent of its classical garment, Vidler suggests, "the traditional sense of a building that embodied beauty in its proportions and in its three-dimensional geometries was gradually subordinated to the idea of a geometrical order that followed the dictates of social or environmental needs."[12]

In Boullee's design for Newton's cenotaph, the sphere is displaced from the realm of platonic ideas and is moved into the concrete domain of cultural discourse. This formal disposition, blended with a discourse on the theme of death, attains an epochal significance like that of J. L. David's paintings. *The Dead Marat* (figure 4.1), for example, illustrates the self-sacrifice and patriotism of the body for a revolutionary soul. Here the grief and tragedy of death are dispersed in the lightness of the soul.

The dialogue between body and soul receives its architectonic language in Boullee's work. In Newton's cenotaph, the sacred is removed from the body of death; its weight evaporates in the lightness of geometry. Did Boullee know that in Newton's theories, as Italo Calvino notes, "what most strikes the literary imagination is not the conditioning of everything and everyone by the inevitability of its own weight, but rather the balance of forces that enables heavenly bodies to float in space?"[13] The floating aspect of Boullee's architecture seemingly differentiated its geometry from that of the classicists. Furthermore, his discourse postulated form, in its totality, as the subject of an autonomous architecture.

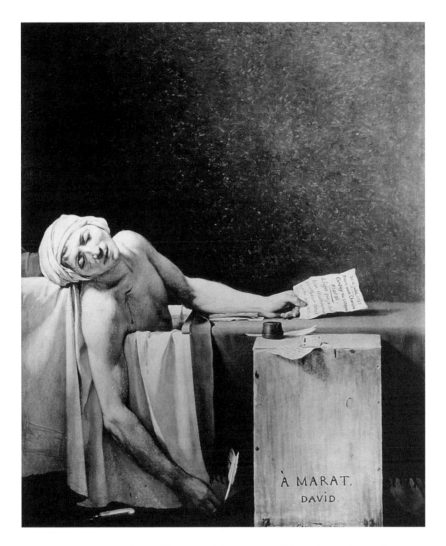

FIG. 4.1. Jacques Louis David, *The Dead Marat*. Courtesy Giraudon/Art Resources, New York.

Certain aspects of Boullee's architecture affirm these hypotheses. In Newton's cenotaph, the relationship between inside and outside is framed by the emblem of the sublime. Vidler writes, "The idea of classical architecture, which had never seen itself as a language, but only as a system of building confronting to laws of beauty, was now definitely superseded by an idea of architecture as expression." And he continues, "The role of architecture 'to construct' was gradually reconstructed to that of 'to speak.'"[14]

This reconstruction also retained the dichotomy between construction and ornament. The criticality of ornament in classical representation is articulated by Leon Battista Alberti. Dividing architecture into the two components of building and design, Alberti saw the function of ornament in elevating building into a phenomenon.[15] Boullee closed the gap between design and building and opened a space for the expressive aspect of his geometrical constructs. In Perrault we see an idea of modernity; Boullee's architecture, instead, departed from the world of similitude through which Alberti could project the image of a triumphal arch into the facade of an existing building.

Such an act of dissociation from "tradition" created a critical situation for artistic production. It is true that eighteenth-century discourse broke from the classical language of architecture; yet, it neither integrated art with politics nor moved toward a concrete realization of an autonomous architecture.[16] This historical threshold introduced a state of anxiety that was nullified by the repression of the Paris Commune. One might speculate that Francisco Goya's *Saturn Devouring His Children* anticipated that tragic event (figure 4.2). The fall of the Paris Commune may have shattered the utopia depicted by Saint Simon or Fourier for the first and, in view of our current political and cultural developments, for the last time.

The eighteenth-century artistic experience and the following sociopolitical development have provided a significant background for Western intelligentsia. Nevertheless, modern art took an ambivalent position in regard to its social context. According to Burger, "Since the middle of the nineteenth century, that is, subsequent to the consolidation of political rule by the bourgeoisie, this development has taken a particular turn: the form-content dialectic of artistic structures has increasingly shifted in favor of form."[17] Burger grounds his argument mainly on the experience of the literary and visual arts. However, his observations can be applied to architectural discourse as well. While Boullee's architecture could speak for certain aspects of its social and natural environment, his modernist heirs conceived form as a practical domain for their subjective intentionalities.[18] The major exponents of modern architecture took the sociocultural structure of the status quo for granted and sought their task in designing its physical environment. Peter Behren's "will to form" and the Bauhaus plan for the "total design" were justified in terms of the *Zeitgeist*. From Le Corbusier's Maison Domino to current postmodern and deconstructivist architecture, form has emerged as the sole content of the architect's analytics.

What divides modernist work from that of the avant-garde is the latter's "attempt to organize a new life praxis from a basis in

FIG. 4.2. Francisco Goya, *Saturn Devouring His Children*. Courtesy Giraudon/Art Resources, New York.

art."[19] Frampton has observed that it was left to the dadaists and the surrealists in art, and to the productivists in architecture to speculate on the integration of art into the practice of life.[20] While the Italian futurists and the Dutch neoplasticists founded their ideas on the physical and perceptual horizons offered by new technologies, the productivists "sought to develop a new rooted culture based on the everyday production of the people themselves and on the fulfillment of their immediate informational needs."[21] Drawing from the experience of the Russian and European avant-garde, Burger agrees with Theodor Adorno that the historical avant-garde's project should be interpreted as a critical discourse against an ongoing drive for autonomous art.[22] For Burger, the dialectic of the avant-garde and the modern movement came to an end when art was institutionalized.[23] This moment also registers the contamination of high art and pop art by each other.[24] This last point should not be taken, as Burger does, for the eclipse of political art, or for that matter, for the end of critical architecture. Instead of pessimism, we need to reassess the experience of modernity with a classificatory mode that would address the present ideological problematic. One should stress, for example, the ways that the failure of the project of the historical avant-garde allowed modern architecture to be criticized from within for the first time. Andreas Huyssen's observation is apt: "The revolt of the 1960s was never a rejection of modernism per se, but rather a revolt against that version of modernism which had been domesticated in the 1950s . . . It no longer opposed a dominant class and its world view, nor had it maintained its programmatic purity from contamination by the culture industry."[25] One should also underline the change taking place in the attitude of the institutions of art in the last four decades. Hal Foster observes that since the 1940s, American museums have promoted a kind of work that in the context of modernity would question the very function of those institutions.[26] Interestingly enough, the show of deconstructivist architecture at MoMA and its reception in different strata of architectural discipline is a reminder of the fact that, in late capitalism, a premature marginal discourse could be (must be?) contaminated by the cycle of production and consumption.

I am not suggesting that postmodern architecture cannot engage in any possible avant-garde practice. But such a practice should give attention to the following two distinctions. First, it is important for architecture to address its differences from the fine arts and literature; architecture is a *métier* whose production is severely tied to the exigencies of capital: land, labor, and building technologies. Any recourse by architects into pure formalist enterprise falls short of searching for a critical discourse and therefore remains either in the transgressive tradition of modernity or in the presentational mode of the historical avant-garde.[27] The strong historicist belief in the metaphysical content of classical forms is as much presentational as was the Russian productivist belief in proletariat as the subject of history. By the same token one could argue that the deconstructivists' internalization of the nihilism of technology into architecture still remains in the modernist transgressive mode.

Second, no discussion of the avant-garde would do justice without highlighting the ways that current simulative technologies differ from the early modern heavy industrial technologies. Indeed, conceptual techniques such as collage and montage, which were instrumental for the sociopolitical content of the historical avant-garde art, are now technologies (machines) at the service of the culture industry. Again Foster: "More than any avant-garde, capital is the great agent of transgression and shock—which is one reason why such strategies in art now seem as redundant as resistance seems futile."[28] Besides (a point already discussed in the last two chapters), at the expense of the tectonic, telecommunication technologies have contributed nothing to modern techniques of construction except camouflaging the latter with spectacular appearances.

The Myth of Technology
After Heidegger, one could not do justice to a discussion of the avant-garde and modern architecture without referring to the development of technology. Mechanization not only opened a new perceptual horizon, it transformed economic and cultural domains. In the nineteenth century, technology was conceived of, and functioned, merely as an economic entity; the influence of scientific discoveries was more visible in the sphere of production and machinery. The production processes of different cultural artifacts became subject to technological change. The depth of this technological infusion depended upon the topological place of an artifact in the overall organization of the production line. While some products were produced by conventional means and materials, others, closely related to the imperatives of the market, became subject to radical technical transformations: we are reminded of the development of new forms of transportation in the years following the Industrial Revolution and their impact on the formal and conceptual aspects of the design of bridges and train stations. In more recent times, the scarcity of housing after World War II introduced the idea of prefabrication to architecture. But already in 1925 Le Corbusier was attracted to the precision of the machine, the beauty of engineering, and the creation of industrial buildings. For him, these works resulted from "the eyes which do see!" Le Corbusier's dreams came true when the

line demarcating the cultural from the technical was blurred by technology. In fact, "technology has come to occupy a destinal horizon, since it no longer represents a variable of economic development but is established as the destiny, both congenital and irremediable, of the Western metaphysical discourse."[29] The point is not to blame modern architects who rethought architecture in conjunction with industrial technology. The criticism should be directed to a postmodernity that does not acknowledge the differences between modern reproductive technologies and the current simulative one.

Yet the question concerning technology is not technological. Rather, it lies in the idea of "enframing," a state of mind that "has the character of a setting-upon, in the sense of a challenging forth."[30] Heidegger's observation posits modern technology outside the domain of *techne*. Technology draws only from its own resources, while *techne* precedes practical knowledge and resides, in significant part, in poetics.[31] In lieu of electronic media, technology has expanded its territory of domination from the technical to the cultural. In a sense, mass production has metamorphosized into mass culture. The technological drive for commodification has deprived the project of the avant-garde from its critical content; these technologies present an understanding of the reality conceived of, and grasped, as picture.[32] Jean Baudrillard articulates the transformation:

> We must remember this: The aim of art was once precisely to posit the power of illusion against reality. There was a time when art was trying to make reality play a game which was different to the game that art itself was playing. . . . But today this is no longer the great game that art is playing. All the art forms are now playing the game at the level of the simulation of reality—and whether the particular art form be painting or architecture makes no difference whatsoever.[33]

The technique that for the futurists and constructivists was a means of social redemption, and for the dadaists and surrealists, a power to invade the spiritual realm, now has turned into technology itself. The essence of technology has not changed, but there has been a structural transformation in the ways that metaphysics folds and unfolds the *logos*. For Heidegger, "only to the extent that man, for his part, is already challenged can the ordering revealing of the challenge occur."[34] Hence, the shock element, once an artistic expression of resistance, has now become a means to mask the nihilism of technology.

The failure of the project of the historical avant-garde, coupled with the nihilism of technology, has problematized current theories of architecture. At stake is the scope of possibilities for a critical discourse of architecture. Tafuri, for example, holds that the experience of the modern movement after the eighteenth century is interrupted by "the very gap that exists between avant-garde ideology and the translation into technique of that ideology."[35] Tafuri suggests that this gap should be turned "into the material of concrete and widespread knowledge." Thus the idea of "history as a project of crisis" becomes the motto for rewriting the history of architecture,[36] and a tool for critical analysis of current architectural practices. Tafuri's reading is informed by the fact that "the thematic of the boundary interior to forms, of the limits of language, is an integral part of a historically determined crisis beyond which (but within the signpost that it has imposed upon us) we are today obliged to situate ourselves."[37] The historicist walls Tafuri sets around contemporary artistic practice leave no room for us to make any assessment about the present architectural practice, except considering them hysterical reactions to the void left by the avant-garde.[38] His ideas recall Burger's conclusions, as interpreted by Jochen Schulte-Sasse:[39] Are we paralyzed before the objective laws of historical determinism independent of human subjectivity? Or should we accept hibernation as the only bastion of art in bad times? Again, one thinks of the power of institutionalized "art" and the simulation of reality by art.

Heidegger offers a different response to the question of technology and its relations to power and art.[40] For him a decisive confrontation with the nihilism of technology "must happen in a realm that is, on the one hand, akin to the essence of technology, and on the other, fundamentally different from it."[41] According to Heidegger, that realm is art. For him the "end" of art creates a historical situation in which the premodern relation between art and truth is deconstructed. Upon the loss of the Kantian "common sense" understanding of art, Heidegger offers the idea that art itself becomes a register for truth.[42] Since the work of art has ontological relation with the instrumental dimension of artifacts, the work of art, Heidegger believed, could disclose the essence of technology. It is this dimension of Heidegger's thought that Tafuri comes short of entertaining. And conversely, it is Frampton's "critical regionalism"[43] that in a complex way comes close to Adorno's idea that modern art mourns over its subjugation to the forces of commodification.

The idea of art as the last bastion of resistance against the weight of the stones of history and the power of the culture industry is crucial for Frampton's oeuvre. Recognizing the negative aspects of the modern movement, Frampton rethinks the project of the historical avant-garde. Emphasizing the tectonic of space making, he advocates an associative understanding of architecture that draws its semantic aspects from the domain of existence, a place where the cultural dynamics of our present condition of life take place. If read in the context of romanticist opposition to modernity, Frampton's position might sound like a nostalgic yearning for the loss of an organic integrity between architecture and community. But in regard to postmodern disenchantment with the transgressive dimension of the historical avant-garde, Frampton thinks of an architecture that, in lieu of such a historical development, becomes an index for disclosing the truth content of such a loss. The mourning involved in experiencing modernization would prepare architecture, first, to apprehend the historicality of modernization, and second, to make the ground to depart for a different architecture. And yet, in a very complex way, critical regionalism entertains the postmodern concept of "both-and." Frampton charges architecture with sociopolitical aims. At the same time, by utilizing the technique of defamiliarization,[44] his critical regionalism induces a semiological understanding of architecture. For him the tactile and tectonic dimensions of the work should display the impact of modernization on the architectonic elements of a given region.

I wish to emphasize here the differences between the mourning implied in critical regionalism and Robert Venturi's architecture of communication. The heterogeneous character of Venturi's work is informed by the collapse of the wall separating kitsch from high art. In the addition to the National Gallery in London, for example, Venturi juxtaposes the architectonic elements of high modernism with classical vocabulary (figures 4.3 and 4.4). The contextualism implied in front facade is a cardboard simulation of the language of the adjacent building. The side facade, instead, is covered by a Miesian steel and glass wall. The balance Venturi maintains between high modernism and the values of the mass culture (which for historical reasons is more at home with conventional ambiances) discloses an aesthetic valorization unleashed in many disciplines since the 1960s. However, one should not criticize him for being sympathetic to the erosion of the boundaries separating high art from pop art. To present a better picture of Venturi's problematic and his difference from critical regionalism a few historical references might be useful. Consider the Bauhaus project and Adolf Loos's position in the context of the early century's drive for modernization. While most advocates of the Bauhaus pursued the alignment of architecture with the production line and others, like Peter Behrens who covered the structure of new building types with classical language, masking the fragmentation launched by the Metropolis, Loos first insisted on the separation of architecture from art and second proposed a dialectical relationship between technology and architecture.[45] I am not suggesting following his tactics for ambiguity or "his attempt to find an ideal synthesis within the dramatically fragmented reality in which he lived."[46] Instead of Venturisque corporatization of architecture, one should think of an architecture that evolves out of the dialectics of rupture and reconciliation with the very conditions of postmodernity. Venturi's architecture dispenses with the experience of modernity and substitutes simulation and image making for both the tec-

FIG. 4.3. Sainsbury Wing, National Gallery, London, 1991. Courtesy Venturi, Scott Brown and Associates, Inc. Photograph by Matt Wargo.

FIG. 4.4. Sainsbury
Wing, National
Gallery, London,
1991. Courtesy
Venturi, Scott Brown
and Associates, Inc.
Photograph by Matt
Wargo.

tonic and haptic dimensions of architectural space. It is in this
paradox that Frampton's critical regionalism comes forward as
both antimodern and antipostmodern. Frampton's architecture
of resistance problematizes the incision forced into the *genius
loci* of a culture by the very process of modernization. He rejects
a modernism that uncritically would subject architecture to the
forces of mechanization, and yet he does not accept the postmodern critique of the project of modernity.

However, the kind of works Frampton has chosen to support his discourse are mostly practiced in regions that, for historical reasons, are not directly engaged with the cultural implications of late capitalism. Praising Frampton's approach, Hal Foster observes, "the principle of 'critical regionalism' is tied to a problem that may not still be our own, not entirely anyway."[47] Frampton stresses the cultural dimension of architecture and, like Heidegger, grounds architecture in the Greek *techne,* suggesting that the work should not be blind to the material used and that, as the art of building, architecture should restore meaning to the life-world. Yet if technology is entered and almost dominating the cultural, can we speak of the values of culture as an entity apart from the nihilism of technology? And more important, can we think of the tactile experience of the body when technology is constantly liquidating the place—both in the West and in other geographic spaces—from the very residue of its premodern life-world? As soon as architecture is separated from craft/place matrix of tradition, it has no choice but to lose or compromise its autonomy under the spell of modernization. This process was accelerated by the general drive of modern architecture for *Sachlichkeit.* And yet if few architects, besides Alvar Aalto, like Walter Gropius of the Residence of Dr. Abele (Mass., 1941) and Le Corbusier of "Petite Maison de Weekend" (figure 2.4), could still entertain sensibilities drawn from the tradition of building and place, by the 1960s, the technological turn had tossed the "cultural" into the orbit of commodification.[48] The nihilism of technology has infiltrated all known geographical spaces, and to assign autonomy to culture might mean to fall back into the discourse of good and evil (national cultures vs. modernization).[49]

Frampton's affinity for Heidegger is well-known.[50] And if there is a residue of romanticism in his position it might come from an early criticism of modernization and a Heidegger who looked back to Greek experience to find a remedy for the suffering of modern art. Between the lines of critical regionalism one should read, as I suggested before, an Adornoesque understanding of modern art's mourning whose criticality comes neither from the loss of an ideal past nor from a Ruskinian dream for a bygone culture where art and technology were reconciled. In fact, critical regionalism mourns because of the process of secularization, a transformation that every contemporary cultural product, including architecture, must face. It is this political potentiality in Frampton's discourse that has made him a good target for both conservative and reactionary postmodernist, while neo-avant-gardism of a deconstructivist bent cunningly avoids it. In this paradox, Peter Eisenman maintains a position peculiar to the historical avant-garde: he pursues the process of total dematerialization of architecture, first by deconstruction of the ethos of humanist discourse and second by withdrawing architecture from its alleged public function. Eisenman wants to "save" architecture not only from the spirit of gravity but from any form/content metaphysics. Yet his "formless" architecture intends to be as political as that of Venturi and Frampton. What makes these major postmodern discourses different from each other has to do with the political color of their architecture. One should indeed gauge their position by asking, as Benjamin would do, what is the work's position in the relations of the production of architecture in late capitalism. (It is this sociopolitical function of architecture that Tafuri found hard to achieve, and thus sought a Hegelian indictment for the end of architecture). To do him justice, it should be stated that after the failure of the project of the historical avant-garde, Tafuri sees no political function for art but a resilient acceptance of commodification.

However, caught in a Heideggerian rift between the "yes" and "no" position to technology, Frampton presents a different reading of the "void" left by the failure of the project of the historical avant-garde. This is implied in concluding remarks of his recent reflection on the subject:

> In this oscillation between doubt and faith, the idea of modernity, along with the process of modernization, has been beset by a cyclical crisis, among which the emergence of the so-called post-modern period is hopefully not the last. At the same time the storm of progress condemns us to wander through the ruins of history like Benjamin's angel, not only the history of the Classic and Gothic, the history of the lost vernacular, but also the history of the historical avant-garde and the history of those colonized, once enchanted civilizations that are now subject to the modernizing law; those others of which, as Ricoeur reminds us, we are but one more other.[51]

This journey into history endorses the inevitability of the process of secularization and a sense of spatiality that alludes to the nonoppositional mode of late capitalism.[52] In this space, one also notices a discursive shift in modernist interest from homogeneity of time and place (historicism) to heterogeneity of space—feminism, ethnic, and gender, just to mention a few considerations that have become topical for current restructuring of space-time-being.[53] In this conjunction, architecture can no longer pursue transgressive and oppositional tactics. There is also no room for eclecticism or stylistic agendas complacent to the conservative side of the status-quo culture.

The historical space Frampton speaks of suggests that architecture be read at two levels. First is a genealogical study of themes accumulated throughout the culture of building.[54] These themes, as will be discussed in the next chapter, are formative for understanding architecture as the tectonic of space making. Second, architecture should be rethought in response to alternatives sought by institutions whose power is exercised in the public spaces. A genealogical work on architecture and its relation to the city unfolds a project of "recollection" that stands for the return of neither history (time) nor place (culture) but for the spatiality of architectural discourse itself.[55] A sense of spatiality analogous to the openings made by telecommunication technologies, it surpasses national and historical boundaries, providing a sense of "total space" in which the opaque historicist walls are replaced by transparent enclosures.[56] Only in this space can one critically apprehend the current return of eclecticism and avant-gardism and their different discursive performances within the project of modernity. This spatiality also encourages one to think of architecture beyond the humanist discourse: since the Renaissance, architecture has been conceived as a self-contained entity theorizing the return of classical forms or deconstruction of the former's ethos. All said, the reader should have no delusion about my proposed spatial transparency: It does not define an *epistemic* rupture. At stake is the modernist mode of disclosure, that things are made and seen to enchant technology, as Heidegger would say. Postmodernity epitomizes a standstill sense of history; itself a spatial enclosure whose power is folded and unfolded in the numerous utterances we postmoderns make with prefixes such as "re," "de," and "post."

Two Textual Levels of Architecture

> Let us therefore agree that the idea of eternal return implies a perspective from which things appear other than as we know them. They appear without the mitigating circumstances of their transitory nature.
> —Milan Kundera,
> *The Unbearable Lightness of Being*

Compared with disciplines such as language, labor, and medicine, architecture maintains what is not yet recognized as a "formation," to use the word coined by Michel Foucault,[1] nor has it been classified as a mere utilitarian artifact. It would do nothing for the complexities of architecture to discuss it as if it were an art whose discourse is canonized by the humanist vision of the fine arts. Yet one cannot deny the thematic sharing among architecture, painting, and sculpture, and more important, the presence of a sense of *métier* in architecture that is essential for craft-oriented industries. This paradox of craft vs. art framed the entire discourse of modern architecture, and it was left to Mies van der Rohe to articulate its dialectics. According to him, architecture, on the one hand, responds to its "intrinsic lawfulness" (the tectonic), and on the other, results from a creative act. This understanding of architecture is in fact embedded in the German word *Baukunst,* meaning "building art." In this respect, architecture neither refers to the sublime beauty of its technique nor connotes the semantic depth of its figure. In a broader scope of consideration, architecture folds and unfolds the conditions of the life-world. Obviously I am speaking for a semiautonomous reading of architecture whose "intrinsic lawfulness" is constantly reinterpreted within prevailing cultural discourses and technological developments.

For a better understanding of Mies's position, it is useful to ask, what are the thematic choices by which one can map the limits of architecture? We are not concerned with those visible boundaries at which something stops but with those "from which something begins its presencing."[2] Martin Heidegger's statement seems to anticipate Louis Kahn's vision: "architecture has limits—and when we touch the invisible walls of the limits, then we know more about what is contained in them."[3]

Both in practice and in theory, the architectural experience of the last century comprised different readings of the limits of architecture. It is beyond the scope of this volume to discuss the response of various sectors of modern architecture to the crisis of the object that was induced by the mechanical reproduction of art.[4] Implied in Walter Benjamin's idea of the loss of aura is the crisis of the subject too. The separation of the work of art from its ritualistic and symbolic world coincided with the alienation of the subject from her/his products. This state of mind was radicalized by the turn of century, and the entire efforts of modern architects were directed to close the gap between the subject and the physical world reshuffled by the industrial revolution. According to Friedrich Nietzsche, the historical malady of the nineteenth century speaks for an excessive historiographic awareness that could not create its own history.[5] The critical implications of the crisis of the subject for architecture were repressed, temporarily, by the humanistic, self-centered subject embedded in the modern utopia. In fact a major facet of postmodern debate is concerned with the possibilities for a new line of thinking about the subject and its tectonic ramifications.

What brings me back constantly to the idea of the tectonic is indeed the place of history in architecture. The criticality of this subject for the experience of modernity and its problematic continuity in present architecture have been discussed throughout this volume. Here I would like to underline the significance of Mies and Adolf Loos, whose work along with Le Corbusier's constitute three major resources for current rethinking of the limits of architecture. Their work helped to recode the tradition of architecture in the context of the experience of modernity.[6]

It is also useful to recall Le Corbusier's *Towards a New Architecture* in order to stress, for the last time, his presence in postfunctionalist architecture. Le Corbusier reformulated the humanist subject in the index of the century's achievements, tracing its creative potentialities in engineering and painting: the one for its truthfulness to the universal laws ("mechanical selection"[7]), and the other, for its aesthetic qualities.[8] In this paradox, Le Corbusier mapped the vicissitudes of an architecture in which the theme of construction is pushed aside in favor of an aesthetic whose sublime beauty would raise emotion in the hearts of those who could see it.[9]

The "erosion" of the theme of construction in Le Corbusier's thought needs attention. It discloses the conclusions he had already made about nineteenth-century architectural discourse. His belief that Gothic architecture was not plastic, and thus devoid of any sentimental nature, is worth mentioning. His position also undermined the work of those architects who stressed the importance of construction. I am thinking of Viollet-le-Duc's, or for that matter, Gottfried Semper's thought on the tectonic. Yet Le Corbusier did not take sides with the classical revivalists of the period either. For him, a new architecture was conceivable only by "translating" the thematic of humanist discourse (including the absence of the concept of the tectonic in Renaissance architecture) by means of an aesthetic abstraction already at work in the purist paintings. Le Corbusier's reduction of the purpose of construction to "making things hold together" has in many ways resurfaced in postfunctionalist architecture. It is not far-fetched to argue that the theme of construction so dear to Kahn and Mies is brushed aside in the work and writings of Robert Venturi, the New York Five architects, and in deconstructivist architecture as well.

In contrast to Le Corbusier's platonism, Mies and Loos redeemed the tradition of architecture by rethinking it according to the imperatives of the process of secularization. While Le Corbusier tried to make homologies between the *Zeitgeist* and those aspects of cultural life that were not yet touched by mechanization, Loos disclosed a complex position: the whitewashed exteriors of his buildings resonated the silence of the Metropolis while their "intimate" interiors were conceived as the ultimate space to recuperate from the toil of the *unheimlich* public realm. And where Le Corbusier's interest in the "right angle" paved the way for the oculus to rise up and stare out of the horizontal openings of the Villa Savoye, Loos turned the back of the seats in the Moller House against the window and created an internal virtual center. Around that center, different rooms were arranged in such a way that each one stands like a stage for the others to watch. Loos's interior spaces held together those aspects of domestic culture that were commonly shared and were critical for the dichotomies between culture and technology. Le Corbusier, instead, introduced the forces of mechanization into the entire body of the domestic culture, siding with the Bauhaus's project for total design.

Nevertheless, it was left to Mies to dramatize the Loosian tradition and to recode the craft of architecture by his ambivalent position on technology. Mies's understanding of technology "as a means of realization and seeing it as a potential threat"[10] did not stop him from underlining the importance of the tectonic as the "linguistic quality" of architecture. I will discuss Theodor Adorno's views on linguistic quality shortly; here I would like to mark the following points: Mies's deterritorialization[11] of the language of modern architecture prompts second thoughts about postmodernists' transparent discourse on tradition and a deconstructivism that, even in light of the failure of the historical avant-garde, cannot hear Adorno's belief that "all social utopias since Plato's merge in a dismal resemblance to what they were devised against. The leap into the future, clean over the condition of the present, lands in the past."[12]

The reappearance of a repressed past seems to be the uncanny state of the postmodern subject. For Sigmund Freud, every repressed emotion is eventually transformed into anxiety, and therefore, the uncanny is nothing but "something familiar and old—established in the mind that has been estranged only by the process of repression."[13] Accordingly, one might argue that the "doubling" of historical forms prevalent in postmodern architecture speaks for the failure of an avant-garde state of mind who took the temporary repression of tradition for its total banishment. What the historical avant-garde sought to push to the outside boundaries of history was indeed their own discursive problematics. In return, one might associate the apparent radicalism of deconstructivist architecture with a state of mental anxiety that cannot accept the failure of the project of the historical avant-garde and thus the return of historicism. Their blindness to this aspect of the postmodern conditions is ideological and not fancying with styles.

Exploring the different manifestations of the uncanny in present architecture, Anthony Vidler states: "The apparently irreconcilable demands for the absolute negation of the past and full representation of the past here meet in their inevitable reliance on a language of architectural forms that seems, in the surface at least, to echo already used-up motifs *enabime*."[14] The psychoanalytical point of view reduces the problematic of architecture to the psychic dimension of the individual and dispenses with the socioideological and technical aspects of architecture. Nevertheless, the historicity of the uncanny is not anterior to the experience of modernity. Whether contemporary artists were conscious of this historical conjunction or able to direct this phenomenon to its critical end is another issue.[15] In retrospect, one might argue that modernity was not supposed to produce the "new" but to dress the old with the new, the "always-the-same." Paradoxically, in a postmodernity where the subject of the death of the author is topical, it seems plausible to discuss architecture either in light of the individual psyche, and thus the importance of the unconscious, or to conceive architecture as an autonomous entity perceived in an isolated environment.[16]

Both postmodernism and deconstructivism advocate a self-autonomous discourse—one by believing in the universality of the classical language of architecture, the other by pressing on deconstruction theory—accelerating the termination of architecture and its reduction to a text. This esteem for the death of architecture is not Hegelian in nature: it discloses the problematic of a point of view that escapes the ghost of historicism and opens the limits of architecture to science, art, and philosophy.

And yet, the recent philosophical interest in architecture performs a twofold task; on the one hand, it is part of the tradition of metaphysics to articulate its epistemological horizon around issues directly concerned with aesthetics in general, and architecture in particular. On the other, the inclusion of architectural topics in recent philosophical texts indicates that philosophy, and especially deconstruction theory, has realized the impossibility of erecting its "ground" without the concurrent deconstruction of architecture.[17] Seemingly, this last point is not of interest to a deconstructivism whose drive to prey upon the corporeality of architecture makes one think of the mutilated bodies depicted in Francis Bacon's paintings.[18] Might this obsession with fragmented and dismembered forms be in part a desire to resist the anthropomorphism that is central to the classical discourse? Or is it a mirror image of the decentered self of the postmodern subject? In the lacuna unfolded by the idea of the "death" of architecture/author, one is tempted to suggest that "the future is secret again."[19]

This aphorism has merit when one recalls architectural thought of the late nineteenth century and the works of the international style. Compare the best buildings built under the principles of the international style with Victor Horta's Hotel Tassel in Brussels. While the former located the limits of architecture in the vicissitudes of technology and the aesthetics of the machine, the latter discloses a complex dialogue between architecture and technology. Kenneth Frampton notes that Horta "treated iron as though it were an organic filament insinuated into the fabric to subvert the inertia of stone."[20] Horta's columns are not classical, nor do they anticipate the modern perception of column, a nonfigurative white cylinder. Yet, like Frank Furness, Horta connotes the idea of "beginning": He sees and constructs the column according to the structural and formal potentialities of iron. One might speculate that Horta conceived of architecture through the maze (Benjamin would say "the bloody fog"[21]) surrounding the life of the industrial city and the perceptual domain offered by new technologies. Horta's was the architectonic expression of what Benjamin called a "wish image" by which the collective memory marks the "new nature," the world produced by industrial technology. In addition, "these wish-fulfilling images manifest an emphatic striving for dissociation with the outmoded—with the most recent past."[22] At a glance, it seems the collective memory here performs a conservative role. But upon closer observation, as Susan Buck-Morss reminds us, one should make the following distinction: "In nature, the new is mythic because its potential is not yet realized; in consciousness, the old is mythic, because its desires never were fulfilled. Paradoxically, collective imagination mobilizes its powers for a revolutionary break from the recent past by evoking a cultural memory reservoir of myths and utopian symbols from a more distant ur-past."[23] In other words, the unfulfilled potentialities of the past can be preserved only by rethinking them within the experience of modernity.

If one agrees with Benjamin's reading of the nineteenth century's cultural formation, then an oversimplified analogy might suggest that our very postmodern culture, marked by the loss of center and history, and by the perceptual domains offered by media technology, speaks for a historical threshold too. This analogy attains its critical level when one gives attention to Jean-François Lyotard. For him postmodernity is nothing but a delay in the project of modernity. This temporal delay was caused by the project of the historical avant-garde whose failure unmasked the metaphysical content of the utopia of the modern movement and the return of "tradition," a repressed subject topical for the architecture of the 1960s. This historical awareness has made room for some scholars to speculate on the death of the author, but more important, it has introduced a spatial void in which technology extends its function beyond the realm of the technical and into the cultural. However, the present sociocultural situation presents a state of stillness, a pause, through which one can rethink architecture beyond both traditionalist and neo-avant-garde discourses. Again, one thinks of the uncertainties induced in the early nineteenth century and the impossibility for architects to sustain the totality of the classical language of architecture: For them the time was not ripe to align architecture with technology.[24] Certain aesthetic horizons had to be reached and technical developments made in order for Horta's column to dissociate itself from the "outmoded" and to take its new architectonic form in Le Corbusier's abstract white piloti.[25]

The above association between current architecture with its near past does not imply a linear or cyclical concept of history. Nor am I suggesting wiping the slate clean and starting from scratch. Rather, to use a term popular these days, I speak for a history understood in terms of recycling. In this paradigm, it becomes critical to compare the notion of beginning to that of origin. Implied in the latter is the idea of an end already conceived and planned to be reached by a linear progression. It also relegates the presence of truth into a blank point in history and invigorates a constant desire to return to the origin of the loss. Beginning, instead, is historical: It opens a schemata where there are no directions or preconceived ends. According to Foucault, "History is the concrete body of development, with its moments of intensity, its lapses, its extended periods of feverish agitation, its fainting spells; and only a metaphysician would seek its soul in the distance ideality of the origin." Beginning discloses a state of unknown potentialities, "derisive and ironic, capable of undoing every infatuation."[26]

I contend that capturing the limits of architecture without replicating historical forms leaves us with a major critical option, that is, to engage in a genealogical study of architecture. This focus on history is not a search for origin, nor does it attempt to reactivate historical solutions to current problems. Genealogy is the act of "recollecting," through which the scope of a given discourse is broadened. Genealogy "fragments what was thought unified; it shows the heterogeneity of what was imagined constant with itself."[27] However, there may be different ways to provide substance to this notion of beginning. One might even ask if this subject has not already occupied a formative place in the present architectural theories. A positive response to this question would not dispense with my claim that both postmodern and deconstructivist architecture remain in the vicissitudes of humanist discourse; they designate the formal traits and canonic rules of classical architecture as the only subject for architecture to copy or deconstruct.[28] In this paradox, reduced to a single edifice, architecture is conceived as a representational form stopping short of playing any critical role in the physical construction of the conditions of life.

In chapter 1 I discussed the weight of classical discourse in the neorationalist emphasis on typology, in the postmodern esteem for simulation of historical forms, and finally in the theoretical vigor of deconstructivist architecture. Beyond these three architectural theories, it is possible to think of an alternative discourse of beginning by focusing on what may be called recollection of "the culture of inhabiting."[29] This encompasses themes that have accumulated in historical work, both in theory and practice, including thematic dualities such as inside/outside, structure/ornament, column/wall, and so forth, as well as the hermeneutics of their construction. These themes are historical and suggest an architecture beyond any stylistic consideration. Conceived, theorized, and practiced in various regions, the culture of inhabiting unfolds a semiautonomous architecture whose discourse circulates in the heterogenous spaces left by the death of the author.[30] Here recollection does not intend to correct what went wrong with a certain theme in such a place and time. It also does not construct a nostalgic remembrance of some forgotten past. Recollection is a counter memory that "distorts"[31] any unified cultural experience that attempts to attain a hegemonic position. In this process, architecture accommodates itself to the existing subjective and objective conditions and unfolds its poetics within the limits of the culture of inhabiting. Again, the limits are not perceived in the gradual progression of a certain theme toward its evolutionary peak but are located in the "flashing line that causes the limit to arise."[32]

We must also stress the dialectical relation between architecture and its sociocultural structure. It is true that genealogical study opens a critical view of architectural history; however, we cannot forget our present historical situation: we should conceive architectural knowledge as an indivisible part of its social reality, a structure within another.[33] Manfredo Tafuri is correct in proposing that a genealogical study must, on the one hand, "be made possible of critically describing the processes that conditions the concrete side of the creation of objects, that is to say, the autonomy of linguistic choices and their historical function as a specific chapter in the history of intellectual labor and its mode of reception. On the other hand, genealogical study must fit into the general history of the structures and relations of production."[34] This position implicitly addresses the question of the ontology of the present and its construing.

The problematic of current architectural theories rests in the gaps that sustain the nihilism of technology and the separation of architecture from the city. Mechanization had profound impact on social relations and the metaphysics of humanism. It subjugated those relations to the process of secularization and prepared the ground for the actual realization of Heidegger's idea of "standing-reserve": Technology frames a window through which everything is seen to be nothing but matter at hand for a technical service.[35] Yet the essence of the nihilism of technology is not technical. Various conceptual and scientific discoveries were needed in order to facilitate the departure from techniques of territorial domination for spatial ones. This historical advent transformed the life-world and its physical context. According to Foucault the idea of the city as a cluster of heterogenous institutions was critical for the nineteenth-century technological developments.[36] In this context, the opening of the *Ecol des Ponts et Chaussees* should be underlined: It initiated the dissociation of *techne* from architectural discourse. In return, architecture had no choice but to face the imperatives of a technology whose matrix of development had nothing to do with architecture. The alienation of technology from architecture was accelerated by some factions of the Bauhaus school and by the avant-garde who either strived to postpone the ultimate results of the nihilism of technology or sought to modify it according to the actual needs of people, as was the case with the Russian productivists.[37]

A critical approach to the nihilism of the technology and the city, and their implications for architecture, would complement our genealogical study. Mies's later work commands our attention again. Placed against the chaos of the Metropolis, the strong geometrical configuration of the New National Gallery in Berlin (figure 5.1), for example, recalls Mies's appeal for order as a "definition of meaning and measure of being."[38] Yet the glass enclosure of its void anticipates the silence of the "culture indus-

try." One also thinks of Mies's Friedrichstrasse in Berlin (figure
5.2), where the building functions as a dis-joint, mediating between the culture of building and the loss of center experienced
in the Metropolis. Similarly, in some of his drawings, the human
figure is depicted within a space cleared of any figural dimension.
The void maintains its meaning not in its undecorated surfaces
but in anchoring architecture to the solitude of modern man.
According to Francesco Dal Co, "It is the architecture of Mies
and not the steel constructions of the Bauhaus which tells of the
withering of modern experience."[39] Mies's sheer glass enclosures
nullified the dichotomy between inside and outside spaces and
blurred the otherness of metropolis.

The above painted picture of the relationship between architecture and the city is not sufficient if we do not discuss what was
happening at the same time on the other side of the Atlantic. It is

to Rem Koolhaas's credit that he read the grid of Manhattan as a mental construct embodying solutions for the problems posited by Metropolis. In New York City, the grid disclosed a horizon to supersede both the nostalgic and utopistic visions. One might discuss the grid in terms of the Greek word *techne,* a practical rationality grounded by a conscious goal at work in the dawn of civilization.[40] The grid unfolds a total space, a site for a non-conventional relationship between architecture and the city. In New York, Koolhaas observed, "Beaux Arts sensibility can only

FIG. 5.2. Ludwig Mies van der Rohe, Friedrichstrasse Skyscaper, Berlin, project, 1921. Courtesy Ludwig Mies van der Rohe Archive, Museum of Modern Art, New York.

go where there is no Grid, that is: underground."[41] The grid in Manhattan left the ground empty for the unpredictable tide of construction and deconstruction, a constant recycling process analogous to what was going on in the dawn of this century between Manhattan and Coney Island.[42] However, one might pursue in Koolhaas's reading of the relation of architecture and the city a Miesian project of renunciation, or more specifically, an avant-gardist tactic of "automatic writing," that is to subdue the subject to the point where the process shapes its material substance. Automatic writing was already at work in New York: Here the solution to the problem of congestion, for example, was sought in escalating congestion "to such intensity that it generates—as a quantum leap—a completely new condition where congestion becomes mysteriously positive."[43] Fritz Neumeyer eloquently discusses the presence of such a design strategy in Ludwig Hilberseimer, Mies, and most important, Karl Fredrich Schinkel's concept of the "cubical city"[44] (figure 5.3).

Learning from modern artistic production in general and Mies's work in particular, we might designate two textual levels for architecture. The autonomous aspect of architecture embodies themes and concepts whose particular enunciation characterizes the culture of inhabiting. Architecture as such surpasses the formal boundaries of historicism and establishes its limits in the terrain of its formative themes.[45] Yet, architectural knowledge is

also inspired by thematic modifications taking place within architecture and beyond it. Technological developments, along with the infusion of certain concepts from other discourses, blend architectural autonomy with dependency. To emphasize for a semiautonomous architecture does not imply that architecture should mirror its social and technical realities. The social aspect of architecture is rather measured by the degree of resistance it exerts against the power unleashed by nondiscursive and institutional practices.[46] It is possible to trace the theme of renunciation in Mies's work, in his deterritorialization of the established language of the international style. In return, his architecture of glass and steel left this choice for the coming generation of architects: either to make a fetish out of Mies's idea of "less is more" or to fold back the past in the architecture of postmodern and the neo-avant-garde, each in its own way framing a radical position against modern experience at the expense of consolidating the metaphysics of classical architecture.[47]

The two textual levels of architecture I have discussed so far pertain to two different functions. At one level, it provides a way to read architectural drawings and buildings. In analyzing a planimetric organization, for example, the object is not to decipher its semantic dimension, nor to verify a one-to-one correspondence between spatial organization and the functional needs of a program. In reading an architectural drawing, we are interested in the way a theme's ordering mode differentiates one architectural object from another. One could explore the ways in which contemporary architecture debases the classical discourse on the relationship between column and wall. At another level, one might investigate the implications of ornament and structure in the work of different architects. This strategy transcends the classical notion of composition as well as the deconstructivist interest in the idea of "play." Moreover, beyond the analytical level, the suggested framework attempts to recollect the thematic of the culture of inhabiting divorced from any mitigating conditions and works toward a design economy that is not identified as a "theory," meaning that there is no single solution to the relations between, for example, column and wall. And yet, as long as architecture has to do with the forces of gravity and enclosure, the duality between ornament/structure and column/wall are important topics to be considered for the tectonic.

Finally, the present condition of artistic production, marked as it is by the debate on the validity of the project of modernity and the nihilism of technology, opens a temporal situation that can plausibly be framed as a beginning. Again, for Heidegger, a beginning "contains the undisclosed abundance of the unfamiliar and extraordinary, which means that it also contains strife with the familiar and ordinary."[48] The challenge facing us is not to immortalize Mies but to recollect the limits of architecture, not by previewing the idea of the death of the author but according to Vattimo's discourse on weak thought.

The idea of weak thought is important for a semiautonomous architecture for two reasons. First, the idea of the weak thought unfolds the thematics of a posthistory subject that comes to terms with the failure of the project of the historical avant-garde and the prevailing nihilism of technology. The horizon of weak thought is somewhat like a chronically ill person who not only has to admit the existence and the seriousness of the disease but must live with it. In the context of current intensification of the process of secularization, the idea of weak thought provides an opportunity to heal the self, which witnesses the bankrupting idealogy and the commodification of the life-world. Against the vanguard modernist idea of overcoming, Vattimo suggests the Heideggerian concept of *Verwindung*: "an overcoming which is in reality a recognition of belonging, a healing of an illness, and assumption of responsibility."[49]

In the world of medicine, "healing" has different connotations. A physician cures a patient by fighting the causes of the illness. When necessary, surgery and transplantation are the last resort as an aggressive act of overcoming. It is the main concern of the psychoanalyst to heal the patient by modifying and readjusting the self to the unpleasant given conditions of life. "One of the earliest homages paid to psychoanalysis speaks of healing through consciousness. The phrase is exact," claims Paul Ricoeur, "if one means thereby that analysis wishes to substitute for an immediate and dissimulating consciousness a mediate consciousness taught by the reality principle."[50] Yet the "reality principle" itself is shaped partly by the nihilism of technology and the void left by the failure of the project of the historical avant-garde. From this standpoint, Vattimo beholds the decline of art: "The poetics of the avant-garde reject the limitations which philosophy, especially of the neo-Kantian and neo idealist sort, had previously imposed upon art." He continues, "avant-garde art refuses to be considered as a place of non-theoretical and non-practical experience, and instead claims to be the model for a privileged mode of knowledge of the real, a moment of subversion of the individual and society, and thus an instrument of true social and political action."[51] The experience of modernity convinces us to dispense with any attribute of authenticity or revolutionary function for art. Yet, the idea of weak thought does not resign itself to the idea of the death of art; its objective is to surpass the "strong" art.

Second, the analogy between Vattimo's concept of healing and Freudian therapy could be generalized to include post-Hegelian thought, wherein Hegelian dialectics is questioned and the relation to the past is resumed from the scope of recollection. A major object of Freudian therapy is to neutralize the subject. A radical version of this is the death of the man or the author. In response, Vattimo reactivates the dynamic implication of Nietzsche's view of the death of God—the situation in which "man rolls from the center toward X"—and unfolds the thematic of a post-history subjectivity. In this context, recollection is a project of disarticulation of the sign into "de-sign."[52] De-sign as the hermeneutical deferral of a sign provides other levels of interpretation. The word could be read and pronounced as "design" with a dash inserted in the middle (de-sign). The distance between de and sign sets a different relationship between design and sign (architecture) as understood in current theories of architecture. Design is the very process of architectural production through which the architect manipulates the program and the final product as well. Separated from the domain of construction (practically and conceptually), design veils the presence of metaphysics in architecture. By recoding the limits of architecture, de-sign, instead, disseminates the sign and unfolds an architectural thinking whose limit surpasses both formalism and historicism.

The hermeneutical mechanism of de-sign does not negate or overcome the limits of architecture that are coded in dualities such as ornament and structure. Instead, one comes to terms with these limits not as strict rules but as mere possibilities.[53] It would require another book to investigate such dualities case by case; however, I would like to suggest that the idea of weak thought postulates an architecture in which the dualities essential for my own position on the two textual levels of architecture would eventually be nullified and architecture, as Adorno would say, will turn into "technique," or the Miesian architecture of "almost nothing" (figure 5.4).

FIG. 5.4. Ludwig Mies van der Rohe, "Concert Hall." Project, 1942. Courtesy Ludwig Mies van der Rohe Archive, Museum of Modern Art, New York.

For Adorno, technology plays a problematic role in the art work: The rational and instrumental world of technology stands in sharp contrast to artistic technique whose purposefulness is vested in the work itself and not somewhere outside. "While technique is the epitome of the language of art," Adorno argued, "it also liquidates that language." And he concluded: "This is art's inescapable dilemma."[54] In saying this one should be aware that the case of architecture is more complicated than that of cinematography, for instance, where the best films are those that utilize the language of montage at its highest technical level.[55] The analogy between film and architecture is also important for spatial considerations: through montage, the film discloses a nonhierarchical and nonlinear perception of space. Montage dispenses with the duality between inside/outside and annuls the "other." It also weaves and compresses a scenario (program?) into a spatial whole that has to be unraveled through sectional cuts alleviating part-to-whole economy.[56]

I would like to suggest that such a state of simultaneous compression and fluidity is at work in Mies's discourse on void. In his work, the spatial importance of void is vested not in the plan but in the section. While the Miesian void remained silent, Koolhaas, following Piranesi, entertains a spatiality almost equal to the filmic experience, debunking the space generated by the conventional habit of stacking floors at the top of each other. A different spatiality is at work in the Sea Trade Center or in Deux

Bibliotheques de Jussieu: "instead of simple stacking of floors, sections of each level are manipulated to touch those above and below; all the planes are connected by a simple trajectory, a wrapped interior boulevard that exposes and relates all programmatic elements." And he adds, "The visitor becomes a Baudlerian flanuer, inspecting and being seduced by a world of books and information—by the urban scenario."[57] The interiority invested in these projects can be associated with the filmic space again: In both cases the inability of the eye to see and experience the space in its totality is symptomatic of the postmodern departure from conventional inside/outside duality by which Leonardo, for example, could depict the viewer (himself?) not only in the outside of an edifice but above and in a position of total control. However, our present interest in decentralized and fragmented spaces, depicted by Piranesi and nowadays at work in Koolhaas's architecture, has a price to be paid: Diffusion of the utopian energy from any kind of grand narratives has tossed the subject into a space the external boundaries of which, similar to financial corporations and telecommunication networks, are inaccessible.[58] The enclosure of this virtual space is analogous to the limitations imposed on architecture by what I have discussed to be Mies's deterritorialization of the language of modern architecture. One should not read the premises of my argument in historicist terms but in the context of the ever-expansion of the antinomies of modernity that make us postmoderns unable to see its outside boundaries. Within this epistomological limitations, the prefix "post" becomes meaningful if discussed in the matrix of the idea of the death of the author and the shift occurred in technology.

Nevertheless, Adorno's observation about the impact of technology on artistic technique posits the following questions: how could technology be utilized without opening architecture to the physical and metaphysical rationale of technology? And more important, by what critical means could the constructed world be saved from the ever-expanding domain of cultural commodification? To articulate a tentative response to these questions would mean, first, to dispense with the possibility of a synthesis between technology and art and, second, to avoid reducing the artistic language of architecture, the tectonic as discussed by Gottfried Semper, to the language of technology. Both Mies and Loos were aware of the import of these two points.[59] The limits of their architecture are skillfully drawn within the antinomies of modern artistic production, that is, the destruction of the language of art by technology. "Ornament and Crime" and Loos's polemical remarks against the Werkbund speak for themselves. And Mies, in keeping abreast of the latest technological developments, imparted meaning to architecture without making a fetish of technology.[60] In his architecture, the sharp edges of the steel column and the coldness of stone partitions create a space that is supposed to be not perceived from a distance but received from nearby. Discarding the stylistic dimension of architectural form, Mies's tectonic and tactile sensibilities graft the limits of architecture onto the vicissitudes of body and the nihilism of technology. Mies's concept of the architect as a "servant," who is loyal to the craft of architecture, is a valid topic for investigating architecture in the context of a late capitalism whose every facet ensures another intensification of the processes of secularization; more divisions, more separations, and further distanciation from the ethic and moralities of humanism. Disintegration and demythification of values are indeed the ultimate content of the project of the nihilism of technology, which, after all, gives us the chance to think of the alleged metaphysical values as possibilities, if not "lies." In this paradox, a discussion of the limits of architecture provides the chance to rethink the modifications necessary for the tectonic to express the conflict between the language of architecture and the nihilism of technology.

The conflict also addresses the particular place of architecture among other cultural products. Architecture and painting/sculpture have enjoyed a common discursive horizon since the Renaissance. Part of the reason for this homology was the fact that, in the Renaissance, the work of art had to represent the duality between everyday life and the divine world. Another characteristic of Renaissance art and architecture was their close association with craftwork. In all arts, including architecture, a homology between the skills of hand and the images conceived by the artist was instrumental. Realist painting and its contemporaneous architecture were seen and constructed (composed?) according to a figure/ground relations in which the depth issue was essential for the corporeality of the work. After mechanization of production process, the organic immediacy between the artwork and society is gone, perhaps forever. Since then, painting obtained its autonomy, and the attention of painters shifted from skillful representation of a text or an object into the painting itself. In a sense "what occurs is a new valuation of visual experience: it is given an unprecedented mobility and exchangeability, abstracted from site or referent."[61] The desire to overcome the representational dimension of painting ended with the abstract art, a self-referential work.

Throughout modernization, architecture has also profited from its dissociation from the guild system and craftwork. Before that, technology was mostly identified with a broader concept of fabrication that would include architecture. The vicissitudes of building technology covered all industries: the construction of machines, timepieces, and the tower of winds.[62] In modernity and more so in postmodernity we confront with techniques that have nothing to do with architecture and yet insert certain influence on it. I am thinking of the spatial implications of video and other kinds of mass communication technologies. However, for obvious reasons architecture has not been able to acquire the kind of autonomy peculiar to painting. Regarding the question of autonomy, architecture maintains an in-between position:[63] Architecture is in part a craft and yet falls short of being a mere useful artifact. Architecture is also partly art but not autonomous and "purposeless," to use Loos's word, as is the case with painting. Architecture occupies a middle ground between craftwork and art. In this paradox, it is appropriate to think of a tectonic figuration that discloses the repressed desire of architecture for becoming an art. Obviously, the degree of repression is intensified by the nihilism of technology and commodification of architectural form. If this is a plausible reading of the condition of architecture in late capitalism, then the tectonic (to mention one aspect of the culture of inhabitation I am still concerned with) should mold architecture's repressed desire for autonomy with the mystic character of the world of commodities. I discussed this diffusion in terms of theatricality in previous chapters. In the following remarks I wish to introduce lightness as another facet of theatricality.

A concept of "light" has become formative for our present consumerist culture.[64] In fashion, in diet, and most important, in the floating images of videos, we are witnessing an experience of lightness, fragmentation, and movement. To make something light also means to abandon all preperceived values, alleged truths, and grand narratives.[65] In classical architecture, the tectonic emphasized the heaviness of material and the forces of gravity perpetuating the naturalness of the bond between architecture and the site and the truth of material. Even the lightness expressed in the steel and glass architecture of early modernism remained to be bonded to the earth and to the datum of perspectival regime. The modernist vision of lightness was concerned with purity, transparency, and erosion of ornament. To go beyond the classical understanding of the tectonic, one should think the Semperian division of building into two material procedures of the framework and the earth-work in a way that the final form expresses the optimum connection needed to hold itself firm, and do not fall into topographical absoluteness of high and low territories. There is an uncanny association between the tectonic of the earth-work and the framework with the gesture of the body in dance. Somewhat similar to a ballet dancer, the building might want to break free of the ground, denying the forces of gravity. Such a theatricality does not, however, simulate total weightlessness. Its tectonic figuration recalls the posture of a dancer who after soaring up and twisting around eventually stands firm and maintains the least possible contact with the ground. The point is not to deny weight and gravity or reiterate another transparencies; but to weaken the spirit of gravity and the substitution of one set of values for another. Beyond absolute heaviness or lightness, the theatricality I am pursuing here is not a passive duplication of the fantasy generated by telecommunication technologies. It rather is concerned with fabrication of spatial affects (visual, aural, and tactile) of lightness by demythifying material, technique, and of course light and shade.

Therefore, the modification one is willing to graft onto architecture should entice the communicative function of architecture to ex-pose the conflict between subjective and objective conditions of which architecture itself is a product. This is a project of weak thought architecture (a posthistory subjectivity) that accepts the nihilism of technology in resilience. A feeble messianic subject, if you wish, the Benjaminian angel who seeks redemption not in transparent dialogue with the universal displacement of the world market but in a project whose antinomies would postpone the actual realization of the "event" to the moment when the space is cleared and a place is made, when the fog is gone and the excitement of the shock is annulled.

Notes

Introduction

1. Gevork Hartoonian, *Ontology of Construction: On Nihilism of Technology in Theories of Modern Architecture* (New York: Cambridge University Press, 1994).

2. For the history of this journal see Joan Ockman, "Resurrecting the Avant-Garde: The History and Program of *Oppositions*," in *Revisions 2*, (New York: Princeton Architectural Press, 1988), 180–99. The title of this journal is suggestive of the intellectual inclination toward a basic structuralism of some of its founders. In fact one can speculate that Peter Eisenman's early experimental houses spoke for structuralism's grounding of the truth in the laws of opposition of binary pairs. To muse further upon this idea, one can speculate on the simultaneity of the end of the life of this journal with a shift in Eisenman's work toward a deconstruction theory of architecture.

3. I am alluding to Robert Venturi's *Complexity and Contradiction in Architecture* (New York: Museum of Modern Art, 1966). The book demonstrates the impact of semiotics (a discourse whose synchronic approach to history now seems to be a timely substitute for historicism and the failure of the project of the historical avant-garde) on architecture and an understanding of it as language. Criticizing the logocentrism of the modern movement, Venturi revitalized the rhetorical dimension of the classical language of architecture. The absence of the theme of construction in his text, a subject that since then has remained problematic, has apparently escaped critical notice.

4. The enormous literature on postmodern discourse shares a number of sociocultural, economic, and political developments, among which the position of avant-garde in modernity and the question of technology are central to almost all. These two themes embody discussions concerning "death of the subject," mass media, the high and low arts, and the process of cultural secularization. I discuss these issues in my text not from a deterministic view but exploring the ways that architecture "translates" them into its own thematics.

5. Here I am paraphrasing Jacques Derrida in "Force and Signification," in *Writing and Difference* (Chicago: University of Chicago Press, 1978), 3–30. On Habermas see Richard D. Bernstein, ed., *Habermas and Modernity* (Cambridge: MIT Press, 1985), especially Richard Rorty, "Habermas

and Lyotrad on Postmodernity," 161–76. Habermas's insistence on "speech" (a public act) is the bedrock of his political liberalism and a means to question the poststructuralist interest in "text," the communication of which does not necessarily takes place in a public realm.

6. In this short and concise piece, Jurgen Habermas presents the ontology of modernity and underlines the importance of the tenets of the enlightenment for any deployment beyond modernity. What is interesting in Habermas's later work is the idea of "communicative consensus," from which one might develop the ethical environment of a secularized society. Habermas, "Modernity: An Incomplete Project," in *The Anti-Aesthetic: Essays on Postmodern Culture,* ed. Hal Foster (Washington, D.C.: Bay Press, 1983), 3–15.

7. For Jurgen Habermas on aesthetics and his position in the debate between Theodor Adorno and Walter Benjamin concerning the impact of mechanization on art, see Martin Jay, "Habermas and Modernism," in *Fin.De.Siècle Socialism* (New York: Routledge, 1988), 123–36.

8. "The decentering of traditional notion of identity, the fight of women and gays for a legitimate social and sexual identity outside the parameters of male, heterosexual vision, the search for alternatives in our relationship with nature, including the nature of our own bodies," all these phenomena that, according to Andreas Huyssen, "are key to the culture of the 1970s, make Habermas's proposition to complete the project of modernity questionable, if not undesirable." Andreas Huyssen, "The Search for Tradition: Avantgarde and Postmodernism in the 1970s," in *After the Great Divide* (Indianapolis: Indiana University Press, 1986), 160–78, 175. The normative dimension of Jurgen Habermas's theoretical model is a hindrance for a discussion of gender and ethnicity and the public space. Concerning current state of public sphere in Germany, Peter Uwe Hohendahl argues that Habermas's theory "contained a superior understanding of the problematic of the welfare state and its impact on the public sphere, but it was predicated on a questionable normative notion of a pure and unified bourgeois sphere." Hohendahl, "Recasting the Public Space," *October* 73 (Summer 1995): 54. For an interdisciplinary discussion of theories of sexuality in architecture see Beatriz Colomina, ed., *Sexuality and Space* (New York: Princeton Architectural Press, 1992).

9. Jean-Francois Lyotard, *The Postmodern Explained* (Minneapolis: University of Minnesota Press, 1993).

10. Peter Burger, *Theory of the Avant-Garde* (Minneapolis: University of Minnesota Press, 1984).

11. For the idea of the death of the author see Michel Foucault, *Language, Counter-Memory, Practice* (Ithaca: Cornell University Press, 1972). To question the role of the author doesn't mean literary "death" or the banishment of meaning in art. The idea of the death of the subject opens a space for the post-avant-garde era, through which the meaning of a work is embedded neither in the work itself nor in the symbolic/formal intention of the artist. The death of the author could also be seen as an inevitable discursive development of the crisis of the grand narrative. For Fredric Jameson the concept of the death of the author is critical for an understanding of postmodern discourse. See Jameson, "Periodizing the 60s," in *The 60's Without Apology,* ed. Sohnya Sayers and Andres Stephanson (Minneapolis: University of Minnesota Press, 1984), 178–209.

12. A minor language does not operate outside of an existing major one. Rather it uses the major language's potentialities for unexpected purposes. According to Gilles Deleuze and Felix Guattari, such an act of deterritorialization of language could result either in reterritorialization (James Joyce) or deterritorialization of a given hegemonic language (Kafka). See Deleuze and Guattari, *Kafka: Toward a Minor Literature* (Minneapolis: University of Minnesota Press, 1986), 16–27. One might also read Mies van der Rohe in light of what Manfredo Tafuri calls "a moment of shock" through which one dehistoricizes a given dominant architectural language by translating it into the purview of current ideological demands. See Tafuri's reading of Brunelleschi in *Theories of History of Architecture* (New York: Harper and Row, 1980).

13. Interestingly enough, in a piece written in the 1950s, Adorno suggests that the artistic material of music is turned into "material fetishism," that is to say, neoclassicism occurring in Strawinsky's work could have alluded that the artistic material of music has run to its internal limits. Peter Burger draws the same conclusions for Picasso's painting after 1917. See Peter Burger, *The Decline of Modernism* (University Park: Pennsylvania State University Press, 1992), 32–47.

14. From a different point of view, Joseph Masheck sees the following factors important for a postmodern architecture: "the detached post-romantic experience of classical forms as sheerly visual . . . the phenomenon of sixteenth-century mannerism is just such a caesura, noticed sympathetically in modern time; a passively conservative nonmodernist classicism that went underground with the emergence of modern architecture . . . and an explicitly vernacular elastic clause opened by pop art, especially as concerns the partying junk architecture of the strip." See Joseph Masheck, *Building-Art: Modern Architecture Under Cultural Construction* (New York: Cambridge University Press, 1993), 173.

15. I have discussed the importance of Mies van der Rohe in the context of the failure of the project of the historical avant-garde and the nihilism of technology in "Mies van der Rohe: The Genealogy of Column and Wall," *Journal of Architectural Education* 42, no. 2 (Winter 1989): 51–55, an expanded and revised version of which is published in *Ontology of Construction*; see note 1, above. On the importance of Mies for current architecture see Michael Hays, "Critical Architecture," *Perspecta* 21 (1984): 14–24, and the brilliant work of Fritz Neumeyer, *The Artless Word* (Cambridge, Mass.: MIT Press, 1992). While revising this manuscript, I had the chance to read *The Presence of Mies*, ed. Detlef Mertins (New York: Princeton Architectural Press, 1994). The text collected here discloses a poststructuralist reading of Mies, among which I found Ignasi de Solá-Morales Rubio's case quite in line with the premises of my argument. According to him, since the 1960s, faced with the crisis of modern tradition, "there were those who sought, through a return to origins, to the pure wellspring of enlightened architecture of the purism of the Modern Movement. . . . Others, in marked contrast, believed that they saw in the diffusion of the popular or in the prestige of classical architecture a fountain with the power to renew signification" (149). Most engaging, however, is Michael Hays's "Afterword," which discusses Theodor Adorno's ideas on mimesis and expression. I have appropriated these themes in my last chapter to disclose Mies's critical understanding of the relationship between architecture and metropolis.

16. Fredric Jameson has this to say on this historical closure: "There is another sense in which the writers and artists of the present day will no longer be able to invent new styles and words—they have already been invented. . . . So the weight of the whole modernist aesthetic tradition— now dead—also 'weighs like a nightmare on the brains of the living,' as Marx said in another context." Fredric Jameson, "Postmodernism and Consumer Society," in Foster, *Anti-Aesthetic*, 111–25, 115.

17. Such a discourse has its roots in the radical factions of modernity, such as the futurists, who thought that technology could solve sociocultural problems. One should rather read Jean-Francois Lyotard as part of the poststructuralist discourse that conceives technology as a harbinger of Western metaphysics, and the tradition of literary avant-garde that sees the question of modern aesthetic not in "what is beautiful?" but in "what is art to be (and what is literature to be)?" See Lyotard, *Postmodern Explained*, 7.

18. The concept of second nature derives from Hegel and later was appropriated by Theodor Adorno and Walter Benjamin. See Susan Buck-Morss, *The Origin of Negative Dialectics* (New York: Free Press, 1977), 52–57.

19. Fredric Jameson, *Postmodernism, or, the Cultural Logic of Late Capitalism* (Durham: Duke University Press, 1991), esp. 1–66.

20. Sensitive to some aspects of Fredric Jameson's discourse on the postmodern, Hal Foster disagrees with any analysis that draws a definite line between modern and postmodern, denying the space for thematic overlapping between the past and the present. Foster sees modernity's loss of identity in its simultaneous advent in discovering the "other," the colonial territories, registering the post of postmodernism in discursive shifts taking place around three themes: the subject, the cultural other, and technology. See Foster, "Postmodernism in Parallax," *October* 63 (Winter 1993): 3–20.

21. Regionalism and organicism have philosophical and political connotations for American architecture. From the early theoretical reflection on "frontier" to Frank Lloyd Wright's and Lewis Mumford's esteem for regionalism there resides an aversion for the Metropolis and the nihilism of technology. See Giorgio Ciucci, "The City in Agrarian Ideology and Frank Lloyd Wright: Origins and Development of Broadacres," in *The American City* (Cambridge, Mass.: MIT Press, 1979), 293–388.

22. I am alluding to Serge Guilbaut, *How New York Stole the Idea of Modern Art* (Chicago: University of Chicago Press, 1983), and T. J. Clark, "In Defense of Abstract Expressionism," *October* 69 (Summer 1994): 23–48.

23. I am alluding to Roland Barthes, *Writing Degree Zero* (1953; rpt., New York: Noonday, 1967).

24. Martin Jay expresses his caution in the context of the opposition between two themes of differentiation and *differance*. Against any evolutionary view of a totalized history, poststructuralist theory underline "a network of proliferating and incommensurable differances, which escape reduction to a finite number of common denominators" (*Downcast Eyes*, 148).

25. Fredric Jameson sees this as a sign of "the disappearance of a sense of history, the way that our entire contemporary social system has little by little begun to lose its capacity to retain its own past, has begun to live in a perpetual present and in a perpetual change that obliterate traditions of the kind which all earlier social formations have had in one way

or another to preserve." Jameson, "Postmodern and Consumer Culture," in Foster, *Anti-Aesthetic*, 125.

26. Fredric Jameson, "Postmodernism, or, the Cultural Logic of Late Capitalism," *New Left Review* 146 (July–Aug. 1984).

27. According to Manfredo Tafuri, since the Enlightenment, the task of architecture was to accomodate itself to the exigencies of the bourgeois city. For him, Piranesi is exception to this role: in *Campo marzio* Piranesi declared: "the great new problem was that of the equilibrium of opposites, which in the city finds its appointed place: failure to resolve this problem would mean the destruction of the very concept of architecture." Tafuri, *Architecture and Utopia: Design and Capitalist Development* (Cambridge, Mass.: MIT Press, 1976), 25. Shall we go further and speculate that various current declarations of the death of architecture or the latter's resort into the libidinal world of pleasure are scapegoats for the struggle between architecture and the city?

28. From its early Dutch settlement, New York City has evolved without a preconceived totalizing project, which was at the top of the plan of the historical avant-garde. Instead, what was erected today was destroyed the next day mainly for practical reasons in which commerce and communication were the two indexes that eventually generated the gridiron. "Manhattan is a *theater of progress*" where "performance can never end or even progress in the conventional sense of dramatic plotting; it can only be the cyclic restatement of a single theme: creation and destruction irrevocably interlocked, endlessly re-enacted." Rem Koolhass, *Delirious New York* (New York: Oxford University Press, 1978), 10. The irony of history is that almost a century after the arrival of the first Dutch settlers into the new world the history of New York City should be written by a Dutch architect.

29. As early as 1910 Max Weber underlined the significance of Metropolis in general and the implications of modern technology for "formal aesthetic values." According to him, "the distinctive formal values of our modern artistic culture could only have come to be through the existence of the modern metropolis" (quoted in Charles W. Haxthausen and Heidrun Suhr, ed., *Berlin Culture and Metropolis* [Minneapolis: University of Minnesota Press, 1990], 43). Michael Hays has recently argued for the critical incorporation of the theme of metropolis in the architecture of Mies and Hans Meyer. See Hays, *Modernism and the Posthumanist Subject* (Cambridge, Mass.: MIT Press, 1992).

30. This seems to be Susan Buck-Morss's concluding remarks on a recent article on Walter Benjamin's thought on the city. Buck-Morss says, "In this cynical time of the 'end of history', adults know better than to believe social utopias of any kind" ("The City as Dreamworld and Catastrophe," *October* 73 [Summer 1995]: 26).

31. Jacques Derrida, *Specters of Marx* (New York: Routledge, 1994), 50.

Chapter 1

1. The differences between a Weberian approach to the dichotomies generated by the rift between civilization and *Kulture* and that of the Werkbund is discussed by Francesco Dal Co. Confronting "the plurality of power, the multiplicity of specialized function as" the Werkbund, according to Dal Co, assumed the "task of building an ideological apparatus and a systematic of design aimed at exorcising, overcoming,

or concealing precisely the inescapable deep-rootedness of such dia-metrical oppositions." See Dal Co, *Figures of Architecture and Thought: German Architecture Culture, 1880–1920* (New York: Rizzoli International Publications, 1990), 176.

2. In his preface to the third edition of *The Society of the Spectacle* (originally published amid social upheavals of the 1960s), Guy Debord has this to say about the 1960s: "The biggest dupes of that time have since received a clear object lesson—in the form of their own shattered existences—as to what exactly was meant by the 'negation of life become visible,' by the 'loss of quality' associated with the commodity-form or by the 'proletarianization of the world'" ([New York: Zone, 1994], 8). Debord sees the fall of Russian statehood, the dictatorial freedom of the market, as "the most unfavorable portent for the future development of capitalist society" (80).

3. Matei Calinescu argues: "At the dawn of modernity the myth of progress emerged based on a secularized concept of linear and irreversible time. . . . But the alliance between modernity and progress turned out to be only temporary, and in our age the myth of progress appears to have been largely exhausted." *Faces of Modernity: Avant-Garde, Kitsch and Decadence* (Bloomington: Indiana University Press, 1977), 246. For "culture industry" see note 49, below.

4. Peter Burger states that the avant-garde's challenge to art as an institution has failed. Therefore, there is no perceptible sublation of art in a changed context; "the means by which the avant-gardists hoped to bring about the sublation of art have attained the status of works of art." *Theory of the Avant-Garde,* trans. Michael Shaw (Minneapolis: University of Minnesota Press, 1984), 58.

5. "The principle of montage was supposed to shock people into realizing just how dubious any organic unity was. Now that the shock has lost its punch, the products of montage revert to being indifferent stuff or substance." Theodor Adorno, *Aesthetic Theory,* trans. C. Lenhardt (New York: Routledge and Kegan Paul, 1984), 223. Also see Matthew Teitelbaum, *Montage and Modern Life, 1919–1942* (Cambridge, Mass.: MIT Press, 1993).

6. On Mies van der Rohe and Adolf Loos, see Gevork Hartoonian, *Ontology of Construction: On the Nihilism of Technology in Theories of Modern Architecture* (New York: Cambridge University Press, 1994).

7. Ernest Bloch, "Building in Empty Spaces," in *The Utopian Function of Art and Architecture,* trans. Jack Zipes and Frank Mecklenburg (Cambridge, Mass.: MIT Press, 1988), 187.

8. Mies van der Rohe, in Fritz Neumeyer, *The Artless Word* (Cambridge, Mass.: MIT Press, 1992), 332.

9. Robert Stern, "The Temple of Love and Other Musings," *Historic Preservation* 34 (Sept./Oct. 1982): 28–31.

10. Charles Jencks, *The Language of Post-Modern Architecture* (New York: Rizzoli International, 1977).

11. See my discussion of the implications of the Dom-ino for postmodern architecture in chapter 2.

12. Martin Heidegger, "The Age of World Picturing," in *The Question Concerning Technology and Other Essays* (New York: Harper Torchbooks, 1977), 115–54. Heidegger is concerned with the disappearance of the "mythical distance" between a person and the world that has

occurred through the process of objectification and bringing everything close into the picture.

13. I am thinking of Edward W. Soja, who, following Michel Foucault, directs our attention to space and spatiality understood in terms of various topographies as well as spatial structures formed by minority groups. Considering the nineteenth-century obsession with time and history, Soja defines "historicism as an overdeveloped historical contextualization of social life and social theory that actively submerges and peripherializes the geographical and spatial imagination." Edward Soja, *Postmodern Geographies* (London: Verso, 1989), 15.

14. Kenneth Frampton, *Modern Architecture: A Critical History* (New York and Toronto: Oxford University Press, 1980), 84.

15. Ulrich Conrads, "De Stjil," Manifesto I, *Programs and Manifestoes on Twentieth-Century Architecture* (Cambridge, Mass.: MIT Press, 1975), 39.

16. Massimo Cacciari, *Architecture and Nihilism: On the Philosophy of Modern Architecture* (New Haven: Yale University Press, 1993), 24. For Cacciari the idea of Metropolis is critical not only for an understanding of the concept of modernity but of the very problematic of various tendencies within the broader scope of modern architecture.

17. This was the new function of "intellectual work of the avant-garde at the beginning of twentieth century." Manfredo Tafuri, "Idealogy and Utopia," in *Architecture and Utopia,* trans. B. L. Penta (Cambridge, Mass.: MIT Press, 1976), 50–77. This position is further elaborated in "history as a project of crisis." See Tafuri, *The Sphere and the Labyrinth* (Cambridge, Mass.: MIT Press, 1987).

18. This phenomenon is extensively discussed in Paul Ricoeur's insightful article, "Universal Civilization and National Cultures," that was essential for Kenneth Frampton's "The Prospects for a Critical Regional Architecture," *Perspecta* 20 (1983): 147–62. This article was revised and published as "Towards a Critical Regionalism: Six Points for an Architecture of Resistance," in *The Anti-Aesthetic: Essays on Postmodern Culture,* ed. Hal Foster (Washington, D.C.: Bay Press, 1983).

19. In this historical background one should consider Lewis Mumford's discourse on regionalism as a resistance to the Beaux Art's historicism and the white architecture of the International Style. I am referring to Mumford's lecture at the occasion of a seminar held by the Museum of Modern Arts titled "What Is Happening to Modern Architecture?" See *Museum of Modern Arts Bulletin,* Spring 1948, 4–21.

20. According to Gianni Vattimo, the crisis of history as a unitary course does not mean that we are no longer able to reconstruct the past. A distinction between what has happened in the past and its subjective interpretation is different from metanarrative, a unified view of the course of events leading to an expected result, a utopia indeed. Vattimo, "The End of (Hi)story," *Chicago Review* 35, no. 4 (1986).

21. Gianni Vattimo, "Myth and the Fate of Secularization," *Res* 9 (Spring 1985): 29–34.

22. Ibid.

23. Roland Barthes, *Mythology* (New York: Hill and Wang, 1982).

24. Jean-Francois Lyotard, *The Postmodern Condition: A Report on Knowledge* (Minneapolis: University of Minnesota Press, 1984), 18. For

a comparative critique of Lyotard's discourse and other postmodern attitudes toward art and architecture see, Alan Colquhoun, "Postmodern Critical Attitudes," *Modernity and the Classical Tradition* (Cambridge, Mass.: MIT Press, 1989), 235–41.

25. This phenomenon could be associated with the historical malady of the nineteenth century: an obsession with historiography, which according to Friedreich Nietzsche, "destroys the capacity to create new history," and therefore affirms the split between theory and practice. See Gianni Vattimo, "Hermeneutical Reason/Dialectical Reason," in *The Adventure of Difference* (Baltimore: Johns Hopkins University Press, 1993), 9–39.

26. Vattimo, "Myth and the Fate of Secularization."

27. Paul Ricoeur suggests that Marx, Nietzsche, and Freud demystified hermeneutics by setting up the rude discipline of necessity, and thus dispensing with the grace of imagination. Ricoeur, *Freud and Philosophy: An Essay on Interpretation* (New Haven: Yale University Press, 1970), 35. See also Gevork Hartoonian, "A Monument to the End of Modernity," in *On Architecture, the City and Technology,* ed. Marc M. Angelil (Butterworth-Heinemann, Mass.: Butterworth Architecture, 1990), 77–79.

28. Regarding the idea of the new in modernism, and Theodor Adorno's analogy between modern art's infatuation with newness and commodity, see Peter Burger, *Theory of the Avant-Garde,* 59–63. For a historical account of the battle between the ancients and the moderns, see Matei Calinescu, *Five Faces of Modernity* (Durham: Duke University Press, 1987), 23–33. According to Calinescu, "the *Quarrel* proper started when some modern-minded French authors, led by Charles Perrault, thought fit to apply the scientific concept of progress to literature and art" (27). For the implication of the "Quarrel" for architecture see Joseph Rykwert, *The First Moderns* (Cambridge, Mass.: MIT Press, 1983), 22–53.

29. Consider the following debates taking place simultaneously at both sides of the continent. In June 1993, Jeffery Kippnis and others were discussing the implications of the "fold" for enthusiastic students of the Association of Architecture in London and the ways in which those students might plant the concept of fold in their designs. At home, Mark Taylor reminds us that neither the Derridian difference nor the Deleuzian fold can tackle the problems of architecture. According to him, architecture may be able to rediscover "its ethic-political mission" by means of the idea of seem/seam, a "seamy architecture." For a brief on the claim of both sides, see "Seaming," *Newsline* 6, no. 1 (1993): 5.

30. To save Friedreich Nietzsche's discourse on the eternal return from a conservative interpretation, Massimo Cacciari suggests that "the idea of the return must be understood as the idea of destiny, and as the idea of going *beyond,* as well as the negation of nostalgia, as the culmination of the negative: in other words, as tragic theory." *Architecture and Nihilism,* 26.

31. "The past carries with it a temporal index by which it is referred to redemption. There is a secret agreement between past generations and the present one. Our coming was expected on earth. Like every generation that preceded us, we have been endowed with a weak Messianic power to which the past has a claim. That claim cannot be settled

cheaply. Historical materialists are aware of that." Walter Benjamin, "Theses on the Philosophy of History," in *Illuminations,* trans. Harry Zohn (New York: Schocken, 1969), 254.

32. Manfredo Tafuri considers the opening of architecture to other fields to be part of a "plan of development," through which capital extends the use of science and other achievements in the communications industry into other disciplines. Tafuri, *Architecture and Utopia.*

33. According to Alan Colquhoun, in *Complexity and Contradiction* Venturi "oscillates between the effect of a building on the perceptions of the observer and the effect intended by the designer, as if these were historically the same thing." "Sign and Substance: Reflections on Complexity, Las Vegas, and Oberlin," *Oppositions,* no. 14 (Fall 1978): 26–37.

34. Robert Venturi, "A Definition of Architecture as Shelter with Decoration on It, and Another Plea for a Symbolism of the Ordinary in Architecture," in Venturi and Denise Scott Brown, *A View from the Campidoglio* (New York: Harper and Row, 1984), 63.

35. Jean Baudrillard, *For A Critique of the Political Economy of the Sign,* trans. Charles Levin (St. Louis: Telos Press, 1981), 185–203.

36. See Walter Benjamin, "Paris, Capital of the Nineteenth Century," in *Baudlaire: A Lyric Poet in the Era of High Capitalism* (New York: Harcourt Brace Jovanovich, 1978), 146–62, and "Surrealism, the Last Snapshot of the European Intelligentsia," ibid., 177–92. According to Haim N. Finkelstein the greatest exponent of architecture that "violates" the rational functionalism of modernity is Antoni Gaudi. The author's discussion is mostly motivated by Salvador Dali's reflections on Gaudi. H. Finkelstein, *Surrealism and the Crisis of the Object* (Ann Arbor: University Microfilms International, 1979), 111–18. For a provocative reading of surrealism see Hal Foster, *Compulsive Beauty* (Cambridge, Mass.: MIT Press, 1993).

37. The phrase was first used by Andre Breton in 1932. Breton and other surrealists presented a project of reconstitution of the object that in one way or another problematized the total and "clean" transformation of traditional object into a new one. The result was what Walter Benjamin would later call "wish-image." On Breton see Finkelstein, *Surrealism.* For the idea of wish-image see Benjamin, "Paris." My own discourse throughout this book might be read as a reflection on the crisis of the object induced by the nihilism of technology, the death of the author, and the failure of the project of the historical avant-garde.

38. For Walter Benjamin's discourse on technology see "The Work of Art on the Age of Mechanical Reproduction," in *Illuminations,* 217–52. And John McCole, *Walter Benjamin and Antinomies of Tradition* (Ithaca: Cornell University Press, 1993). My argument here and in concluding paragraphs draws extensively from McCole's discussion in chapters 4 and 5.

39. "Today the Paris arcades are being restored like antiques to their former grandeur; . . . When trying to reconstruct what the arcades, expositions, urbanism, and technological dreams were for Benjamin, we cannot close our eyes to what they have become for us." Susan Buck-Morss, *The Dialectics of Seeing* (Cambridge, Mass.: MIT Press, 1989), 340. For the political function of kitsch see Clement Greenberg's "The-Avant-Garde and Kitsch," first published in *Partisan Review* 6, no. 5 (Fall 1939): 34–

49; republished in *Kitsch: The World of Bad Taste,* ed. Gillo Dorfles (New York: Bell, 1975), 116–26.

40. Clement Greenberg, "Avant-Garde and Kitsch," in Dorfles, *Kitsch,* 116–26. For the quotation here see Serge Guilbaut, *How New York Stole the Idea of Modern Art* (Chicago: University of Chicago Press, 1984), 36. According to Guilbaut, by depoliticizing art Greenberg paved the way for the American abstract expressionism and a sense of universal intellectualism. The postwar intellectual life in America dissociated itself from the left's cultural agenda, grouped around Meyer Schapiro and Andre Breton, and utilized surrealist technique for pure formalistic ends. This metamorphosis is important since one could associate it, as we will do shortly, with deconstructivist architecture.

41. Gianni Vattimo, *The Transparent Society* (Baltimore: Johns Hopkins University Press, 1992), 73. This metamorphosis was anticipated by Vittorio Gregotti. Discussing the new developments in contemporary architecture he disclosed that "as a result of these new attitudes the demarcation line which separated kitsch and the avant-garde about thirty years ago now appears broken and ill-defined." Gregotti, "Kitsch and Architecture," Dorfles, *Kitsch,* 255.

42. Giorgio Agamben, "Without Classes," in *The Coming Community,* trans. Michael Hardt (Minneapolis: University of Minnesota Press, 1993), 62–64.

43. T. J. Clarck, "In Defence of Abstract Expressionism," *October 69* (Summer 1994): 23–48.

44. Ibid., 47.

45. Leo Steinberg, *Other Criteria* (New York: Oxford University Press, 1972), 80. Implied in Steinberg's reading is the return of avant-garde. According to him, "something happened in painting around 1950—most conspicuously (at least within my experience) in the work of Robert Rauschenberg and Dubuffet. We can still hang their pictures—just as we tack up maps and architectural plans . . . Yet these pictures no longer simulate vertical fields but opaque flatbed horizontal." What Rauschenberg invented was "a pictorial surface that let the world in again" (82–91).

46. Kenneth Frampton, "America, 1960–1970: Notes on Urban Image and Theory," *Casabella* 359–60 (Dec. 1971): 24–38. Frampton maps Robert Venturi and Scott Brown's discourse in the populist and advocacy-planning policies of the early 1960s, a school of thought whose implicit attitude remains to be "one in which the design professions are to be reactivated only through greater conformity to the sacrosanct 'populist' goals of our affluent society" (33). For Dennis Scott Brown's response see ibid., 39–46.

47. On postmodern politics of search for meaning and its political implications see Mary McLeod, "Architecture and Politics in the Reagan Era: From Postmodernism to Deconstructivism," *Assemblage* 8 (1989): 23–60.

48. Alan J. Plattus, "Toward a Post-Analytical Architecture," in *Thinking the Present: Recent American Architecture,* eds. K. Michael Hays and Carol Burns (New York: Princeton Architectural Press, 1990), 45–60. Speaking of Wu Hall at Princeton, Plattus suggests that "this new 'old Gothic hall' is subjected to the constraints imposed by the 'frozen section' of modern architecture while its perimeter shows evidence of a flirtation with the 'free plan'" (48). Can one speak of the imposed

"frozen section" of modern architecture after the experience of Villa Savoye and Carpenter Center?

49. "For American popular culture in the 1950s had, on its own, so to speak, become as technologically advanced as anything modernism could have hoped for." Michael Hays, "Odysseus and the Oarsmen, or, Mies's Abstraction Again," in *The Presence of Mies*, ed. Detlef Mertins (New York: Princeton Architectural Press, 1994), 243. See also my last chapter here, where I draw similar conclusions in regard to Hays's discussion of the dialectics between city and Mies's architecture.

50. Written almost half a century ago, the culture industry discloses those aspects of life that we take for granted today—a world filled with soap operas, situation comedies, and TV and radio channels that frames the consumers' choice, and, more important, the exclusion of the new and the fusion of movies into life and vice versa. Max Horkheimer and Theodor Adorno, "The Culture Industry: Enlightenment as Mass Deception," *Dialectic of Enlightenment* (New York: Herder and Herder, 1972), 168–208.

51. Henry Russell Hitchcock, *Modern Architecture, Romanticism and Reintegration* (New York: Dacapo Press, 1993), 8. Important for my conclusion in this chapter is a distinction Hitchcock makes between the "New Tradition" and the "New Pioneers." The former, characteristic of a Richardsonian architecture, intends to integrate modern building technology with the tradition of architecture.

52. Theodor Adorno, *Aesthetic Theory*, 340.

53. Robert Venturi, *Complexity and Contradiction in Architecture* (New York: Museum of Modern Art, 1966), 44.

54. Guilbaut, *How New York Stole the Idea of Modern Art*, 143. Among historical factors important for this metamorphosis, mention should be made of the spread of fascism in Western Europe and Stalin's banishment of Russian constructive art and architecture.

55. Charles Jencks, "The Ressurection and Death of the New Moderns," *Architectural Design* 60, no. 7/8 (1990): 20–25.

56. Demetri Porphyrios, "The Meaning of Atlantis," in Lâeon Krier, *Atlantis* (Bruxelles: Archives d' architecture moderne, 1988) 15–22. Of course, postmodern architecture here refers to Venturi's or M. Graves's work, in which the concept of the tectonic has no place.

57. Vattimo, "Myth and the Fate of Secularization." Also see Piero Derossi, "Project II," *Domus International* 48–49 (1986): 126–33. In criticizing Paolo Portoghesi's historicist position, Derossi asserts that "this obsession with making the present harks back to the historicist procedure of reconstructing the origins of a certain state of things in order to get a better grip on them, according to the traditional notions of knowledge, as knowledge of causes and of beginnings."

58. Barthes, *Mythology*, 109.

59. See Andrea Ponsi, "Contemporary Italian Architecture," *Archetype* 3, no. 1 (Winter 1983): 10–12. Also see Manfredo Tafuri, *History of Italian Architecture, 1944–1985* (Cambridge, Mass.: MIT Press, 1989), esp. chs. 4 and 5.

60. Aldo Rossi, *The Architecture of the City* (Cambridge, Mass.: MIT Press, 1982).

61. According to Peter Eisenman, type is an apparatus that "allows urban elements to be perceived as having a meaning that is always original and

authentic and its logic, then, exists prior to form, but also comes to constitute the form in a new way." See Rossi, *Architecture of the City*, 8.

62. According to Michel Foucault "the heterotopia begins to function at full capacity when men arrive at a sort of absolute break with their traditional time." Again one thinks of the collapse of History and simultaneity of time and space that, according to Foucault, is implied in structuralism. Michel Foucault, "Of Other Spaces," *Diacritics* 16, no. 1 (Spring 1986): 22–27.

63. See Giulio Argan, "On the Typology of Architecture," *Architectural Design* 33, no. 12 (1963): 565. For a thorough survey of the debate on typology, see Micha Bandini, "Typology as a Form of Convention," *AA Files* 6 (1986): 72–82. And Rafael Moneo, "On Typology," *Oppositions*, no. 13 (Summer 1978): 23–45. On the place of type in modern architecture, see Anthony Vidler, "The Third Typology," in *Rational Architecture* (Brussels: Archives d'Architecture Moderne, 1978), 28–32. David Leatherbarrow reminds us of the ambiguities in Rossi's discourse on type: "Type is supposed to be logically prior to embodiment and rule articulation, but never is one known or seen except when present as an existing building or number of existing buildings, which are, because existing *in* time, permanently changing." *The Roots of Architectural Inventions* (New York: Cambridge University Press, 1993), 72.

64. Aldo Rossi, *A Scientific Autobiography* (Cambridge, Mass.: MIT Press, 1981).

65. Peter Eisenman, "The House of the Dead as the City of Survival," in *Aldo Rossi in America* (New York: Institute for Architecture and Urban Studies, 1976), 9. Eisenman rejects Tafuri's belief that architecture has lost its public significance and instead reads Rossi in the context of "posthistory" where the choice between "imminent or eventual mass death, heroism, whether individual or collective, is untenable: only survival remains possible." Ibid., 5. Eugene J. Johnson sees Rossi's interest in the cube, the cone, the triangle, and the U-shaped buildings in association to Boullée, for whom "to give character to a work means not to make us experience sensations other than those intrinsic in the subject; the character constitutes the evocative, emotional part." Johnson, "What Remains of Man: Aldo Rossi's Modena Cemetery," *Journal of Society of Architectural Historians* 41, no. 1 (March 1982): 38–54.

66. For a poetic and yet concise reading of "Modena Cemetery," see Rafael Moneo, "Aldo Rossi: The Idea of Architecture and the Modena Cemetery," *Oppositions*, no. 5 (Summer 1976): 1–30.

67. Tafuri, *History of Italian Architecture*, 135.

68. Jacques Derrida, *Writing and Difference* (Chicago: University of Chicago Press, 1978), 5.

69. This observation is implied in Yve-Alain Bois's review of Manfredo Tafuri's "Theories and History of Architecture," *Oppositions*, no. 11 (Winter 1977): 118–23. I am well aware of my own inclination for metadiscourse on architecture in this book.

70. This development has also changed the relationship between theory and practice. Before the 1960s, most schools of architecture would follow the practical implications of the so-called Masters and their firms. With unfoldings made possible by postmodern discourse, the academia and schools of architecture have taken the lead in architectural theory

inducing a critical practice that has left no choice for the major architectural firms but to follow these institutions. This disposition is accelerated by deconstructivist architects who explore the impact of technology on perception and the formal horizons opened by computer technologies.

71. Norman Bryson, *Tradition and Desire* (Cambridge: Cambridge University Press, 1987), 77. On the importance of Velazquez's painting for representation, see Michel Foucault, *The Order of Things* (New York: Vintage Books, 1973), 3–16. Also see John R. Searle, "Las Meninas and the Paradox of Pictorial Representation," *Critical Inquiry* 6, no. 3 (Spring 1980): 477–88.

72. Discussing Marcel Duchamp in the general context of the historical avant-garde, Manfredo Tafuri suggests that the painter's "asserted dominion over form was but a cover for something he could still not accept: that is, that by now it was the form which dominated the painter." After almost half a century, deconstructivist architects are facing the same dilemma. See Tafuri, *Architecture and Utopia*, 91.

73. Peter Eisenman, "Cardboard Architecture: House I," in *Five Architects* (New York: Oxford University Press, 1975), 25.

74. Ibid., 16. In retrospect, one might associate the mentioned dual structures with the ways that unconsciousness relates to consciousness. These ideas of Eisenman were first developed in an earlier text called "Notes on Conceptual Architecture: Towards a Definition," *Casabella* 359–60 (1971): 49–57.

75. The Five Architects were Peter Eisenman, John Hedjuk, Charles Gwathmey, Michael Graves, and Richard Meier, who worked separately articulating the language of postfunctionalist architecture.

76. Colin Rowe, introduction to *Five Architects*, 7.

77. Manfredo Tafuri, 'American Graffiti: FiveXFive=Twenty-five," *Oppositions*, no. 5 (Summer 1976): 35–74.

78. Peggy Deamer explores the theoretical shift in Michael Graves, whose early work was informed by the expression of the subject from his/her inhabited space. Graves departed from a phenomenalogical interest in the interdependence of see-er and the seen object in favor of an architecture that because of being reduced into a sign negates any engagement of the subject except a distance reading and recognition of the familiarity of the given sign. Deamer, "Michael Graves, Body Builder?" *Thinking the Present: Recent American Architecture* (New York: Princeton Architectural Press, 1990), 6–22.

79. For a discussion of the antiocular position of deconstruction theory, see the significant work of Martin Jay, *Downcast Eyes* (Berkeley and Los Angeles: University of California Press, 1994), esp. the last chapter.

80. Michael Hays discusses the Cannaregio project as the point by which Peter Eisenman shifts from his early isolated formal investigations in favor of site and text as informative factors for signification. Hays, "From Structure to Site to Text: Eisenman's Trajectory," *Thinking the Present*, 61–71.

81. One way of doing justice to Kahn is to read his work in the context of a Semperian discourse on the tectonic. With all his debt to Le Corbusier, Kahn withdrew from seeing architecture in the formal potentialities embedded in the Dom-ino house.

82. According to Jacques Derrida, there are two readings of the theme of play: one is disclosed in the structuralist search for origins, presenting

the "play of repetition and the repetition of play, a nostalgia for an ethic of the archaic and natural." The other, "which is no longer turned toward the origin, affirms play and tries to pass beyond man and humanism, the name of man being the name of that being who, throughout the history of metaphysics or of ontotheology—in other words, throughout his entire history—has dreamed of full presence, the reassuring foundation, the origin and the end of play." Derrida, "Structure, Sign, and Play," in *Writing and Difference,* 292. See also Derrida's remark in *The Ear of the Other,* ed. Christine McDonald (New York: Schocken, 1985), 67–71.

83. Hal Foster continues, "[Play] replicates the circulation of signs characteristic of our cultural-political economy." See *Recodings* (Washington, D.C.: Bay Press, 1985), 157–79.

84. Mark Wigley, *Deconstructivist Architecture* (New York: Museum of Modern Art, 1988), 18.

85. For Jurgen Habermas's criticism of deconstruction see Habermas, "Modernity-An Incomplete Project," *The Anti-Aesthetic: Essays on Postmodern Culture,* ed. Hal Foster (Washington D.C.: Bay Press, 1983), 3–15.

86. Deconstruction of classical architecture might end up strengthening the consolidation of classical architecture. See Jacque Derrida, "The Ends of Man," *Philosophical and Phenomenological Research* 1 (1969): 56.

87. This also alludes to the ways that Marcel Duchamp would explain the difference between his work and that of the Dada. See Octavio Paz, *Marcel Duchamp* (New York: Arcade, 1978), 81.

88. Gianni Vattimo, *The End of Modernity* (Baltimore: Johns Hopkins University Press, 1988), 33.

89. Walter Benjamin, "Paris, Capital of the Nineteenth Century," in *Reflections,* trans. E. Jephcott (New York: Harcourt Brace and Jovanovich, 1978), 148. Again recalling the political content of Russian constructivism, one can see in deconstructivist and postmodernist architecture a transformation of dream into delusion. The playfulness and redemptive formal potentialities of current architecture actualize the unknown of modern utopia without mediating between the objective and subjective conditions of late capitalism. However, according to Susan Buck-Morss, "The wish symbols, signposts in a period of transition, can inspire the refunctioning of the new nature [technology] so that it satisfies material needs and desires that are the sources of the dream in the first place. Wish images do not liberate humanity directly. But they are vital to the process." Susan Buck-Morss, *The Dialectics of Seeing,* 120.

90. "These returns are as fundamental to postmodernist art as they are to post-structuralist theory: both make the breaks that they do through such recoveries." Mapping the vicissitudes of the neo-avant-garde in art, Hal Foster presents a critical reading of Peter Burger's *Theory of the Avant-Garde.* I will reflect on Foster's position in my discussion of "Avant-Garde; Re-Thinking Architecture." For Foster see "What is Neo About Neo-Avant-Garde?" *October* 70 (Fall 1994): 5–32.

91. Michel Foucault, *Language, Counter-Memory, Practice* (Ithaca: Cornell University Press, 1977).

92. Peter Eisenman, "A Critical Practice: American Architecture in the Last Decades of the Twentieth Century," *Education of an Architect* (New York: Rizzoli International, 1988), 190–93.

93. Roland Barthes, "The Death of Author," in *Image, Music, Text* (New York: Hill and Wang, 1977), 142–48.

94. Peter Eisenman, "Blue Line Text," *Architectural Design* 58, no. 7/8 (1988): 6–9.

95. The following pages map a theoretical paradigm whose concrete architectural results are further discussed in the last chapter of this volume.

96. The major themes and categories of this debate are: "Dialectical Image," "aura," and what Adorno calls the "unmediated brand of materialism." For a thorough analysis of these issues see Susan Buck-Morss, *The Origin of Negative Dialectics* (New York: Free Press, 1977), esp. chs. 9, 10, and 11. Also see Richard Wollin, *Walter Benjamin: An Aesthetic of Redemption* (New York: Columbia University Press, 1982), 163–212. Yet, the contemporary importance of the debate lies in the relationship between art and technology. As pointed out previously, Benjamin's hope for the redemptive aspect of technology undermines the critical function of art, which can be significant only by keeping a distance from the dominant ideology. One might question whether Benjamin's view could not initiate a false integration of art with social life. Nevertheless, the appeal to convention by postmodern architecture not only unfolds its loss of the critical edge but also heralds a fake sublation of art with social life.

97. Theodor Adorno, *Aesthetic Theory*, 8. According to Peter Burger, such characterization of autonomy differs from the concept of "l'art pour l'art" and the view that autonomy is an entity of the artist's imagination (35–54).

98. Philip D. Verene, *Vico's Science of Imagination* (Ithaca: Cornell University Press, 1982), 55.

99. Martin Heidegger believed that the way out of the impasse of modern technology would take place through a return to the "primal scene"; the site of Greek experience where "productionist metaphysics" began. The purpose of return was to suggest that the Greek experience was not basic and did not embody the essential structure of the human existence. It rather evolved out of an act of violence, or deconstruction of a prior mode of existence. Therefore, one might speculate that the Greek art was metaphysical and that Heidegger's intention was to reverse the course of this historical experience by calling on the work of art to bring forth the nihilism of technology.

100. "Heidegger runs this risk, despite so many necessary precautions, when he gives priority, as he always does, to gathering and to the same (*Versammlung, Fuge, legein,* and so forth) over the disjunction implied in my [Derrida's] address to the other, over interruption commanded by respect which commands it in turn, over a difference whose uniqueness, disseminated in the innumerable charred fragments of the absolute mixed in with the cinders, will never be assured in the One." Jacques Derrida, *Specters of Marx* (New York: Routledge, 1994), 28. I will discuss the critical implications of "disjunction" in Kenneth Frampton's "critical regionalism" in chapter 4.

101. Martin Heidegger, "Building Dwelling Thinking," in *Basic Writings*, ed. D. F. Krell (New York: Harper and Row, 1977), 320–39. In the ever-increasing scarcity of public space, Kenneth Frampton sees in Heidegger the theoretical means to reformulate the dialectics between place and

production, and the possibility to underline the import of the political and ontological aspects of the production of the conditions of life. See Kenneth Frampton, "On Reading Heidegger," *Oppositions*, no. 4 (Oct. 1974). Frampton directs his criticism against both the formalism and contextualism of the late 1960s and their tendency to reduce architecture to a single building: "Autonomous artistic production certainly has many provinces but the task of place production in its broadest sense is not necessarily one of them." This short piece later becomes a pretext for his "Six Points for an Architecture of Resistance." Also see Frampton, "Towards a Critical Regionalism," in Foster, *Anti-Aesthetic*, 16–30.

102. According to Theodor Adorno, "Aesthetics deal with reciprocal relations between universal and particular where the universal is not imposed on the particular from the outside but emerges from the dynamic of particularities themselves." *Aesthetic Theory*, 481.

103. Heidegger, "Building Dwelling Thinking," 339. Delegitimation of harmony between the place and the home is also pursued by Emmanual Levinas. According to him, "The primordial function of the home does not consist in orienting being by the architecture of the building and in discovering a site, but in breaking the plenum of the element, in opening in it the utopia in which 'I' recollects itself in dwelling at home with itself." *Totality and Infinity* (Pittsburgh: Duquesne University Press, 1969), 156.

104. See note 35, above.

105. Gianni Vattimo, "The End of Modernity, The End of the Project?" *Philosophy and Architecture* (New York: St. Martin's Press, 1990), 77.

106. On this subject and its implications for modern architecture see my *Ontology of Construction* and note 5 in this chapter.

107. For further discussion on the concept of the culture of building see the last chapter in this volume.

108. "What the recollection achieves is the recovery of this eventual character of Being: metaphysics appears to Heidegger as the series of the epochs in which Being has opened itself in the form of different *archai*, each one claiming to be a stable (metaphysical) structure while it was just an epochal openness, a sort of *episteme* in Foucault's sense." Vattimo, "The End of (Hi)story," 26.

109. Martin Heidegger, "Art and Space," trans. Charles H. Seibert, *Pratt Journal of Architecture* 20 (Spring 1988): 9–11.

110. Vattimo, *End of Modernity*.

111. Martin Heidegger, "The Origin of the Work of Art," in *Basic Writings*, 169.

112. Massimo Cacciari, "Mies's Classics," *Res* 16 (1988) 9–16. In this rather complex and dense text, Cacciari seems to be presenting Mies's work as a "thing" in which a distinction between sign and signifier is impossible. He also reminds us that Mies believed that one could serve the life not by changing it but by being "faithful to the essence of *Bauen*; construction should be faithful to the unconditional nature of truth and reject seeing the truth as a formal pairing or confronting of the product/thing and the mind that designed it" (10). With regard to Loos, Cacciari recalls Benjamin's angel of history: "it is the loyalty that links Loos to Veillich, and that links both of them to what lasts: the beauty of material, and the happy forms of tradition." Cacciari, *Architecture and Nihilism*, 154.

113. Paraphrasing Theodor Adorno, Susan Buck-Morss wrote, "The thinker reflected on a sensuous and non-identical reality not in order to dominate it, not to butcher it to fit the Procrustean beds of mental categories or to liquidate its particularity by making it disappear under abstract concepts. Instead the thinker, like the artist, proceeded mimetically, and in the process of imitating matter transformed it so that it could be read as a monodological expression of social truth." Buck-Morss, *Origin of Negative Dialectics,* 132.

114. Here, I am paraphrasing Jon R. Snyder's reading of the term *Verwindung,* and its connotation for Vattimo's "weak thought." See Vattimo, *End of Modernity,* xxv.i.

115. Pierlugi Nicolin, "The Secularized Territory," *Lotus International* 65 (1989): 5.

Chapter 2

1. Walter Benjamin discusses the overall mode of appropriation of modern art and architecture. Yet for him architecture differs from other art forms by its capacity to endure and disclose the dynamic conditions of the life-world. "Buildings have been man's companions since primeval times. Many art forms developed and perished." And he continues, "architecture has never been idle. Its history is more ancient than that of any other art, and its claim to being a living force has significance in every attempt to comprehend the relationship between masses to art." "The Work of Art in the Age of Mechanical Reproduction," in *Illuminations,* trans. Harry Zohn (New York: Schocken, 1969), 222.

2. And he continues, "through its interest in technical phenomena, its curiosity about all kinds of discoveries and machinery, every childhood ties technological achievement to the old symbol-worlds." Walter Benjamin, "N [Re the Theory of Knowledge, Theory of Progress]," in *Walter Benjamin,* ed. Gary Smith (Chicago: Chicago University Press, 1989), 49.

3. I am paraphrasing Walter Benjamin in, "N," 45.

4. On several occasions, Walter Benjamin spoke about Le Corbusier's work positively. Yet according to John McCole, Benjamin "found this fierce parsimony [the parsimony demanded by the new poverty of experience] best incarnated in the figure of Loos, the inveterate enemy of ornament." John McCole, "Benjamin and Weimar Modernism," *Walter Benjamin and the Antinomies of Tradition* (Ithaca: Cornell University Press, 1993), 185.

5. Of course this was not a new concern for architects. Since 1850, and especially with the erection of the Crystal Palace, most German architects have spoken and discussed the importance of engineer's work and the place of iron in a new style. In his introduction to the newly published English translation of Sifried Giedion's *Building in France* (1928), Sokratis Georgiadis presents a brief and concise account on this subject. See *Building in France, Building in Iron, Building in Ferroconcrete,* trans. J. Duncan Berry (Santa Monica: Getty Center for the History of the Art and Humanities, 1995).

6. Le Corbusier, *The Decorative Art of Today* (Cambridge, Mass.: MIT Press, 1987). For the implication of "mechanical selections" in the context of French decorative arts, see Nancy Troy, *Modernism and the Decorative Arts in France* (New Haven: Yale University Press, 1991).

7. McCole, "Benjamin," 181.

8. These topos are central for current revisions on Le Corbusier. I am
   thinking of Beatriz Colomina's discussion of the gender aspect in Le
   Corbusier's spatial configuration. Colomina, "The Split Wall: Domestic
   Voyeurism," in *Sexuality and Space,* ed. Beatriz Colomina (New York:
   Princeton Architectural Press, 1992), 73–128. Also see Mark Wigely's
   reading of Le Corbusier's white architecture in light of Gottfried
   Semper's ideas on the principle of cladding, in "Architecture After
   Philosophy: And the Emperor's New Paint," *Journal of Philosophy and
   the Visual Arts* (1990): 84–95.

9. Alberto Pérez-Gómez, for example, locates the origin of the continuing
   critical situation of Western architecture in the late eighteenth century
   and sympathizes with an architecture of the past in which "the primacy
   of perception as the ultimate evidence of knowledge was never questioned." Pérez-Gómez, *Architecture and the Crisis of Modern Science*
   (Cambridge, Mass.: MIT Press, 1983).

10. See Martin Heidegger, "The Age of the World Picture," in *The Question
    Concerning Technology,* trans. W. Lovitt (New York: Harper and Row,
    1977). The concept of world-picture does not mean a picture of the
    world but the world grasped as a picture. The German word for "pic-
    ture" can be understood as "we are in the picture," or "we get the
    picture." See Michael Zimmermann, *Heidegger's Confrontation with
    Modernity* (Bloomington: Indiana University Press, 1990), 86.

11. Leon Battista Alberti, *On Painting* (New Haven: Yale University Press,
    1966).

12. "The desire to integrate painting and architecture, to establish a perfect
    coincidence between the basic elements of painting (the color plants)
    and architecture (the wall), led to a major architectural discovery—
    walls, floors, ceiling as surfaces without thickness that can be dupli-
    cated, or unfolded like screens and made to slide past one another in
    space." Yve-Alain Bois, *Painting as Method* (Cambridge, Mass.: MIT
    Press, 1993), 116.

13. Colin Rowe, "Chicago Frame," *The Mathematics of the Ideal Villa and
    Other Essays* (Cambridge, Mass.: MIT Press, 1982), 107. Here Rowe
    criticizes the implementation of the Dom-ino frame for the International
    Style, arguing that the Chicago frame was developed based on pragmatic
    needs and not as an "idea," which according to him was the driving
    force for the entire modern movement.

14. Several authors have discussed the relationship between painting and
    architecture in Le Corbusier. To utilize painting in architecture, Le
    Corbusier used the method of *recherche patiente,* by which one trans-
    forms certain motives into signs using them in diverse contexts. Thus Le
    Corbusier would transplant elements like *piloti, brises-soleil* and ramp
    in different cultural and environmental conditions. See Edward F. Sekler,
    "Le Corbusier's Use of a 'Pictorial World' in His Tapestry La Femme et
    le Moineau," in *Vision and Artifact,* ed. Mary Hesnle (New York:
    Springer, 1976), 119–29. Also see Katherine Fraser Fischer, "A Nature
    Morte, 1927," *Oppositions,* no. 15/16 (Winter/Spring 1979): 157–65.
    For an analogy between the concept of house and still life in Le
    Corbusier's painting see Kurt W. Forster, "Antiquity and Modernity in
    the La Roch-Jeanneret House of 1923," *Oppositions,* no. 15/16 (Winter/
    Spring 1979): 131–52. Also important is Kenneth Frampton's observa-

tion in the project of Palace of the Soviets, where "the hyperbolic arch solution finally adopted also relates to Le Corbusier's Purist habit of transposing a plan configuration into a section and vice versa, so that the arch trajectory reflects almost directly the hyperbolic plan of the auditorium." Kenneth Frampton, "Le Corbusier's Design for The League of Nations, the Centrosoyus, and the Palace of the Soviets, 1926–1931," in *Le Corbusier,* ed. H. Allen Brooks (Princeton: Princeton University Press, 1987), 52–82.

15. M. Merleau-Ponty, *Phenomenology of Perception,* trans. C. Smith (New York: Humanities Press, 1962).

16. Rowe, *Mathematics of the Ideal Villa.*

17. My stress on technology should be read in the context of a modern architecture that in search for a new style had no choice but to rely heavily on industrial techniques and materials. In painting, however, I agree with Jonathan Crary's contention that "a reorganization of the observer occurs in the nineteenth century before the appearance of photography. What takes place from around 1810 to 1849 is an uprooting of vision from the stable and fixed relations incarnated in the camera obscura." Crary, *Techniques of the Observer* (Cambridge, Mass.: MIT Press, 1991), 14.

18. Fischer, "A Nature Morte, 1927," 162.

19. Le Corbusier, *Towards a New Architecture,* trans. Frederick Etchelles (New York: Praeger, 1974), 210. In a passage of *La Peinture moderne,* Le Corbusier paints the differences between purism and cubism in terms of their choice of objects. Purism drew their choices "preferably from among those that serve the most direct human uses; those which are like the extensions of man's limbs, and thus of an extreme intimacy, a banality that makes them barely exist as subjects of interest in themselves" (quoted in Forster, "Antiquity and Modernity," 142).

20. Peter Eisenman, "Aspects of Modernism: Maison Dom-ino and the Self-Referential Sign," *Oppositions,* no. 15/16 (Winter/Spring 1979): 121. The literature on the Dom-ino is limited. In the above-mentioned issue of *Oppositions,* Eleanor Greg reminds us of Le Corbusier's concern for the place of architecuture in a technical world occupied by engineers, and maps the technical and sociocultural environment of the early century to disclose their impact on Le Corbusier's thought in general, and the evolution of the Dom-ino in particular. See Greg, "The Dom-ino Idea," 61–87. The idea of "mechanical selection," present both in nature and machine products, leads Le Corbusier to see, as discussed before, the Dom-ino frame as the matter-of-factness of an architecture to be realized. This last point is extensively discussed, also in that issue of *Oppositions,* by Barry Maitland, "The Grid," 91–117. According to Maitland, in Le Corbusier's architecture an antithetical dialectic operates between two systems of structural and nonstructural "enclosing and defining just those volumes which the particular building requires" (96).

21. Le Corbusier, *Towards a New Architecture,* 11–12. This idea was important for Le Corbusier because, through Purist painting and the formal potentialities provided by the Dom-ino frame, he could transpose horizontal planes for the vertical and vice versa. The reader will notice shortly why such a transposition was not possible for a masonry construction. Thus Frank Lloyd Wright, for example, could not attain the perceptive qualities invested in Le Corbusier's villas. Or for that

matter, Mies van der Rohe's interest in the tectonic would not allow him to disintegrate the architectural elements as Le Corbusier did.

22. Le Corbusier, *Towards a New Architecture,* 166.

23. For Rudolf Wittkower, see *Architectural Principles in the Age of Humanism* (London: Academy, 1973), Colin Rowe, *Mathematics of the Ideal Villa* (1984).

24. Gilles Deleuze and Felix Guattari, *A Thousand Plateaus* (Minneapolis: University of Minnesota Press, 1987), 475.

25. Andrea Palladio, *The Four Books of Architecture,* trans. M. H. Morgan (New York: Dover, 1960), 27.

26. Leon Battista Alberti, *On the Art of Building in the Ten Books,* trans. Joseph Rykwert (Cambridge, Mass.: MIT Press, 1988), 7.

27. Ibid.

28. In "A Picturesque Stroll around Clara-Clara," Yve-Alain Bois examines the importance of geometrization and the plan for the spatial journey taking place in the eighteenth-century picturesque gardens, in Richard Serra's sculptures, and in Le Corbusier's Villa Savoye. Bois considers the idea of *promenade architectural* as a means for Le Corbusier to undermine his own strong belief in the plan. See Bois, *October* 29 (Summer 1984) 33–62. For an association between filmic visual experience and the Carpenter Center building see Stan Allen, "Le Corbusier and Modernist Movement," *Any* 5 (Mar./Apr. 1994): 42–47.

29. Along this space the eye of the ascending person monitors different spatial cues according to the posture of the body. Robert Slutzky has extensively discussed the implications of an elevated oculus in Le Corbusier's work. One might speculate that the elevation of the eye to the horizontal slot of the facade of the Villa Savoye is another reminder of the painterly need to posit the vanishing point and the eye of the beholder in the same plane. Yet at a representational level, Slutzky argues that the elevation of the oculus intends to disregard the mechanism of one-point perspective in favor of flattening the depth field, and making the facade "a two-dimensional space of the Cubist still-life." Slutzky, "Aqueous Humor," *Oppositions,* no. 19/20 (1980): 29–51.

30. Peter Eisenman, "The Futility of Objects," *Harvard Architectural Review* 3 (Winter 1984): 65–82.

31. Kenneth Frampton correctly observes that Le Corbusier's Maison Week-End, built at St. Claud near Paris, "announces a totally fresh departure, one that was to be as much at variance with the ideology of Purism as with the fuctionalism of the Neue sachliechkeit." Frampton, *Studies in Tectonic Culture* (Cambridge, Mass.: MIT Press, 1994), 344.

32. Manfredo Tafuri and Francesco Dal Co, *Modern Architecture,* trans. E. Wolf (New York: Harry N. Abrams, 1979). For Tafuri's reading of Walter Benjamin's discussion of the crisis of the object and Le Corbusier, see Francoise Very's interview with Tafuri in *Casabella* 619–20 (1995): 37–45.

33. Leo Steinberg, *Other Criteria* (New York: Oxford University Press, 1972), 192–223.

34. For the significance of this separation in the history of architecture and the place of the subject in Peter Eisenman's work, see Mario Gandelsonas, "From Structure to Subject: The Formation of an Architectural Language," *Peter Eisenman House III* (New York: Rizzoli International, 1982), 7–31.

35. On the role of the notion of "erosion" in the Five Architects, see Kenneth Frampton, "Frontality vs. Rotation," in *Five Architects* (New York: Oxford University Press, 1975), 9–13. For the ways in which Michael Graves utilizes Le Corbusier's experience, see Peggy Deamer, "Michael Graves: Body Maker?" in *Thinking the Present,* eds. K. Michael Hays and Carol Burns (New York: Princeton Architectural Press, 1990), 6–22.

36. Robert Venturi, *Complexity and Contradiction in Architecture* (New York: Museum of Modern Art, 1966), 30.

37. Manfredo Tafuri, *The Sphere and the Labyrinth,* trans. P. d'Accierno and R. Connolly (Cambridge, Mass.: MIT Press, 1987), 301.

38. Michel Foucault, *The Order of Things* (New York: Vintage, 1973), 46–50. The split between things and words is given a theological dimension by Walter Benjamin. To him "the Fall marks the birth of the human word, in which name no longer lives intact, and which has stepped out of name language." As a result there occurred a chasm between name and thing. See "On Language as Such and on the Language of Man," in *Reflections,* trans. E. Jephcott (Harcourt Brace Jovanovich, 1978), 314–32.

39. Peter Eisenman, "miMisses READING: does not mean A THING," *Mies Reconsidered* (Chicago: Art Institute of Chicago, 1986), 86.

40. Jean Baudrillard, *Simulation* (New York: Semiotex, 1983), 142.

41. Peter Eisenman, "The End of the Classical," *Perspecta* 21 (1984): 154–72.

42. Walter Benjamin, "The Author as Producer," *Reflections,* 220–38. Also see Tafuri, *Sphere and Labyrinth,* 287.

43. Jean Baudrillard, *The Evil Demon of Images* (Sydney: Power Institute of Fine Arts, 1987), 47.

44. Demetri Porphyrios, "Invention and Convention," *Architectural Design* 58, no. 1/2 (1988).

45. I am referring to Gilles Deleuze's reading of what Michel Foucault has framed as "internal conditions of differences." See Gilles Deleuze, *Foucault,* trans. Sean Hand (Minneapolis: University of Minnesota Press, 1988), 23–44.

46. Discussing the role of the observer in the modern techniques of visuality, Jonathan Crary contends that "a recognition of the observer occurs in the nineteenth century before the appearance of photography." Crary, *Techniques of the Observer,* 14.

47. According to Martin Jay, Theodor Adorno insisted on "the importance of utopian thought as a negation of the status quo even as he argues against the possibility of fleshing out its contours." See Martin Jay, *Adorno* (Cambridge, Mass.: Harvard University Press, 1984), 65.

48. Jean-Francois Lyotard, "Re-Writing Modernity," *Substance,* no. 7 (1987). Here, Lyotard restates his hopes for a technological revolution. Nevertheless, he separates his discourse from a postmodernism whose conditions he had mapped before. This latest theoretical development gave Peter Eisenman the chance to refine his position against postmodernists in general and Michael Graves in particular. See P. Eisenman, *Architecture and Urbanism,* no. 202 (July 1987): 18–22.

49. "This 'postmodernist suicide' as a metaphor for writing differs from 'modern suicide' in that it posits the death of the narrator in *tandem* with annihilation of the world. It thus makes suicide a collective act instead of an individual subjective one." Alan Wolfe, "Suicide and the

Japanese Postmodern: A Postnarrative Paradigm?" in *Postmodernism and Japan,* eds. Massap Miyoshi and H. D. Harootunian (Durham: Duke University Press, 1989), 226.

50. Robin Evans, "Eyes It Took Time to See," *Assemblage* 20 (April 1993): 36–37. In revising this text I noticed the following statement by Evans, which implicity speaks for some of the themes presented throughout this book, specifically my stress of the idea of "both-and." In *The Projective Cast* (Cambridge, Mass: MIT Press, 1995), the late Evans observes: "The distinguished feature of deconstructive architecture is its exaggeration of a property already recurrent in twentieth-century architecture. Reviving the disruptions presaged in cubist and constructivist painting and sculpture, it raises, once again, specific technical problems of realization ignored in its public presentation, or quite deliberately flouted as insignificant by its promoters. In order to overcome them architects will either have to become conservative, in the sense of having to undertake a long, maturing travail, or they will have to retreat into Derridian graphology from which increasingly violent representations will produce decreasing effects, or the effects achieved through the labor, skill, and ingenuity of others" (92).

51. Since Le Corbusier, the theme of the city has been an important subject for a postmodern architecture that is indulged with the place of history and tradition in architecture. Besides Colin Rowe's *The Collage City,* mention should be make of Aldo Rossi's seminal work, *Architecture and the City,* which revitalized the idea of type and of the morphological relationship between architecture and the city. Robert Venturi's *Learning from Las Vegas,* on the other hand, was an important observation on consumerist values of American mainstream architecture. Facing the failure of the project of the historical avant-garde, Venturi sought no other way for architecture to function except by assimilating itself into the process of commodification. A less pessimistic reflection on such a historical condition is the point of departure for Rem Koolhaas in *Delirious New York.* Here Koolhaas implements a surrealist position toward an urban context that is framed by the logic of late capitalism. While touched by the wide spectrum of current historicism, Koolhaas's insistence of seeing architecture as a part of a larger totality is suggestive to think of architecture beyond any ideological and typological reduction.

52. See J. Baudrillard's argument in *For a Critique of the Political Economy of the Sign* (St. Louis: Telos Press, 1981), esp. pp. 198–203.

53. Colin Rowe, *Five Architects,* 3. Interestingly enough, Le Corbusier found New York City "utterly lacking in order and harmony and the comforts of the spirit which must surround humanity." Quoted in Rem Koolhaas, *Delirious New York* (New York: Oxford University Press, 1978), 220. According to Manfredo Tafuri, Le Corbusier came to have second thoughts on his impracticable utopias. Recalling Aragon's reflection on the steering wheel as the emblem of modern tragedy, Tafuri suggests that the "Ville Radieuse wanted to guide such a mythological steering wheel; its ceaseless motion is what the Open Hand opposed with its oscillating metaphors, which are endowed, to use Walter Benjamin's phrase, 'with a feeble messianic strength.'" See Tafuri, "'*Machine et memoire*': The City in the Work of Le Corbusier," in *Le Corbusier,* ed. H. Allen Brooks (Princeton: Princeton University Press, 1987), 214.

54. This is not to say that Louis Kahn did not use frame in his architecture, but the tectonic of his constructs utilized frame as a means for spatial expression. I discuss this aspect of Kahn in chapter 3.

55. Tadao Ando, "Nature and Architecture," in *Tadao Ando and Sketches,* ed. Werner Blaser (Germany: Verlag Basel, 1990), 15.

56. Rosalind E. Krauss, *Passages in Modern Sculpture* (Cambridge, Mass.: MIT Press, 1981), 262. Rosalin Krauss's phenomenological reading of minimalism (her emphasis on the nature of meaning and the status of subject) contradicts, according to Hal Foster, "the two dominant models of abstract expressionism—that of the expressive artist and that of the formal critique of the medium—presented respectively by Harold Rosenburg and Greenberg." See Foster, "The Crux of Minimalism," in *Individuals: A Selected History of Contemporary Art,* ed. Howard Sigerman (New York: Abbeville, 1986), 162–93. For the implications of minimalist art for post-1960s architecture, see Ignasi de Solá-Morales Rubio, "From Autonomy to Untimeliness," *Anyone* (New York: Rizzoli International, 1991), 173–85. Also see Vittorio Gregotti, "A Path to Explore," *Casabella* 582 (1991): 60.

57. In minimal art the work itself is figure, meaning that, in minimalism literal shape is predominant. See Michael Fried, "Art and Objecthood," in *Minimal Art: A Critical Anthology,* ed. Gregory Battcock (New York: Dutton, 1968), 116–47.

58. Tadao Ando, "New Relations Between the Space and the Person," *Japan Architecture,* Oct./Nov. 1977, 11.

59. According to Tadao Ando: "Light is mediator between space and form. Light changes expressions with time. I believe that the architectural materials do not end with wood and concrete that have tangible forms, but go beyond to include light and wind which appeal to our senses." Quoted in Kenneth Frampton's remarks on Tadao Ando's exhibition catalog at Museum of Modern Art, New York: MoMA, 1991.

60. Tadao Ando, "The Wall as Territorial Delineation," in *Tadao Ando: Buildings Projects Writing,* ed. Kenneth Frampton (New York: Rizzoli International, 1984), 6.

61. Kenneth Frampton, "Tadao Ando's Critical Modernism," in *Tadao Ando,* 6.

62. Tadao Ando, "From Self-Enclosed Modern Architecture Towards University," *Japan Architecture,* no. 301, (May 1982): 8–12. Ando's words recalls Tony Smith, who wanted "form to be made of space light and not material." Quoted in Frances Colpitt, *Minimal Art: The Critical Perspective* (Seattle: University of Washington Press, 1993), 10.

63. I am thinking about the debate between high and popular art and the ways Robert Venturi appropriated popular art both for his architecture and the polemics directed against high modernism. Yet, according to M. Christine Boyer, "the boundaries between high and popular art are never so clearly separated nor carefully maintained. The witty and the vernacular, or the mannered and the decorous, have always been contaminated by imitations and translations stolen from each other. . . . architects of the 1970s and 1980s hoped that lost traditions would be regained, that history and everyday visual reality once rejected could be reinscribed in new projections of the comic theatrical stage." Boyer, *The City of Collective Memory* (Cambridge, Mass.: MIT Press, 1995), 125.

64. Frances Colpitt, *Minimal Art,* 17. Discussing the "objecthood" in minimalist art, Colpitt suggests: "Attention is paid to what the work of art actually does rather than what it communicates about its creator—that is, what its creator 'put' into it or intended it to do" (72).

65. Comparing different ethical and aesthetic aspects of Japanese culture with that of the West, Jun'ichiro Tanizaki states, "we happen to find ourselves, to content ourselves with things as they are, and so darkness causes us no discontent, we resign ourselves to it as inevitable." Tanizaki, *In Praise of Shadow* (Ne Have: Leete's Island Books, 1977), 31. Tanizaki's text was originally published in 1933, and some of his ideas resurfaced in an academic gathering to discuss "overcoming the modern" in 1942. According to H. D. Harootunian, some participant in the conference insisted that "beauty never evolved in a progressive, purposeful manner, and can never be understood from the historically motivated perspective of the modern." However, "overcoming the modern" was not a yearning for a new period, nor a demand to return to an agrarian order. It meant to secure an autonomous sphere for culture: "a reunion outside of history with the eternal forms of truth and beauty." Harootunian, "Visible Discourses/Invisible Ideologies," in *Postmodernism and Japan,* eds., Harootunian and Masao Miyoshi (Durham: Duke University Press, 1989), 69. I will come back to the subject of aporia of modernization and tradition in chapter 4, discussing Kenneth Frampton's critical regionalism.

66. I am thinking of Fredric Jameson's correct response to Charles Jencks's classification of late modern and postmodern architecture based on modernists' obsession with technology. According to Jameson, "this characterization earns its credentials precisely on account of the historicist impulse at work within the technological obsession, namely the reference to an essentially modernist technology, an older kind of technology than the one currently predominant." Jameson, "Tadao Ando and the Enclosure of Modernism," *Any* no. 6 (May/June 1994): 22.

67. Tadao Ando, "The Wall as Territorial Delineation."

68. Koji Taki, "Minimalism or Monotonality? A Contextual Analysis of Tadao Ando's Method," in Frampton, *Tadao Ando,* 16.

69. I am alluding to Jacques Derrida's discussion of the fetish of commodities in which the laborer cannot recognize his/her labor. "These ghosts that are commodities transform human producers into ghosts. And this whole theatrical process (visual, theoretical, but also optical, *optician*) sets off the effect of a mysterious mirror: if the latter does not return the right reflection, if, then, it phantomalize, this is first of all because it naturalizes." Derrida, *Specters of Marx* (New York: Routledge, 1994), 156. On fetish and its implications for various disciplines see *Fetish* (New York: Princeton Architectural Press, 1992). See also my concluding remarks on Louis Kahn in the next chapter. My reflections on theatricality also benefit from Charles Bernstein's "Artifice of Absorption." According to Bernstein "theatricalizing or conceptualizing the text, removing it from the realm of an experience engendered to that of a technique exhibited." The implied communicative quality of an artifice differs from the spellbinding replication of the historical forms because "the more intensified, technologized absorption made possible by nonabsorptive means may get the reader absorbed into a more ideologized or political space." Bernstein, *A Poetics* (Cambridge, Mass.:

Harvard University Press, 1992), 53. To me, the tectonic is a nonabsorptive means whose architecture communicates with the beholder on a more critical level than those engaged in simulation of historical forms. See also my discussion of theatricality and montage in *Ontology of Construction: On Nihilism of Technology in Theories of Modern Architecture* (New York: Cambridge University Press, 1994).

70. Theodor Adorno, *Aesthetic Theory* (New York: Routledge and Kegal Paul, 1986), 468.

Chapter 3

1. Louis Kahn's statement is important because it can be associated with the postmodern discourse of the death of the author and with Mies van der Rohe's view of the task of the architect as a servant who humbly does what is intrinsic to *Belkidung.* For Mies's concept of servant, see note 27, below.

2. For a general phenomenological interpretation of architecture see Christopher Norberg-Schultz, *The Concept of Dwelling* (New York: Rizzoli International, 1985). On his association between Louis Kahn and Martin Heidegger see Norberg-Schultz, "Kahn, Heidegger and the Language of Architecture," *Oppositions,* no. 18 (Fall 1979): 29–47.

3. For Jacques Gubler the determinist element in Kahn is not type but a kind of Gothicism, "in the primacy of vertical structure, in the figurative coexistence of the plan and the constructional system." Implied in Gubler's argument is Kahn's pursuit of the tradition of the nineteenth-century rational functionalists, like Viollet le Duc. Gubler, "Lacampata é un tipo?" *Casabella* 509–10 (1985): 76–81.

4. In contemporary discourse, the idea of the crisis of the object was first discussed in Surrealist circles. Walter Benjamin tuned the subject with technological unfoldings of the turn of the century, suggesting that the age of mechanical reproduction is the beginning of the end of the aura of the work of art. Others, including Tafuri and Frampton, have discussed the periodic crisis of the object in architecture. Tafuri links the end of classical object to the eclipse of history implied in Piranese's work. Frampton predicates the crisis of the object in three historical instances; first occurring in 1747 and in A. Laugier's writings, then in 1851 with the Industrial Revolution and the emergence of mass culture, and finally in 1918 by the work of Russian constructivist and the Bauhaus experience. From a phenomenological view, Pérez-Gómez sees the crisis of the object as a by-product of a positivism that celebrates the separation of logos from mythos. See Haim N. Finkelstein, *Surrealism and the Crisis of the Object* (Ann Arbor: University Microfilms International, 1979); Benjamin, "The Work of Art in the Age of Mechanical Reproduction," in *Illuminations*); Tafuri, *Theories and History of Architecture* (New York: Harper and Row, 1979); Frampton, "Industrialization and the Crisis of the Architecture," *Oppositions,* no. 1 (September 1973): 57–82; and Pérez-Gómez, *Architecture and the Crisis of Modern Science* (Cambridge, Mass.: MIT Press, 1983). In contemporary cultural discourse, one should discuss the crisis of the object in the purview of ideas developed around the death of the subject and infusion of technology into the life-world. These last two points are absent from current phenomenological readings of architecture and therefore fall short of fully entertaining the implications of poststructuralist discourse for architecture.

5. Paul Shepard reminds us that for Vitruvius architecture included both buildings and machines: "The machines, which in Vitruvius's book are simply dedicated to building or destroying buildings, have now come into their own . . . The biggest change came when they pulled away from the mother art [architecture] entirely and went subperceptual." Shepard, *What is Architecture?* (Cambridge, Mass.: MIT Press, 1994), 60.

6. Discussing the differences between speech and writing in Western philosophy, Jacque Derrida suggests that "the supplement adds itself, it is a surplus, a plentitude enriching another plentitude, the *fullest measure* of presence." Derrida, *Of Gramatalogy* (Baltimore: Johns Hopkins University Press, 1976), 144. In the void opened by the death of the author, Louis Kahn's "what the building wants to be" works as a supplement, adding itself in-the-place of the subject. But supplement does not work as an explicit addition; it represents itself as natural to what is put in-place-of. The tectonic of theatricality is the embodiment of what is alleged to be the poetics of Kahn's architecture. On this last point see my concluding remarks here.

7. Robert Venturi, *Complexity and Contradiction* (New York: Museum of Modern Art, 1966), 20.

8. The concept of return is significant for posthistoricist discourse of culture. From a Freudian discussion of "repetition and the pleasure of return, one could argue that the line dividing postmodern from modern is not total. There is always a possibility for the same to return in difference." Only through this paradigm one could do justice to a discussion of the aesthetic, cognitive, and political contribution of the neo-avant-garde. See Hal Foster, "What is Neo about the Neo-Avant-Garde?" *October* 70 (Fall 1994): 16.

9. Mario Gandelsonas, Editorial, *Oppositions,* no. 5 (Summer 1976).

10. Peter Eisenman, "Post-Functionalism," *Oppositions,* no. 6 (Fall 1976).

11. Fredric Jameson, *Postmodernism, or, The Cultural Logic of Late Capitalism* (Durham: Duke University Press, 1991), 1–54; in particular, pp. 6–11. For Martin Heidegger's reading of Van Gogh's painting see, "The Origin of the Work of Art," in *Basic Writings,* 143–88.

12. For a deconstructivist reading of these paintings see Jacques Derrida, "Restitutions," in *The Truth of Painting* (Chicago: University of Chicago Press, 1987), 255–383. The focus of Derrida's reading is a restitution that is rendered around topos like pairedness, seriality, and the milieu of the shoes in Van Gogh's painting. Interestingly enough, Derrida also recalls Magritte's Le Modele Rouge to remind us that "you can see," in Magritte's painting, "the disposition of the toes which form one and the same body with the boots. They form both the pair and the join" (134).

13. Mannfredo Tafuri and Francesco Dal Co, *Modern Architecture* (New York: Harry N. Abrams, 1979), 407. To place Kahn in the context of the historical loss of the center recalls Freud's belief that "the finding of an object is in fact a refinding of it." Quoted in Paul Ricoeur, *Freud* (New Haven: Yale University Press, 1970), 273. Kenneth Frampton is more explicit on this subject by suggesting that the phenomenological aspect of Kahn's work could be explained partly "by the perennial frontier conditions obtaining in the cultural ethos and the socio-psychology of the United States" but also because "of its ever-receding frontier of an abandoned culture and history, which by definition was the

condition of its foundation." See "Louis Kahn and the French Connection," *Oppositions,* no. 22 (Fall 1980): 48.

14. Theodor Adorno, *Aesthetic Theory* (New York: Routledge and Kegan Paul, 1984). Adorno discusses mimesis in numerous parts of his text. This particular quotation is from appendix 2, p. 453. For a comprehensive reading of Adorno's concept of mimesis, see Lambert Zuidervaart, *Adorno's Aesthetic Theory* (Cambridge, Mass.: MIT Press, 1991), 110–12 and 181. Zuidervaart articulates Adorno's discussion of the differences between magic, instrumental reason, and art: "Unlike magic, art does not make itself similar to specific things. Unlike science, art does not reduce things to their being controllable. Instead, art imitates itself, and it contrasts its pure image to reality, art works seek the appearance of the whole in the particular" (133).

15. Gottfried Semper, *The Four Elements of Architecture and Other Writings,* trans. Harry Francis Mallgrave and Wolfgang Herrmann (New York: Cambridge University Press, 1989), 249. For my reading of Semper's tectonic see *Ontology of Construction: On Nihilism of Technology in Theories of Modern Architecture* (New York: Cambridge University Press, 1994).

16. Adorno, *Aesthetic Theory,* 44.

17. Anthony Vidler, *The Writing on the Walls: Architectural Theory in the Late Enlightenment* (Princeton: Princeton Architectural Press, 1987), 3.

18. Adorno, *Aesthetic Theory,* 164–68.

19. Ibid., 162.

20. Reflecting on Adorno, Lamber Zuidervaart reminds us that "an artwork's 'objective ideal' is not a Platonic form of beauty, but the *telos* of the artwork alone. 'Objective' means 'not posited by the artist,' and 'ideal' means 'what an art work itself wants to be and become.'" Zuidervaart, *Adorno's Aesthetic Theory,* 181.

21. Adorno, "Functionalism Today," *Oppositions,* no. 17 (Summer 1979): 31–41.

22. See Vittorio Gregotti, "Modern Connection," *Rassegna* 21 (1985): 4–5; and Kenneth Frampton, "The French Connection," *Oppositions,* no. 27 (Fall 1980): 21–53.

23. Adorno, "Functionalism Today," p. 35.

24. Again, this might explain why a whole post-Kahn generation of American architects has turned to the kitsch of Las Vegas for inspiration.

25. Gevork Hartoonian, "Louis Kahn: Permanence and Change," *Symposium on Architecture, and ACSA Technology Conference* (Baton Rouge: Louisiana State University, 1989), 217–20.

26. From Mies's lecture, "With Infinite Slowness Arises the Great Form," published in Fritz Neumeyer, *The Artless Word* (Cambridge, Mass.: MIT Press, 1991), 325. This was in part Mies's rethinking of architecture after Carl Botticher's distinction between the core-form and the art-form. According to Fritz Neumeyer, this fissure could only be bridged "by a fundamental reappraisal. Either function had to be legitimized and had to be viewed as an art form in its own right, as had been advocated by the Deutsche Werkbund before 1919, or one had to draw the uncomfortable conclusion, with Karl Kraus and Adolf Loos, that with respect to the serviceable things in life one simply had to suspend artistic demand" (35).

27. Sandor Randoti, "Benjamin's Dialectic of Art and Society," in *Benjamin,* ed. Gary Smith (Chicago: University of Chicago Press, 1989), 134.

28. Walter Benjamin, "Surrealism: The Last Snapshot of European Intelligentsia," in *Reflections,* trans. E. Jephcott (New York: Harcourt Brace Jovanovich, 1978), 180.

29. Here Ernest Bloch makes analogies between the abstract emptiness of glass surface with the hollow spaces surrounding bourgeois nothingness. Bloch, "Building in Empty Spaces," in *Utopian Function of Art and Literature,* trans. Jack Zipes (Cambridge, Mass: MIT Press, 1988), 189.

30. According to Michel Foucault "the sixteenth century superimposed hermeneutics and semiology in the form of similitude. To search for a meaning is to bring to light a resemblance." He continues, "There is no difference between the visible marks that God has stamped upon the surface of the earth, so that we may know its inner secrets, and the legible words that the Scriptures, or the sages of Antiquity, have set down in the books preserved for us by tradition." For Foucault the discourse of representation brought an end to the resemblance between words and things. Foucault, *The Order of Things* (New York: Vantage, 1973), chs. 2 and 3.

31. Again, Christopher Norberg-Schultz picks up this dimension of Kahn's thought for his own interest in phenomenology. Drawing analogies from spoken language, Norberg-Schultz insists on the import of archetypes for architectural language and makes correlations between Michael Graves and Kahn. See Christopher Norberg-Schultz, "The Demand for a Contemporary Language of Architecture," *Art and Design,* Dec. 1986, 14–21.

32. Bloch, *Utopian Function of Art and Literature,* 16.

33. This reading of Kahn seems to be in Manfredo Tafuri's mind when he attributed a school of mysticism in Kahn's architecture. See Tafuri and Dal Co, *Modern Architecture.*

34. Discussing architectural analogies in literature, Ellen Eve Frank suggests that, etymologically, the word "window" "is actually a combined form of wind (weather, air in motion, formless or unembodied, external energy) and eye (the seeing or perceiving edge of mind)." Frank, *Literary Architecture* (Berkeley and Los Angeles: University of California Press, 1979), 263.

35. The pure window-view is a romantic innovation—neither landscape nor interior but a curious combination of both. It brings the confinement of an interior into the most immediate contrast with an immensity of space outside." Lorenz Eitener, "The Open Window and the Stormed-Tossed Boat: An Essay in the Ichnography of Romanticism," *Art Bulletin* 37 (Dec. 1955): 285. For a general account of the characteristic of window in painting see Kyra Stomberg, "The Window in the Picture—The Picture in the Window," *Daidalos* 13 (September 1984): 54–64.

36. Emmanuel Levinas, *Totality and Infinity* (Pittsburgh: Duquesne University Press, 1969), 156.

37. Rainer Maria Rilke, *The Complete French Poems* (Saint Paul, Minn.: Graywolf, 1986), 31.

38. Speaking about the Salk Institute, Louis Kahn had this to say about the study rooms: "the studies have one idea which I am not sure was such a good idea, but every study had to look out to the sea." Louis Kahn,

Louis I. Kahn: Writings, Lectures, Interviews, ed. Allessandra Latour (New York: Rizzoli International, 1991), 215.

39. The concept of opening is important for an understanding of Kahn's architectonic articulation of the threshold between inside and outside. In his latest work, openings provide light and air without framing the window. For the significance of opening in architecture since Leon Battista Alberti's discourse on *aperito* see Werner Oschlin, "Leon Battista Alberti's *aperito* the Opening Absolute," *Daidalos* 13 (Sept. 1984): 29–38.

40. Bloch, *Utopian Function of Art and Literature,* 73.

41. Karl Marx, "Commodities," *Capital,* vol. 1 (New York: International Publishers, 1967), 35–93. Thus, to enter the world of exchange-value the commodity first has to become anonymous: Its total separation from the sensuous and bodily realm of a craft-person, an essential phenomena for the aura of craftsmanship.

42. This is Manfredo Tafuri's reflection on Peter Eisenman's House II. One can extend his reading to Eisenman's latest work too. See Tafuri, 'American Graffiti: FiveXFive=Twenty-five."

43. I am using these words in regard to their conceptual load invested in surrealism. Also one should be reminded of Walter Benjamin's assessment on phantasmagoria of the Paris of exhibition halls, the flaneur, and the crowd. For automatism, see Hal Foster, "Exquisite Corpses," *Compulsive Beauty* (Cambridge, Mass.: MIT Press, 1993), 125–56. For Benjamin see "Paris, Capital of the Nineteenth Century," in *Reflections,* 146–62. I will present a concept of theatricality evolving out of the revealed poetics of construction shortly.

44. According to Jacques Derrida, "if a work of art can become a commodity, and if this process seems fated to occur, it is also because the commodity began by putting to work, in one way or another, the principle of an art." Jacques Derrida, *Specters of Marx* (New York: Routledge, 1994), 162. This I believe is also suggested in Gianni Vattimo's discourse on secularization. See Gianni Vattimo, "Myth and the Fate of Secularization," *Res* 9 (Spring 1985): 29–34. My concluding remarks on Louis Kahn are indebted to Derrida's argument here, especially his last chapter.

45. "If you talk to a brick and ask what it likes, it'll say it likes an arch. And you say to it, look arches are expensive and you can always use a concrete lintel to take the place of an arch. And the brick says, I know it's expensive and I am afraid it probably can not be built these days, if you ask me what I *like* it's still an arch." Louis Kahn, in *Louis I. Kahn,* 296. The phantasmagoria Kahn created in Dacca is indeed the result of a marriage between what the brick wanted to be and what it could be by the help of concrete lintel. Ironically, in a passage of *Capital,* K. Marx also speculates that "could commodities themselves speak, they would say: Our use-value may be a thing that interests men. It is no part of us as objects. What, however, does belong to us as objects, is our value." We see here another expression of the inevitability of metamorphosis unleashed by modernization: A graft insinuated into the body of tradition which in return makes the possibility for tradition to survive, though in a different form. See Marx, *Capital,* 83.

46. Adorno, *Aesthetic Theory,* 453. Adorno has this to say about what history has grafted into a material: "Clearly there exists, perhaps imperceptible in the materials and forms which the artist acquires and

develops something more than material and form. Imagination means to *innovate* this something . . . for the forms, even the materials, are by no means merely given by nature." According to him, artistic imagination should awaken what "history has accumulated in them [materials], and spirit permeates them." Adorno, "Functionalism Today", *Oppositions,* no. 17 (Summer 1979): 37. The *passe,* or tactile grafting, is also dramatized by Renzo Piano at Menil Center, where wood panel cladding—a vernacular element—is juxtaposed with the tectonic of a Miesian frame.

47. See Hartoonian, *Ontology of Construction,* 23 and 85–90.

48. For Evans, see *The Projective Cast* (Cambridge, Mass.: MIT Press, 1995), 228, and for Benjamin see "The Work of Art in the Age of Mechanical Reproduction," *Illuminations* (New York: Schocken, 1969), 224. And Paul Virilio has this to say on this subject: "along with construction techniques, there's always the construction of techniques, that collection of spatial and temporal mutations that is constantly reorganizing both the world of everyday experience and the esthetic representations of contemporary life." Virilio, *Lost Dimension* (New York: Semiotext(e), 1991), 21. Here I am also thinking of Charles Bernstein's thoughts on theatricality in poetry. Bernstein, "Artifice of Absorption," in *A Poetics* (Cambridge, Mass.: Harvard University Press, 1992).

Chapter 4

1. Peter Burger, *Theory of Avant-Garde* (Minneapolis: University of Minnesota Press, 1984). For a critical review of Burger's theory see Benjamin Buchloh, *Art in America* 11 (November 1984): 19–21. Buchloh points to Burger's reduction of the historical avant-garde's contention to "one overriding concern—the dismantling of the false autonomy of the institution of art," and the functionary nature of Burger's view in regard to the ways that the totality of ideological discourses influence the institution of art. According to Buchloh, one should rather "define avant-garde practice as a continually renewed struggle over the definition of cultural meaning, the discovery and representation of new audiences, and the development of new strategies to counteract and develop resistance against the tendency of the ideological apparatus of the culture industry." This last position is discussed by Hal Foster in "What's Neo about the Neo-Avant-Garde?" See *October* 70 (1994): 5–32. Foster's critical reading is motivated by objective developments of American postwar art. According to Foster, in America, the historical awareness of the prewar avant-garde "was further complicated by the reception of the avant-garde through the very institution that it often attacked. If artists in the 1950s had mostly recycled avant-garde devices, artists in the 1960s had to elaborate them critically" (10).

2. Matei Calinescu, *Five Faces of Modernity* (Durham: Duke University Press, 1987), 95–148. Also, see Renato Poggioli, *The Theory of the Avant-Garde* (Cambridge, Mass.: Belknap Press of Harvard University Press, 1968). His idea of the "two Avant-gardes" is useful in understanding the sociopolitical roots of the avant-garde in the twentieth century.

3. Burger, *Theory of Avant-Garde,* 49.

4. Manfredo Tafuri, *Architecture and Utopia* (Cambridge, Mass.: MIT Press, 1976), 50–103.

5. Kenneth Frampton, "Avant-Garde and Continuity," *Architectural Design* 7–8 (1982): 21.

6. For Poggioli the coincidence of the two avant-gardes resides in the character of Rimbaud and Verlaine. It is worthwhile to mention here that Theodor Adorno rejected the chronological interpretation of modern art in favor of one that "answers to Rimbaud's postulate that, in relation to its own time, art must be the most advanced consciousness where sophisticated technical procedures and equally sophisticated subjective experiences interpenetrate." *Aesthetic Theory,* (London: Routledge and Kegan Paul, 1984), 49.

7. Jean-Francois Lyotard, "The Sublime and the Avant-Garde" in *The Inhuman,* trans. by G. Bennington and R. Bowly (Stanford: Stanford University Press, 1991), 92.

8. Michel Foucault, *The Order of Things* (New York: Vintage, 1970), 218.

9. See Joseph Rykwert, *The First Moderns: The Architects of the Eighteenth Century* (Cambridge, Mass.: MIT Press, 1983). Also Alberto Pérez-Gómez, *Architecture and the Crisis of Modern Science* (Cambridge, Mass.: MIT Press, 1983). Pérez-Gómez argues that after the seventeenth century the dialogue between logos and mythos of architecture was not maintained, and "scientific thought came to be seen as the only serious and legitimate interpretation of reality" (11). I am more in agreement with Robin Evans, who does not think Perrault took mystery out of architecture by "treating proportion as a convenience rather than the source of true beauty." According to Evans, Perrault "took mystery out of architecture's explanation," and in doing so "he moved attention from invisible causes to the visible constitution of building." Evans, *The Projective Cast* (Cambridge, Mass.: MIT Press, 1995), 271. In the English translation of Perrault's *Ordonnance,* Pérez-Gómez folds the nihilism of present architectural theory into Perrault's discourse and correctly concludes that the latter "must be de-structured, not simply nostalgically denied or falsely overcome." Here Perrault's doubt about the attributed coherency between *logos* and *mythos* is not presented negatively but is suggestive of a possible development of a meaningful architecture. Pérez-Gómez, "Introduction" to *Claude Perrault Ordonnance for the Five Kinds of Columns after the Methods of the Ancients* (Santa Monica: Getty Center for the History of Art and the Humanities, 1993), 38. One should make the distinction between a phenomenological reading of "the crisis of the object," implied in Pérez-Gómez's discussion, and Walter Benjamin's discourse on the idea of the loss of aura. Benjamin was concerned not only with the technological reproduction of the work of art but with the ways that "reality" is represented in traditional art. According to Benjamin, the life-world in the premodern era was not yet touched by the nihilism of technology. I have benefited from both views throughout this volume. In the last chapter I will draw my conclusions primarily from Benjamin's discourse. For Benjamin see "The Work of Art in the Age of Mechanical Reproduction," in *Illuminations,* trans. Harry Zohn (New York: Schocken, 1969), 217–52.

10. I am thinking of Michel Foucault's discourse on the relationship between constructed space and knowledge: "spaces were designed to make things seeable, and seeable in a specific way." See John Rajchman, "Foucault's Art of Seeing," *October,* no. 44 (Spring 1988): 89–117.

11. Etienne-Louis Boullée, "Architecture, Essay on Art," in Helen Rosenau, *Boullée and Visionary Architecture* (New York: Harmony, 1976), 89.
12. Vidler, *The Writing on the Walls*, 3.
13. Italo Calvino, *Six Memos for the Next Millennium* (Cambridge, Mass.: Harvard University Press, 1988), 23.
14. Anthony Vidler, "Notes on the Sublime: From Neo-classicism to Postmodernism," *Canon* 3 (1988): 172.
15. Joseph Rykwert, "Inheritance or Tradition," *Architectural Design Profile* 49, no. 5/6 (1979): 2–6.
16. Kenneth Frampton distinguished the differences between art and architecture, claiming that "what was true of art and literature was always less true in the case of architecture, for where architecture was restrained by power and material production from being fully liberating or liberative in its expression, it was at the same time resistant to the separation of art and politics suffered by the other arts, for architecture was suffused with power." Frampton, "Avant-Garde and Continuity." Michel Foucault suggests that by the end of eighteenth century, architecture became the subject matter of statements made by various power organizations. The empowerment of architecture was part of the discovery of the idea of society: "That is to say, that government not only has to deal with a territory, with a domain, and with its subjects, but that it also has to deal with a complex and independent reality that has its own laws and mechanism of reaction." See "Space, Knowledge, and Power," an interview published in Paul Rabinow, ed. *The Foucault Reader* (New York: Pantheon, 1984), 239–56. Here Foucault stresses the contemporary shift of power techniques from territorial to spatial. Dialectically, one could argue that it was in the spatiality opened by the idea of society that the avant-garde artists could practice their techniques of resistance.
17. Burger, *Theory of Avant-Garde*, 19.
18. In saving Mies van der Rohe from the mainstream of modern architecture, Massimo Cacciari asserts, "Whether one makes pure form one's purpose, or whether the goal is to achieve a perfect conformity between the work and the technical and economic form of contemporary social relations, the theoretical propositions are identical. Both operations presume that the purpose is the simple result of the agent's intentionality, that the work is nothing but the product of this intentionality, that the object—insofar as it is a purpose/telos to be attained—must depend exclusively on the subject that produces it." Cacciari, "Mies's Classics," *Res* 16 (Autumn 1988): 9–16.
19. Burger, *Theory of Avant-Garde*, 49.
20. Frampton, "Avant-Garde and Continuity." Dismissing Burger's last point, Giorgio Grassi charges "all artistic avant-gardes" with the practice of borrowing slogans or inventing their own forms regardless of the specific character of architecture and the history of that specificity. However, one cannot disagree with his critical assessment of the existing cultural "super structure" and the need for architecture to emphasize "collective meanings."
21. Frampton, "Avant-Garde and Continuity," 23.
22. Martin Jay, *Adorno* (Cambridge, Mass.: Harvard University Press, 1984), 65.

23. For the historical implications of this observation in painting, see Serge Guilbaut, *How New York Stole the Idea of Modern Art* (Chicago: University of Chicago Press, 1983). This reading could be applied not only to the institutionalization of the international style in architecture but also to the most recent exhibition of the work of deconstructivist architecture at MoMA, which immediately promoted a fashionlike imitation of deconstructivist architecture in schools and in corporate architectural firms.

24. For Benjamin H. D. Buchloh, Andy Warhol's work marks the moment when the line separating high and pop art was blurred. Since then, Buchloh maps three distinct artistic trends: First one erodes "the high art-mass culture dialectics" and affirms the imperatives of commercial line. The second still holds on the high position of art and its distance from mass culture. And the third, artificially maintains a balance between the high art and the pop culture. Buchloh, "The Andy Warhol Line," in *The Work of Andy Warhol,* ed. Gary Garrels (Seattle: Bay Press, 1989), 66–67. I am not suggesting a one-to-one application of Buchloh's analysis for architecture. I am more intrigued with the historicality of post-avant-garde artistic production, the fact that, similar to Warhol, Mies van der Rohe moved architecture to a historic threshold from where three distinctive architectural discourses, discussed throughout this book, emerged.

25. Andreas Huyssen, "Mapping the Postmodern," *New German Critique* 33 (Fall 1984): 18.

26. For Hal Foster see note 1, above.

27. For a distinction between transgression and resistance see Hal Foster, "For a Concept of Political in Contemporary Art," *Recodings* (Washington: Bay Press, 1985), 139–56. Drawing from Gramscian and Foucauldian discourses, Foster argues: "This passage from a model of avant-garde transgression to one of critical resistance is not merely theoretical; it must be seen historically in relation to the different conditions that have shaped the production and reception of art over the past 100 years" (150).

28. Hal Foster, *Recodings,* 147. In his later work, Walter Benjamin had already noticed the change in ruling class attitude toward any tactic of resistance: "Baudelaire had the good fortune to be the contemporary of a bourgeoisie which could not yet use the social type that he represented as an accomplice. It was left to the bourgeoisie of the twentieth century to incorporate nihilism into its apparatus of domination." Quoted in Buchloh, "Andy Warhol Line," 61.

29. Giovanna Borradori, *Recoding Metaphysics,* ed. G. Borradori (Evanston: Northwestern University Press, 1988), 17. Also see Jean Baudrillard, *The Transparency of Evil* (New York: Verso, 1993), 119.

30. Martin Heidegger, *The Question Concerning Technology and Other Essays* (New York: Harper Torchbooks, 1977), 35.

31. For further discussion of *techne* and implication of technology for architecture see Gevork Hartoonian, *Ontology of Construction: On Nihilism of Technology in Theories of Modern Architecture* (New York: Cambridge University Press, 1994).

32. Heidegger, *Question Concerning Technology,* 129.

33. Jean Baudrillard, *Evil Demon of Images* (Australia City: Power Institute of Fine Arts, 1987), 49.

34. J. M. Bernstein, *The Fate of Art: Aesthetic Alienation from Kant to Derrida and Adorno* (State College: Pennsylvania State University Press, 1992), 112.

35. Manfredo Tafuri, *The Sphere and the Labyrinth* (Cambridge, Mass.: MIT Press, 1987), 1–21.

36. Manfredo Tafuri, *Humanism, Technical Knowledge and Rhetoric: The Debate in Renaissance Venice* (Cambridge, Mass.: Harvard University Press, 1986). Tafuri reflects on the physical transformation of Venice in light of technical developments, and the role this played in the crisis of the unity of knowledge as conceived in the figure of "universal man." In conclusion, he argues that Palladio's architecture remained on the outskirts of the Venetian context because of Palladio's new form of rationality, "which projects its own theories beyond the contingent historical time."

37. Tafuri, *Sphere*, 6.

38. Fredric Jameson suggests that "the sense of Necessity" of closure binds three important contemporary texts together: Besides Manfredo Tafuri's *Architecture and Utopia*, one is reminded of R. Barthes's *Writing Degree Zero* and T. Adorno's *Philosophy of Modern Music*. For Tafuri's account, Jameson has this to say: "of the increasing closure of late capitalism (beginning in 1931 and intensifying dialectically after the war), systematically shutting off one aesthetic possibility after another, ends up conveying a paralyzing and asphyxiating sense of the futility of any kind of architectural or urbanistic innovation on this side of that equally inconceivable watershed, a total social revolution." Jameson, *The Ideologies of Theory Essays, 1971–1986* (Minneapolis: University of Minnesota Press, 1988), 40. For Jameson, Tafuri and R. Venturi present the two sides of one coin, the impossibility of any change. A neo-Gramscian position is crucial to Jameson's reading of the problematics of current architecture. A point of view already touched by Kenneth Frampton. A long overdue attention to "critical regionalism" occupies a chapter in Jameson's most recent work. See Jameson, *Seeds of Time* (New York: Columbia University Press, 1994).

39. See his foreword to Peter Burger, *Theory of Avant-Garde*.

40. On this subject, see Michael Zimmermann, *Heidegger's Confrontation with Modernity* (Bloomington: Indiana University Press, 1990), especially part 1. According to Zimmermann this subject was essential for German thinkers: "Junger described modern technology better than anyone else, but took his ideas about technology as an aesthetic phenomenon from Nietzsche. Nietzsche's doctrine of art as form-giving activity that restores weight and meaning to life resonated with Heidegger's conviction that only a great work of art could save Germany from the leveling effects of the one-dimensional technological mode of working and producing" (76).

41. Heidegger, *Question Concerning*, 35.

42. See Bernstein, *Fate of Art*, esp. the first two chapters.

43. The subject was first discussed in "Prospect for a Critical Regionalism" and then revised and published in "Towards a Critical Regionalism: Six Points for an Architecture of Resistance," in *The Anti-Aesthetic: Essays on Postmodern Culture*, ed. Hal Foster (Washington: Bay Press, 1983),

16–31. The earliest text was published in *Perspecta* 20 (1983): 147–62. Paul Ricoeur's essay "Universal Civilization and National Cultures," published in 1955, is instrumental for Frampton. What has made the critic skeptical of his discourse on resistance is the ever-increasing marginalization of regional cultures in the wake of current liquidation of boundaries by late capitalism. For Ricoeur, see *History and Truth* (Evanston: Northwestern University Press, 1965), 271–304. Ricoeur's position is touched by a neo-Kantian view that in its explanation of human geographies "emphasized the old environmental 'man/land' tradition and sought associations between physical and human geographies on the visible landscape, either via the influences of the environment on behavior and culture or through 'man's role in changing the face of the earth.'" See Edward W. Soja, *Postmodern Geographies* (London: Verso, 1989), 37. At the turn of the century, a reaction to modernity came from German *Volkisch* movement calling for cosmic forces that "were at work in the common language, traditions, art, music, social customs, religion, blood, and soil which united a particular *Volk*." See Zimmermann, *Heidegger's Confrontation with Modernity*, 8.

44. The technique of defamiliarization was used by Russian formalists to distort the habitual perception of things. According to Alexander Tzonis and Liane Lefaivre, "The poetics of critical regionalism carry out its self-reflective function through the method of defamiliarization." Tzonis and Lefaivre, "Why Critical Regionalism Today?" *Architecture and Urbanism* 236 (May 1990): 23–33. For "defamiliarization" and Russian formalists, see *Russian Formalist Criticism*, eds. Lee T. Lemon and Marion J. Reis (Lincoln: University of Nebraska Press, 1965), 12.

45. I have elaborated on these issues in *Ontology of Construction*, specifically chapters 2 and 3.

46. Manfredo Tafuri, "The Chicago Tribune Competition," in *The American City from the Civil War to the New Deal*, ed. Giorgio Cucci, et al. (Cambridge, Mass.: MIT Press, 1979), 403.

47. Hal Foster, "Architecture, Development, Memory," *Thinking the Present*, eds. Michael Hays and Carol Burns (New York: Princeton Architectural Press, 1990), 116.

48. Guy Debord sees the end of culture in "the project of culture's self-transcendence" and "its management as a dead thing to be completed in the spectacle." Debord, *The Society of the Spectacle* (New York: Zone, 1994), 131–32.

49. I am thinking of both the romanticist reaction to modernity and their counterparts in some German intellectual circles at the turn of the century. According to Jeffry Herf, "The reactionary modernists were modernist in two ways. First, and most obviously, they were technological modernizers, . . . Second, they articulated themes associated with the modernist vanguard." Herf, *Reactionary Modernism* (New York: Cambridge University Press, 1984), 12. Michael Zimmermann also reminds us that by 1940, Ernst Junger "was conceiving of technology in terms of the same dualism that had been expressed by critics at the turn of the century: cultural world vs. technological civilization; personal productivity vs. the mechanical performance of work; the true and natural vs. the technological and perverted life." Zimmermann, *Heidegger's Confrontation*, 63. Interestingly enough, in his 1929 lecture at Buenos Aires, Le Corbusier correctly explained "the destruction of

regional cultures" posited by mass communications and transportation. "You hear and see on the screens of all the movie houses of Buenos Aires the voice of Mr. Hoover addressing his citizens, and you will learn English. . . . And the locomotive has brought you the suits of London and the fashions of Paris. You are wearing bowlers!" And he continued, "Only events beyond the power of mechanization seem to resist: the blacks stay black and the Indians red. And even then! Everywhere black blood creeps into white, and red into black or white." Le Corbusier, *Precisions* (Cambridge, Mass.: MIT Press, 1991), 26.

50. Kenneth Frampton, "Heidegger," *Oppositions,* no. 2 (1976). In this short piece Frampton draws conclusions merely from Martin Heidegger's early search for the essential structures of being-in-the-world and dismisses Heidegger's later attempt to deconstruct the Western metaphysics; that is, *Dasien*'s presuppositions about its own existence. It is this later work of Heidegger that discloses the nature of modern technology and its differences with the Greek instrumentalism. See Zimmermann, *Heidegger's Confrontation,* 146–49.

51. Kenneth Frampton, from an unpublished manuscript presented to the entire academic body of the Columbia University. Frampton seems here to be recalling Edward W. Soja's observation that "modernization can be directly linked to the many different 'objective' processes of structural change that have been associated with the ability of capitalism to develop and survive, to produce successfully its fundamental social relations of production and distinctive divisions of labour despite endogenous tendencies towards debilitating crisis." Soja, *Postmodern Geographies,* 26.

52. In postmodernity, culture functions differently than it used to do at high modernism. The operative mode of the latter was "oppositional and marginal within a middle-class Victorian or philistine or gilded age culture." According to Fredric Jameson, postmodernism "constitutes the very dominant or hegemonic aesthetics of consumer society itself and significantly serves the latter's commodity production as a virtual laboratory of new forms and fashions." Jameson, "Periodizing the 60s," in Sohnya Sayers and Andres Stephanson, eds., *The Sixties Without Apology* (Minneapolis: University of Minnesota Press, 1988), 196.

53. This development has opened a new chapter in the current rewritings of the history of modern architecture. For gender implications and architectural space, see Beatriz Colomina, ed., *Sexuality and Space* (New York: Princeton Architectural Press, 1992), and for various views on weaving architecture into fashion, see D. Fausch et al., ed., *Architecture: in Fashion* (New York: Princeton Architectural Press, 1994). At the expense of dispensing with other dimensions of a statement made at the turn of the century, most of these writings correctly disclose the sexist aspect of modern architectural discourse.

54. This latter point is implied in Kenneth Frampton's above statement and in his most recent work, *Studies in Tectonic Culture* (Cambridge, Mass.: MIT Press, 1995).

55. Here "spatiality" connotes a departure from historicism; things or concepts do not occur once and then fade away. In a standstill conception of history, it seems reasonable to expect the "return" of the same, although in difference. In his critical reading of Peter Burger's *Theory of the Avant-Garde,* Hal Foster argues that Burger's premises fall short of considering the neo-avant-garde's work in extension of the prewar

critique of the institution of art. "It also ignores that in doing so the neo-avant-garde has produced new aesthetic experiences, cognitive connections, and political interventions, and that these openings may make up *another* criterion by which art can claim to be advanced today." Foster, "What's Neo about the Neo-Avant-Garde?" 16. Foster's latest work speculates about a shift occurring in the present critical discourse from a Marxist determinism to a Freudian paradigm of "repetition" and the pleasure of return.

56. Long before current technological developments, the concept of "total space" has been at work in cinematography. Montage deconstructs hierarchial and inside/outside distinctions for a spatial fragmentation that annuls the other. While closing this manuscript, I had the chance to read the articles proliferated at the occasion of the exhibition of the OMA's work in MoMA, and Rem Koolhaas's discourse on "Big." The latter might be a better term for what I mean by total space. Interestingly enough, Sanford Kwinter discusses the fluidity of Metropolis in terms of a spatial whole that is implied both in book and film. Kwinter, "The Building, the Book, and the New Pastoralism," *Any* 9 (1994): 9.16–9.23. Fredric Jameson observes that in *Blade Runner* "the street is somehow inside, so the city as a whole, which has no profile, becomes the immense, amorphous, unrepresentable container that realizes the conceptual essence of the geodesic dome." Jameson, "Demographies of the Anonymous," *Anyone* (New York: Rizzoli International, 1991), 56. The total space of film is experienced in section—that is, sequential cuts—and not in plan. For more on this subject and its importance for architecture, see the next chapter.

Chapter 5

1. Michel Foucault, *Archaeology of Knowledge* (New York: Harper and Row, 1972).
2. Martin Heidegger, "Building Dwelling Thinking," in *Poetry, Language, Thought* (New York: Harper and Row, 1975), 154.
3. Heinz Ronner and Sheerad Jhaveri, eds. *Louis I. Kahn: Complete Work, 1935–1974* (Boston: Birkhauser, 1987), 89.
4. See Walter Benjamin, "The Work of Art in the Age of Mechanical Reproduction," *Illuminations* (New York: Schocken, 1969), 217–52. According to Benjamin, the dialogical relationship between logos and mythos is essential for an auratic object. For him, such an object possesses the marks of both the subjective (desire) and the objective (hand/tool) life of the subject. A desire to reconcile these two facets of an auratic object was the force behind the nineteenth-century search for style. It was also the motive for the Werkbund and the Bauhaus schools to reconcile art and technology. On the historical malady of the nineteenth century and Gianni Vattimo's reading of various discourses on the crisis of the subject, see Vattimo, *The Adventure of Difference* (Baltimore: Johns Hopkins University Press, 1993), especially the first three chapters. It is not difficult for the reader to detect my interest in Vattimo's idea of the weak thought and its importance for my discussion of "the two textual levels of architecture."
5. Gianni Vattimo attributes this line of thinking to a Nietzschian response to the crisis of the bourgeois/Christian idea of the subject. According to Vattimo, Martin Heidegger "represents the crisis of the subject in

reference to its radical and constitutive belonging to a historic-social world." Vattimo, *Adventure of Difference,* 53. I would like to pursue Vattimo's idea of the weak thought as the postmodern subject and address the antinomies of tradition and the process of secularization.

6. This is an important subject by which one can articulate the problematic relationship between architecture and its recent past. See Stanford Anderson, "The Legacy of German Neoclassicism and Beidermeier: Behrens, Tessonow, Loos, and Mies," *Assemblage* 15 (1991): 63–88.

7. The term "mechanical selection" was introduced by Le Corbusier in the fourth issue of *L' Esprit Nouveau.* See Nancy J. Troy, *The Decorative Arts in France: Art Nouveau to Le Corbusier* (New Haven: Yale University Press, 1991), 216. For Le Corbusier, tradition sustains its continuity through "mechanical selection," an abstract concept referring to the enduring laws of making and the primary needs and the logic of economic selection.

8. For the latter, he said: "To-day, painting has out sped the other arts. It is the first to have attained attunement with the epoch . . . it lends itself to meditation." The engineers, instead, have achieved harmony by respecting the laws of nature and are healthy and forceful mainly because they discarded the old tools and invented new ones that are the direct expression of progress. Le Corbusier, *Towards a New Architecture* (New York: Praeger, 1960), 15–24.

9. Throughout this text I have discussed the importance of the duality between appearance and construction for postmodern architecture. Recent rewritings on modern architecture discuss the Corbusian free-facade in terms of fashion and Gottfried Semper's concept of dressing, which was also addressed by Adolf Loos. Semper's discourse differs from both Le Corbusier and Loos; the latter two architects consider the split between substance (building) and appearance (dressing) in terms of fashion and women's dress. Contrary to men's suit, whose surface refinements usually confirm the lines defining the shoulder or the waist, women's dress fashionably overrides these bodily contours. The facades of Villa Savoye and the Moller House are articulated independent of the physical constructs of their respected buildings. Semper addressed the separation between construction and appearance differently. For him the tectonic is the symbolically revealed construction (the art-form). If nudity is the ultimate statement of fashion, as Robert Altman suggests in *Pret-A-Porter,* then one might trace "nudity" in Mies van der Rohe's steel and glass architecture and in Tadao Ando's concrete constructs. Both architects unfold an architectural discourse that closes the gap between signifier and the signified. One might speculate that Mies and Ando maintain a neutral position on gender issues, whereas Loos and Le Corbusier conceived architecture to be feminine. On the problematic place of body and gender in Western architecture, see Diana I. Agrest, "Architecture from Without: Body, Logic, and Sex," *Assemblage* 7 (Oct. 1988): 29–41. On fashion and architecture, see D. Fousch, P. Singley, and R, El-Koury, ed. *Architecture in Fashion* (New York: Princeton Architectural Press, 1994), especially Mary McLeod's article, "Undressing Architecture: Fashion, Gender, and Modernity," and her concluding remark: "It is not accidental that the term 'deconstructionist' entered the vocabulary of fashion shortly after the Museum of Modern Art's Deconstructivist Architecture Show in 1988. While this recent trend in

architecture lacks the irony and humor of the parallel movements in women's and men's fashion, it has underscored the ambiguities between construction and ornament" (93).

10. Fritz Neumeyer, *The Artless Word* (Cambridge, Mass.: MIT Press, 1991), 201.

11. I am borrowing the concept of deterritorialization from Gilles Deleuze and Felix Guattari and their argument that "a minor literature doesn't come from a minor language; rather that which a minority constructs within a major language. But the first characteristic of minor literature in any case is that in it language is affected with a high coefficient of deterritorialization." See Deleuze and Guattari, *Kafka: Toward a Minor Literature* (Minneapolis: University of Minnesota Press, 1986).

12. Theodor Adorno, "Messages in a Bottle," *New Left Review* 200 (July/Aug. 1993): 5–14. These are part of Adorno's Minima Moralia and were not included in the final publication.

13. Sigmund Freud, "The Uncanny," in *Collected Papers,* vol. 9 (New York: Basic Books, 1959), 394.

14. For Anthony Vidler, the reemergence of the uncanny since the mid-1960s "seems at once a continuation of its privileged position in the 'negative dialectics' of the modernist avant-garde—a role given double force by the self-conscious ironization of modernism by postmodernism —and a product of the new technological conditions of cultural representation." See Vidler, *The Architectural Uncanny* (Cambridge, Mass.: MIT Press, 1992), 9. One might consider the current interest in psychoanalytical readings of cultural texts as a part of the return of the unconscious in the wake of the death of the subject.

15. Hal Foster argues that "the Surrealists not only are drawn to the return of the repressed but also seek to redirect this return to crucial ends." Foster, *Compulsive Beauty* (Cambridge, Mass.: MIT Press, 1993), xvii.

16. This last point pertains to a theory of the subject emerged since the 1960s, articulating an architectural object that, according to Michael Hays, "is shifted away from a distinctively, uniquely visual, or even generally aesthetic mode of perception and valuation—whereby the object is isolated in a purely abstract and idealized realm, freed from the molestations of ideology and resonances, and plays of signification in excess of the object's abstractable visual meaning." Michael Hays, *Modernism and the Posthumanist Subject* (Cambridge, Mass.: MIT Press, 1992), 281.

17. This point is eloquently discussed by Mark Wigely, *The Architecture of Deconstruction, Derrida's Hunt* (Cambridge, Mass.: MIT Press, 1993). Wigely characterizes the dialogue between architecture and deconstruction theory as a kind of translation whose importance is already in the gaps and cuts of each discourse. "The architectural translation of deconstruction, which appears to be the last-minute, last-gap application, turns out to be part of the very production of deconstructive discourse from the beginning, an ongoing event organized by the terms of an ancient contract between architecture and philosophy that is inscribed within the structure of both discourses" (6).

18. The idea of body and architecture still awaits a thorough study. Nevertheless, one should mention Joseph Rykwert's enormous contribution to this subject. Also Anthony Vidler presents a thoughtful framework for further research. See Vidler, "The Building in Plan: The Body and

Architecture in Postmodern Culture," *AA Files* 19 (Spring 1990): 3–10. One also should explore this subject in modern architecture: for example, the ways that Leon Battista Alberti's understanding of building as body is reconstituted in Le Corbusier's three reminders, the surface, mass, and finally the plan. These three reminders speak for the anthropomorphic dimension of his work: the surface that has to move our emotions, the mass that should be perceived, and the plan that not only rationalizes the sensations but also opens and closes the horizon that the eyes should explore. These are my extrapolations from Le Corbusier's remarks on "Three Reminders to Architects," in *Towards a New Architecture.*

19. There are intriguing similarities between what is happening now and then at the dawn of this century. Current ambiguities about the state of architecture and the vistas experienced through virtual "windows" are comparable to the nineteenth-century debate on the future of architecture and the excitement of journey made possible by modern transportation technology. And yet, like then, is not technology the driving force for cultural development?

20. Kenneth Frampton, *Modern Architecture: A Critical History* (New York: Oxford University Press, 1980), 69. To use iron in conjunction with the monumental tradition of stone architecture was a major dilemma for early modern architects. According to Fritz Neumeyer, "The modern condition became acutely visible as the new rail systems and their facilities intruded on the traditional city space, affecting urban monumental spaces governed by tradition and the architectural tradition of stone." Neumeyer, "Iron and Stone: The Architecture of the Grobstadt," in *Otto Wagner,* ed. Harry Francis Mallgrave (Santa Monica: Getty Center for the History of Art and the Humanities, 1993), 116.

21. According to Miriam Hansen, "Benjamin actually conceived of the Artwork as a heuristic construction, a telescope which would help him to look through 'the bloody fog' at the 'phantasmagoria of the nineteenth century' so as to delineate in the features of a future." Hansen, "Benjamin, Cinema and Experience: 'The Blue Flower in the Land of Technology,'" *New German Critique* 40 (Winter 1987): 182.

22. Walter Benjamin, "Paris, Capital of the Nineteenth Century," *Reflections* (New York: Harcourt Brace Jovanovich, 1978), 148. Benjamin's views was also expressed in the surrealists' interest in the "outmoded": the passages, the bourgeois interiors, and art nouveau. See Foster, *Compulsive Beauty,* 173.

23. Susan Buck-Morss, *The Dialectics of Seeing* (Cambridge, Mass.: MIT Press, 1989), 116. In another context, Buck-Morss argues that "19th-Century design may have been technologically reactionary when it hid function and tried to revive dying forms. But the tremendous value of its culture was that it tacked onto the surface of things all kinds of configurations in which historical truth and utopian dreams could be read." Buck-Morss, "Benjamin's Passagen-Werk: Redeeming Mass Culture for the Revolution," *New German Critique* 29 (Spring/Summer 1983): 238.

24. This was left to Le Corbusier, whose work along with that of the surrealists was pursued by Walter Benjamin. He wrote, "To embrace Breton and Le Corbusier. That would mean to span the spirit of contemporary France like a bow out of which the knowledge [of the past] hits to the heart of the present." Quoted in Buck-Morss, *Dialectics of Seeing,*

293. Obviously it was surrealism that exploited the energies invested in the wish-images and the shock technique for radical ends.

25. One might read the I-shape columns in the later work of Mies van der Rohe as the uncanny return of a *heimlich* thing (iron rails) of a bygone past. Here I am profiting from Hal Foster's argument that "the out-moded is uncanny in another way: as familiar images and objects made strange by historical repression." Foster, *Compulsive Beauty,* 126.

26. Michel Foucault, *Language, Counter-Memory, Practice,* trans. D. F. Bouchard and Sherry Simon (Ithaca: Cornell University Press, 1977), 139–47.

27. Ibid., 147.

28. Consider Robert Venturi's Vanna Venturi House, where complexity and contradiction are maintained at the expense of consolidation of the universality of classical language of architecture invested in the overall symmetry of the form and in the broken gable. Peter Eisenman enter-tains these theoretical considerations in his early work, though from the point of view of deconstruction theory. See Eisenman, "The Futility of Objects: Decomposition and the Processes of Difference," *Harvard Architecture Review* 3 (Winter 1984): 65–81.

29. According to Martin Heidegger, inhabiting comes before building a home. In "Building Dwelling Thinking," Heidegger speaks of the ways in which the bridge opens a vista through which the apartness of the banks are visible. In this sense, inhabiting means to make the space clear for another atmosphere to open itself up. The culture of inhabiting differs from Christopher Norberg-Schulz's discourse on "dwelling." The latter presumes a state of mutual belonging between things and dwell-ing. Different views on this subject are the result of various readings of Heidegger's discourse in "Building Dwelling Thinking," 143–63. For Norberg-Schulz see *The Concept of Dwelling* (New York: Rizzoli International, 1985). On the problematic of modern architecture and Heidegger's thoughts on dwelling, see Massimo Cacciari, "Eupalinos on Architecture," *Oppositions,* no. 21 (1980): 106–15.

30. I have discussed some aspects of these issues in *Ontology of Construc-tion: Nihilism of Technology in Theories of Modern Architecture* (Cambridge: Cambridge University Press, 1994), especially the chapters on Mies van der Rohe and Adolf Loos. Obviously the aim here is not to purify these dualities from their metaphysical content. One should rather recode them in the process of secularization, or to forget them forever, if possible at all, as metaphysical entities.

31. Reflecting on Martin Heidegger's discourse on recollection, Vattimo asserts, "What the recollection achieves is the recovery of this eventual character of Being: metaphysics appears to Heidegger as the series of the epochs in which Being has opened itself in the form of different *archaei,* each one claiming to be a stable (metaphysical) structure while it was just an epochal, opens a sort of *episteme* in Foucault's sense." Gianni Vattimo, *The End of Modernity* (Baltimore: Johns Hopkins University Press, 1988), 26.

32. Foucault, *Language, Counter-Memory, Practice,* 35.

33. Considering the form/content relations, Walter Benjamin suggested that rather than asking "what is the *attitude* of a work to the relations of production of its time?" one should ask, "what is its *position* in them?" See Benjamin, "The Author as Producer," *Reflections,* 222. Seemingly

Benjamin's position differs from the orthodox Marxist view of the base/superstructure duality and the deterministic interpretation of the work of art. For Benjamin, art does not reflect the base but is positioned within it.

34. Manfredo Tafuri, *The Sphere and the Labyrinth* (Cambridge, Mass.: MIT Press, 1987), 1–21.

35. One implication of the nihilism of technology could be discussed in terms of the constant discharge of construction materials from their organic content. The building industry replaces the tradition of craftsmanship with industrial materials and techniques. This development posits a spatial experience that has no historical precedent. Current simulation technologies elevate the tactile experience of architecture to the realm of distraction. Walter Benjamin anticipated this unfolding: Emphasizing on habit and tactile experience of architecture, Benjamin did not neglect the fact that "the distracted person, too, can form habit. More, the ability to master certain tasks in a state of distraction proves that their solution has become a matter of habit. Distraction as provided by art present a covert control of the extent to which new tasks have become soluble by apperception." Benjamin, "The Work of Art in the Age of Mechanical Reproduction," 240.

36. These heterogenous institutions were organized to control the spread of epidemic diseases and accelerate the advent of the railroad and electricity. See Michel Foucault, "Space, Knowledge, and Power," in *The Foucault Reader*, ed. Paul Rabinow (New York: Pantheon, 1984), 243. On the importance of Foucault's discourse for architecture, see Paul Hirst, "Foucault and Architecture," *AA Files* 26 (Autumn 1993): 52–60. Hirst believes that Foucault's approach "avoids the problem of the declared intentions of the architect-author, and side-steps the *cul-de-sac* of their absence," p. 57.

37. Like a lone actor who enacts an absolutely different play from that of the actors on the stage, modern architecture wants to perform without belonging to the scheduled performance: even in its most aggressive campaigns of realization it insists on its own otherworldliness." Rem Koolhaas, *Delirious New York* (New York: Oxford University Press, 1978), 206. Most critics have admired Koolhaas for characterizing the work done in New York between 1890 and 1940 as the unconscious dimension of the avant-garde. Hubert Demish compares Koolhaas's work in Manhattan with Walter Benjamin's "Paris, Capital of the Nineteenth Century." See Demish, "The Manhattan Transfer," *OMA—Rem Koolhaas* (New York: Princeton Architectural Press, 1991), 21–33.

38. Franz Schulze, *Mies van der Rohe: A Critical Biography* (Chicago: University of Chicago Press, 1980), 35.

39. Francesco Dal Co, "Notes Concerning the Phenomenology of Limit in Architecture," *Oppositions*, no. 23 (Winter 1981): 37–51. See also Dal Co, "Mies," in *Figure of Architecture and Thought: German Architectural Culture, 1880–1920* (New York: Rizzoli International, 1990).

40. According to Joseph Rykwert, orthogonal planning "is the product of a tight discipline and its adaptation by a people like the Etruscans was not in the least likely to have occurred as a simple matter of convenience." Rykwert, *The Idea of a Town* (Cambridge, Mass.: MIT Press, 1988), 87. Besides orientation, Rykwert underlines the cosmological content of an orthogonal grid that was first perceived in "the templeum of the sky."

One might associate the grid of Manhattan with the global space at work beneath the networks of current telecommunication technologies.

41. Koolhaas, *Delirious New York*, 170.

42. Rem Koolhaas reminds us of the re-erection of the Latting Observatory, the Crystal Palace, and the Centennial Tower of Philadelphia in Coney Island, and their ever-new incarnation in Manhattan as part of the process of "democratization of pleasure." If life in "the metropolis creates loneliness and alienation, Coney Island counter attacks with the Barrel Love." Koolhaas, *Delirious New York*, 29. Koolhaas also reminds us of the exemption of "pleasure" from the utilitarian planing of modern functionalism: "In a laughing-mirror-image of the seriousness with which the rest of the world is obsessed with Progress, Coney Island attacks the problem of Pleasure, often with the same technological means" (24).

43. Koolhaas, *Delirious New York*, 103.

44. OMA's recognition of the aesthetics of modernism displays a far more sensible and intelligent reaction to the complex reality of Berlin's context and its historic characteristics than contextualist postmodern ideology can produce with its return to classical typology." Fritz Neumeyer, "OMA's Berlin: The Polemic Island in the City," *Assemblage* 11 (Apr. 1990): 51. Interestingly enough, in an interview, Koolhaas bases his skepticism of deconstructivists in "their presumption that this naive, banal analogy between supposedly irregular geometry and a fragmented world or a world where values are no longer anchored in a fixed way. It is hopelessly visual, compositional and therefore, in a very traditional sense, architectural." See Alejandro Zaera Polo, "Finding Freedom: Conversation with Rem Koolhaas," *El Croquis*, Feb./Mar. 1992, 29.

45. For different views on the notion of "autonomy," see *Harvard Architectural Review* 3 (Winter 1984): 6–12. My argument on architectural autonomy is indebted to Demetri Porphyrios's discourse on "critical history." See *Architectural Design* 51, no. 617 (1981): 96–104.

46. On this subject, see Adorno, *Aesthetic Theory* (New York: Routledge and Kegan Paul, 1984), 320, and F. Dal Co, "Notes Concerning the Phenomenology of Limit in Architecture."

47. I am thinking of Jacques Derrida's argument that, as a strategic position, deconstruction might "confirm, consolidate, or 'relever,' at a depth which is ever more sure, precisely that which we claim to be deconstructing. A continuous explication which precedes the opening risks falling into a closed autism." Derrida, "The Ends of Man," *Philosophical and Phenomenological Research* 1 (1969): 56.

48. Heidegger, "The Origin of the Work of Art," in *Poetry, Language, Thought*, 76.

49. Vattimo, *End of Modernity*, 40.

50. Paul Ricoeur, *Freud and Philosophy: An Essay on Interpretation* (New Haven: Yale University Press, 1970), 35. According to Ricoeur, the three figures responsible for demystifying hermeneutics are Marx, Nietzsche, and Freud. They set up the rude discipline of necessity and thus dispensed with the grace of the imagination. Drawing from certain aspects of what Ricoeur terms the mythos-poetic core of imagination, Vattimo, instead, bridges the gap between the two schools of interpretation, the "suspicion" and the "recollecting," as defined by Ricoeur.

51. Vattimo, *End of Modernity*, 53.

52. Giovanna Borradori, *Recoding Metaphysics*, ed. G. Borradori (Evanston: Northwestern University Press, 1988), 17.

53. I am benefiting here from Gianni Vattimo's remarks on Heidegger's concept of play. See Vattimo, *Adventure of Difference*, 124.

54. Adorno, *Aesthetic Theory*, 310. Adorno believed that the mimetic impulse of art could resist the rational and instrumental dimension of technology. In the context of current intensification of technology's domination on culture, one wonders if the system has not already internalized the "irrational" into its nihilistic unfoldings?

55. Discussing Sergei Eisenstein's ideas on montage, Manfredo Tafuri concludes that Eisenstein considers the form of montage to be the "law of the structure of the object." Repudiating the historical avant-garde's interest in shock, Eisenstein favored a "structural consideration of the work where, principally, what is recuperated is precisely the concept and value of the work." Tafuri, "The Dialectics of the Avant-Garde: Piranesi and Eisenstein," *Oppositions*, no. 11 (Winter 1977): 76. For Eisenstein, it is the *unifying principle* that should determine both "the content of the shot and that content which is revealed through a given *juxtaposition of these shots*." See Sergei Eisenstein, *The Film Sense*, trans. Jay Leyda (New York: Harcourt, Brace, 1942), 10. Theodor Adorno also emphasized the role of montage in renouncing meaning and hierarchical compositions in the art. Adorno could not see the spatial implication of montage as it occurs in the filmic experience and its impact on architecture. When the shock aspect of montage was incorporated into advertisement industry, Adorno concluded that now "montage revert to being indifferent stuff or substance." Adorno, *Aesthetic Theory*, 223.

56. I have discussed the importance of montage for architecture in Hartoonian, *Ontology of Construction*.

57. Rem Koolhaas quoted in the pamphlet published at the occasion of OMA's exhibition at MoMA, 1994. The idea of an interactive total space was at work in Tilyou's design in Coney Island, where, according to Koolhaas, "The single roof dramatically reduces the opportunities for individual facilities to display their own characters; now that they do not have to develop their own skins, they blur together like many molluscs in one gigantic shell in which the public is lost." Koolhaas, *Delirious New York*, 37.

58. Fredric Jameson is still the best critic who discusses these issues and yet deconstructs their foundation for a way out of postmodern epistemological enclosure. In the introduction to *The Seeds of Time*, Jameson has this to say about the objectives of his restless critical work: "What it seemed to me useful to do, in an ambitious idea that here remains the merest sketch, is to suggest an outside and an unrepresentable exterior to many of the issues that seem most crucial in contemporary (that is to say, postmodern) debate." Jameson, *The Seeds of Time* (New York: Columbia University Press, 1994).

59. In his brilliant comments on Adolf Loos, Massimo Cacciari states that against the Werkbund ideological inclination to unify langue and language, Loos considered "the language of the relation of exchange is inherent to the structure and modes of exchange." Cacciari, *Architecture and Nihilism: On the Philosophy of Modern Architecture* (New Haven: Yale University Press, 1993), 105. Interestingly enough, Cacciari suggests that this esteem for synthesis was not foreign to Semper. I have

argued for montage and dis-joint as concepts of making that recode Semper's discourse on the tectonic. See Hartoonian, *Ontology of Construction.*

60. Modifying Manfredo Tafuri's position on Mies van der Rohe's hope to neutralize the social, Michael Hays argues for the presence of a sense of abstraction in Mies that is not self-referential but imposed by the American consumer culture of 1950s: "with its newly devised strategies of advertising—the technique of large-scale color printing on outdoor billboards and the use of electric lighting for advertisement, both of a scale and pervasiveness not previously imaginable—changed the very nature of the experience of urban public space." Hays, "Odysseus and the Oarsmen, Or, Mies's Abstraction Once Again," in *The Presence of Mies,* ed. Detlef Mertins (New York: Princeton Architectural Press, 1994), 224. One should read Hays's position in the context of his own observation that the postwar cultural developments have made a split "between the world of quality building, in the European tradition of *bauen* or *Baukunst,* and the everyday world of American popular environment; and this would later (with Venturi and others) become a fundamental split in architectural theory" (24). Hays's observation is a reminder of the fact that since the advent of American abstract expressionism, there has been the tendency to rewrite American art and architecture beyond the thematics of modern discourse, formulated in Europe. It also discloses the drive of postmodern and deconstruction architecture to dispense with the tradition of *Baukunst* in favor of an architecture that is thought in the oblivious space, redeemed from any constrains (metaphysics?), and floating like a spaceship in the infinity of postmodern geographies. Should we recall here Le Corbusier's infatuation with ships as an emblem of both technology and a floating construct?

61. Jonathan Crary, *Technique of Observation: On Vision and Modernity in the Nineteenth Century* (Cambridge, Mass.: MIT Press, 1991), 14.

62. The sides of this octagonal tower were covered by inscriptions, not only describing the direction of each particular wind but mapping the shape of the town itself and the location of various buildings within it. Viturvius, *De Architectura,* bk. 1, trans. F. Granger (Cambridge, Mass.: Harvard University Press, 1983), 57.

63. I am making the following analogies from Martin Heidegger's distinctions among a thing, equipment, and the work of art. According to him "the piece of equipment is half thing, because characterized by thingliness, and yet it is something more; at the same time it is half of art work and yet something less, because lacking the self-sufficiency of the art work." Heidegger, "Origin of the Work of Art," 29. This distinction can be expanded to Theodor Adorno's discussion of Schonberg's mediation between the artistic and the logic of music's construction. Adorno wrote, "Schonberg worked neither as a 'blind craftsman' nor with the 'arbitrariness and optional choice of a subjectively unrestrained artist.' Instead, the composition emerged out of an unresolved contradiction between the subjective freedom of the composer and the objective demands of the material." From Susan Buck-Morss, *The Origin of Negative Dialectics* (New York: Free Press, 1977), 129. The implied analogy between music and architecture and my following remarks on architecture and dance are motivated by Gottfried Semper's definition of

the tectonic as a cosmic art analogous to dance and music. For Semper "Tectonic deals with the product of human artistic skills, not with its utilitarian aspect but solely with that part that reveals a conscious attempt by the artisan to express cosmic laws and cosmic order when molding the material." See Wolfgang Herrmann, *Gottfried Semper in Search of Architecture* (Cambridge, Mass.: MIT Press, 1984), 151.

64. Lightness has also been an important subject for our best recent literary work. Besides Milan Kundera's *The Unbearable Lightness of Being*, I am thinking of the beautiful chapter on lightness in Italo Calvino's *Six Memos for the Next Millenium* (Cambridge, Mass.: Harvard University Press, 1987). There is also a sense of lightness in Sergei Eisenstein discussion of montage, a subject equally important for my discourse on the tectonic. Montage is not a synthetic mounting of one image on top of another but, according to Eisenstein, an act of explosion and disjoint: "When the tension within a movie frame reaches a climax and cannot increase any further, then the frame explodes, fragmenting itself into two pieces of montage." See Eisenstein, *Film Sense*.

65. Italo Calvino wrote: "Whenever humanity seems condemned to heaviness, I think I should fly like Perseus into a different space. I do not think escaping into dreams or into irrational. I mean that I have to change my approach, look at the world from a different perspective, with a different logic and with a fresh method of cognition and verification." Calvino, "Lightness," *Six Memos for the Next Millennium,* p. 7.

Index